MW00528802

Propelled by Hope

My friend Rex attended Perspectives Lesson 1 with his arms folded, wondering when the class would be over. By the end of the evening Rex was leaning forward, asking himself, "Why have I never heard this Biblical overview of missions before?" By Lesson 15 Rex and his wife Anna heard God's call "to give up their smaller ambitions" and "go ahead as far as they could see." They trained to become Perspectives coordinators and brought Perspectives to their home church. Rex and Anna then sold their possessions and moved with their children to one of the most remote regions of the world. Yvonne Huneycutt has told the Perspectives story in this superb book. As Ralph D. Winter said, "We should be on tiptoes to see what is about to happen next."

ROBERT BLINCOE, PHD | President Emeritus, Frontiers US

Propelled by Hope is a story for our time and for a new generation. Now from the advantage point of some fifty years, Yvonne, in looking back has helped "join the dots" of two significant Holy Spirit movements—the Frontier Missions Movement and the Perspectives on the World Christian Movement course—together with the family of courses that has flowed out of Perspectives. Yvonne Huneycutt has done a masterful job. This informative book is riveting, extremely well researched, highly inspirational, and well written. It carries a prophetic element that will help a new generation to be "propelled by hope" and engage enthusiastically with God on mission, as their meaningful expression of worship for God's eternal Glory.

MAX CHISMON | International Director, Simply Mobilizing International
Author, *Kairos* course

In her book *Propelled by Hope*, Yvonne Huneycutt has shown the Perspectives movement to reflect the power and vision of our missionary God. She shows how Perspectives is deeper than a trend and wider than one place and one time. At a time when algorithms and "best practices" can dull our minds and imaginations, her work allows us to see the fingerprints of our missionary God and invites us to join. The invitation takes us closer to the grace of God. The movement changed my calling in 1993. Under the tutelage of my friends David Garrison and David Barrett, I founded Anglican Frontier Missions. While others continue that work, the truths of Perspectives continue to teach me and take me in new paths.

REV. CANON TAD DE BORDENAVE | Founder, Anglican Frontier Missions

Surprisingly, this book shows us more than just the history of the Perspectives movement. It is about the fulfillment of our ultimate hope: to bring praise and worship to God from every people, nation, and language. The Perspectives movement has expanded beyond English-speaking countries to become a global movement. As readers will discover in these pages, Perspectives is spreading as Global South churches, formerly mission fields, begin to actively participate in global missions. Through this book, we can imagine what amazing things God will do through the global churches in the future. The publication of this book would not have been possible without the author's persistence, spirit of inquiry, insight into history, and deep love for the Perspectives movement.

CHULHO HAN | Director, Mission Partners Korea and Perspectives Asia

Here is the story of how the Perspectives course has been helping thousands to step into the great story of God fulfilling his global purpose.

STEVE HAWTHORNE, PhD | Lead Editor, *Perspectives*

Propelled by Hope is the sweeping narrative of a global movement that started from a seemingly small beginning when Perspectives was launched fifty years ago. Huneycutt's inspiring book reveals how God himself is the movement maker. Today, Perspectives is rapidly spreading through the non-Western world. This excellently researched book reveals why thousands around the world have experienced a radical paradigm shift and have now joined this movement of making his glory known. This global God story is continuing into future generations.

MARY HO, DSL | International Executive Leader, All Nations

Dr. Huneycutt has given us a marvelous gift by expertly recounting the fifty-year history of what is now a global missions education movement. While she aptly puts this account in the context of frontier missions, she also recognizes that, since 1974, Christianity itself was transformed as it shifted to the Global South. Both trends have brought greater diversity to the global church while moving us nearer to the Revelation 7:9 vision of all peoples so eagerly anticipated by Perspectives graduates around the world. A compelling and life-changing read!

TODD M. JOHNSON, PhD | Co-Director, Center for the Study of Global Christianity, Gordon-Conwell Theological Seminary

Yvonne Huneycutt pulls back the curtain on the connections between the origin and development of the paradigm shifting Perspectives course and the frontier mission movement that has dominated mission thinking for the last fifty years. Many are aware Perspectives has played a significant role in stimulating, expanding, and sustaining that movement, but few have been privy to the stories of the ordinary men and women used by God to do extraordinary things to align God's church with his purpose for his people within history. Countless thousands have given themselves sacrificially for the sake of his name within every segment of humanity. They are propelled by the hope that they are not just making history, they are fulfilling it.

The cover depicts with stunning vibrancy the fleet of nationally led programs that have emerged around the world, taking their direction from the Son, and although exposed and vulnerable, they boldly seek to capture the wind of the Spirit to mobilize and unite the church around an ancient promise that is an anchor for our souls and the ultimate hope for all nations.

BRUCE KOCH | Director, Perspectives Global Service Office, Frontier Ventures

Before Jesus ascended to the right hand of the Father, Jesus proclaimed to his followers that they would be empowered to bear witness of him to the ends of the earth. Unfortunately, the church today has relegated Christ's mission to a peripheral program emphasis. Yvonne Huneycutt has blessed us with a glimpse of how God graced his church through a curriculum that he has used to awaken his church around the world to the central mission of Jesus Christ and his bride. Thank you, Yvonne, for giving us a history of the God-given vision and people he used through the Perspectives movement to bring his church to repentance and obedience.

JEFF LEWIS | Mobilization/Discipleship Specialist, sixteen:fifteen

A book like *Propelled by Hope* has never been written. Ever! Yvonne has interwoven the story of Perspectives with the history of missions over the last five decades. I couldn't put it down! She traces the development of Perspectives as a worldwide phenomenon—in the context of seemingly every major mission milestone during the past fifty years! *Propelled by Hope* pulls no punches. It describes sodalities and modalities that are real, raw, and yet, redeemed. As it turns out, this book isn't a commercial for a missions course. It's the true story of a tapestry called Perspectives becoming a global movement, changing the lives of course developers and leaders just as radically as it transforms students into missional world changers.

DOUG LUCAS, DBA | President, Team Expansion and Founder/Co-Editor, *Brigada*

For the past two decades I've watched Perspectives and the people that steward it have an outsized impact on the expansion of the gospel around the world. I've often thought, "someone needs to document what's happening!" Yvonne is the one! She knows the movement from every angle. She knows the tactical aspects of running classes and the biblical intricacies of Perspectives' vision and content. She's hands on with the extraordinary global phenomenon of mission mobilization as it's expressed in numerous languages and contexts. This book will help you see the importance of Perspectives and its context in the broader frontier mission movement. You will become inspired to participate; more importantly, the book will leave you in awe of God and of his astonishing activity and purpose!

JAMES MASON | CEO, Perspectives USA

I was freshly inspired by Yvonne Huneycutt's *Propelled by Hope*. Here is a well-crafted collection of stories honoring scores of individuals in frontier mission mobilization. It stretches across decades inside a larger drama: God's movement through the Perspectives course to mobilize individuals, local churches, and organizations around the world toward fulfilling his singular ancient purpose: *blessing all the peoples of the earth through Jesus Christ*. This book is a Christ-centered worship offering. It gives historical witness to the multitudes who've been "ruined" away from the ordinary by the Perspectives course and "The Story of His Glory."

WERNER MISCHKE, D.D. (Hon. Causa) | VP, Mission ONE and Author, *The Global Gospel*

Perspectives on the World Christian Movement was life-altering for the church I pastored and for me. It provided the education and motivation we needed! I've long appreciated Yvonne Huneycutt's friendship and partnership. She's a humble, hard-working missiologist who keeps her finger on the pulse of Gospel advance! Her book about the Perspectives movement is an exceptional and readable addition to the missionary history that's unfolding in our lifetime!

ROBERT J. MORGAN, D.D. (Hon. Causa) | Author, Speaker, Bible Teacher

Propelled by Hope is remarkably and inspiringly focused on the glory of God among all peoples. The writer tells the Perspectives story in a way that is as enjoyable to read as it is academically factual. Yvonne's *Propelled by Hope* is a story of human efforts and Spirit guidance in developing a dynamic movement worth narrating, worth participating in, and worth propagating. It is fitting that Yvonne is the one authoring this story. She brings to this work, what she often does while teaching the historical section of the Perspectives course—life! This book is a welcome addition to our quest to herald the glory of God as championed by those who truly hope for his appearing.

REV. CANON TIMOTHY O. OLONADE, PhD
Pioneer Executive Secretary, Nigeria Evangelical Missions Association
Founding President, El-Rehoboth Global Leadership Foundation

I've been curious about how certain things thrive and others never get traction. Having been near the Perspectives movement since 1982, I have often wondered, "How did this happen?" What a joy to read the story about this ministry tool, which helps people get *into* the story themselves. And it's still happening! Such is the case when you have a course designed to instill globally informed discipleship in people who are committed to do whatever the Lord calls them to. They tend to want to pass it on!

GREG H. PARSONS, PHD | Global Connections Specialist, Frontier Ventures

Incredible! Yvonne Huneycutt has expertly and sensitively condensed fifty years of the Perspectives course and international movement into an exciting and fast paced narrative full of vision, passion, teamwork, setbacks, victories, and most of all, changed lives. Be inspired by what God has done in and through Perspectives, and let it motivate you to make a difference in this ever-growing world Christian movement.

STEVE SHADRACH, DMIN | Global Ambassador, Via (formerly Center for Mission Mobilization)

The Perspectives on the World Christian Movement course changed my life. I first took the course in 1981 with Ralph Winter, Don Richardson, and other pioneers in the frontier mission movement. I lead a mission that is mobilizing artistic and innovative ministry practitioners in fifty countries. As I look back over forty years, I see that the dynamic insights in the Perspectives course have laid the biblical and contextual groundwork that has given me great confidence and courage for innovative efforts in God's world mission. Reading it will give you renewed vision, historical perspective, deep enjoyment, and an enlarged passion for what is still an unfinished task.

BRYRON SPRADLIN, DMIN | President, Artists in Christian Testimony Int'l.

It is amazing what God has done through the Perspectives course! In 2001 we hosted the course at the church I pastored. One of the instructors, David Watson, exposed us to the amazing things he had seen God do in India in a disciple making movement. An African pastor staying with me at the time was enrolled in the course. Together we wondered, "Would God do something like this in Africa?"

With David's mentorship, we gathered other African leaders to implement disciple making movement principles in three regions of Africa. God has blessed the work with 39,565 new churches, including 18,284 among Unreached People Groups. Through Perspectives we met a long-term mentor and learned the importance of partnership and building on what others have done. *Propelled by Hope* is filled with such fascinating stories of the works of God through the quiet faithful labors of many.

JERRY TROUSDALE | Final Command Ministries
Author, *Miraculous Movements* and *The Kingdom Unleashed*

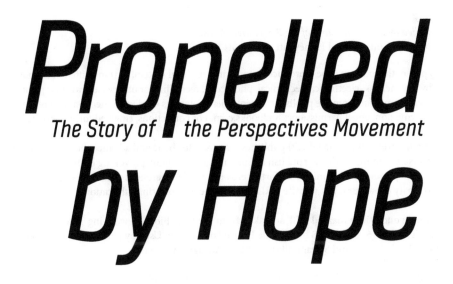

Propelled

The Story of the Perspectives Movement

by Hope

Yvonne W. Huneycutt

WILLIAM
CAREY
PUBLISHING
visit us at missionbooks.org

Propelled by Hope: The Story of the Perspectives Movement
© 2024 by Yvonne Wood Huneycutt. All Rights Reserved.

No part of this book may be reproduced, stored in a retrieval system, or transmitted in any form or by any means—electronic, mechanical, photocopy, recording, or otherwise—without prior written permission from the publisher, except brief quotations used in connection with reviews. For permission, email permissions@wclbooks.com. For corrections, email editor@wclbooks.com.

William Carey Publishing (WCP) publishes resources to shape and advance the missiological conversation in the world. We publish a broad range of thought-provoking books and do not necessarily endorse all opinions set forth here or in works referenced within this book. WCP can't verify the accuracy of website URLs beyond the date of print publication.

Scripture quotations marked NLT are taken from the Holy Bible, New Living Translation, copyright ©1996, 2004, 2015 by Tyndale House Foundation. Used by permission of Tyndale House Publishers, Carol Stream, Illinois 60188. All rights reserved.

Scripture quotations taken from the NASB® New American Bible®, Copyright © 1960, 1971, 1977, 1995, 2020 by The Lockman Foundation. Used by permission. All rights reserved. lockman.org.

Published by William Carey Publishing
10 W. Dry Creek Cir
Littleton, CO 80120 | www.missionbooks.org

William Carey Publishing is a ministry of Frontier Ventures
Pasadena, CA | www.frontierventures.org

Cover and Interior Designer: Mike Riester
Cover image by Flatiron from freepik.com.

ISBNs: 978-1-64508-464-8 (paperback)
         978-1-64508-466-2 (epub)

Printed Worldwide
28 27 26 25 24   1 2 3 4 5   IN

Library of Congress Control Number: 2024930159

DEDICATION

To my Perspectives colleagues and friends who no longer walk beside us, but are now with the Lord. You lived for the name of Jesus and the glory of God to be shed abroad among the nations. We miss you.

Lee Purgason—Perspectives USA director

Victor Ibagón—*Perspectivas* Colombia and *Perspectivas Consejo* director

Melissa Barron—Perspectives USA and Perspectives Global staff

Sussi Servant—Perspectives USA and *Perspectivas* Peru staff

Rory Clark—Perspectives Global staff and co-editor of the French version of the Perspectives curriculum

———————

To Dan Davis, the first pastor to see in me and call forth the calling God placed on my life in missions so many years ago at Hope Chapel in Austin, Texas. I am forever grateful.

———————

To all the servants of God who serve the Perspectives movement around the world. Thank you for your dedicated labor of love for his name.

———————

Most especially to my husband, Steve. Thank you for all the dinners you cooked when I was so focused in my office that I lost track of time! Your support through all the years of ministry, education, travel, and writing have been the wind beneath my wings.

CONTENTS

PREFACE

It is incredible to me that a complete history of this amazing course called Perspectives and the movement surrounding it has never been documented. The course is fifty years old, the reach and impact of the course is widespread, and yet no one has fully recorded its origins, motivations, and development. Due to my thirty-year involvement with Perspectives in a variety of roles, I reckoned that I am as equipped as any to attempt a recorded history.

The primary audience I had in mind as I wrote were the Perspectives directors, coordinators, instructors, and students who have encountered this movement in its developed stages and have no idea of the history or even the *why* of the course. Nor do they know the historical milieu, both in the church and in the world, surrounding the origin and expansion of the course. Most were not even born yet! What I consider second nature concerning the historical events of my lifetime and the important people and issues in missions are unfamiliar to them, requiring definition and explanation. Most participants in Perspectives outside North America have encountered the course in its maturity, so unfolding the Perspectives lineage becomes significant for them as well.

I initially intended to research and document only the history of the Perspectives movement. Once knee-deep in the project, however, I realized that to understand the why and what of Perspectives, one needed acquaintance with the frontier mission movement. Perspectives was birthed out of—and at the same time was a substantial contributor to—the genesis and development of frontier missions. Through the decades, Perspectives and the frontier mission movement have matured in tandem.

Researching authors and periodicals from each era of frontier mission development, I have documented in very brief format key issues, trends, people, events, and organizations. I am well aware that informed people will be dissatisfied with this overview; it leaves out many names and events and does not do justice to the ideas and issues involved. Volumes could be written on the history of frontier missions alone. My objective is to provide enough of an overview to grant context, to reveal the scope of innovation flowing out of frontier missions, and to disclose the breadth of the movement globally.

If you are one of the few who read footnotes, you will notice that the research for this book has occurred over a very long time! Initially begun as part of a doctoral project, I worked on the book in fits and starts over the years. Like many of my readers, I have been employed in the marketplace much of my life, while simultaneously contributing a chunk of my time to volunteering for Perspectives. I have only served Perspectives as a staff member slightly more than a decade. Due to job and ministry responsibilities, and a very long season of parental caregiving, this book has taken far longer to complete than I wanted.

I interviewed over sixty individuals in researching the history of Perspectives. In the process of conducting those interviews, I was struck by how many sensed a very clear call from God to serve the Perspectives movement. Their stories resonated with me, as I also experienced such a distinct call. There is great joy and fulfillment in serving with Perspectives, as ordinary people laboring together toward the same goal realize how a seemingly inconsequential contribution can have far-reaching eternal impact.

For so many, completing a Perspectives course marks the beginning of a new journey with God. Periodically, as I tell the story of the Perspectives movement, I will pause and share individual journeys, including bits of my own. Tens of thousands of personal stories could be told which illustrate the dramatic impact of this course. Most stories that I will share are drawn *from one single area*—the Perspectives students I served in Tennessee—*during one single decade*. When I reflect that such stories are multiplied across decades and thousands of locations, I stand in awe of God's amazing works.

In uncovering Perspectives' history, I have been impacted by the impetus the historic Student Volunteer Movement has bestowed upon the course. The sense that another student mission movement was in the making was a defining motivation to the early founders and students. Now a fresh generation of young people has arisen. They are at home in an intercultural world and are the first truly global generation. Many desire to give their lives to a cause greater than themselves. Would God do it again? Is he raising up a new student volunteer movement passionate for his name to be known among the nations?

To that end, I offer this volume. My desire is that you, my readers, may not merely learn the history of Perspectives and the frontier mission movement, but that you will be inspired to join the movement! For those who are already a part of this movement, may you be sustained in your labor for Christ's name, seeing that you are part of something much grander than your small corner of the world. Together let us press on, co-laboring with God until Jesus receives the full reward of his suffering and God is rightfully glorified through the worship and adoration of a redeemed people from every tribe, language, people, and nation.

INTRODUCTION

I sat bewildered and amazed. What is this teaching? How could I just now be hearing such significant information? After all, I was raised in the church—in a strong, mission-minded denomination. I served in church staff positions. I had a seminary degree, for goodness' sake! How did I miss this? This is revolutionary. My perception of missions was shattered in the space of two hours. My insight into Scripture was enlarged in the space of two weeks. My understanding of God, myself, the world, and my role in it was transformed over the course of a semester.

Welcome to the *Perspectives on the World Christian Movement* course! My experience may be radical, but it is not unusual. Thousands bespeak a testimony that echoes my own. From college students to college professors, from business executives to stay-at-home moms, from pastors to lay leaders, from missionary candidates to seasoned missionaries—we have done more than take a class, we have entered a movement. A movement that has reshaped more than just our lives. A movement that has reshaped the mission endeavors of churches and organizations. A movement that is reshaping the world through the kingdom advance of God's people.

Launched in 1974, Perspectives has intersected the lives of an estimated three hundred thousand course alumni across the globe. In addition to the myriad who have taken the Perspectives course or derivatives of the Perspectives course, tens of thousands have used the Perspectives *Reader* as a textbook in college and seminary classes. There is no way to calculate the additional hundreds of thousands of individuals who have been directly influenced by those who have studied the Perspectives material and embraced the call and promise of God for world evangelization.

Perspectives on the World Christian Movement is a course comprised of fifteen lessons woven together into an integrated paradigm which unfolds God's declared purpose in this world and his active work toward the fulfillment of that purpose. Although often described as a missions course, in reality it is not; it is a vision and discipleship course. The intended purpose of the Perspectives course is to awaken God's people to his purpose, mobilizing his church to strategic engagement with him in the outworking of his purpose.

The uniqueness of Perspectives that undergirds its enduring legacy is found in two surprising elements. The first is that it is almost entirely a volunteer movement. It is propelled forward by millions of volunteer hours supplied by thousands of eager volunteers promoting, organizing, teaching, and conducting courses around the world. Most of the full-time staff raise their own support to have the privilege of serving the ministry. The course produces an outcome of God's people voluntarily engaging God's purpose in a multitude of ways for the rest of their lives.

Why would so many give so much of their time to this movement? The answer is found in the second sustaining element—the paradigm of the course—which often catches believers by surprise. The paradigm, which will be explored in greater detail in this book, is essentially the unfolding of a grand story. A *Great God* is writing a *Great Story*, in which he creates a *Great People of Blessing* within every people, inviting them into his Story to co-labor with him in bringing about his *Great and Global Purpose*.

God's people are not objectivized into useful tools to dutifully accomplish his mission; rather, God grants dignity and purpose to his people by gracing them with a *Great Work* in a relational partnership with himself. The outcome of this story is *Great Glory for God*. Because God's purpose is certain, God's people engage with him in *Great Hope*, knowing that they are giving their lives to an ancient and eternal and sure purpose. They are *propelled by hope*.

This, then, is the Perspectives story: a volunteer movement of God's people propelled forward by hope in the sure completion of God's purpose.

The Perspectives movement and the frontier mission movement are inextricably intertwined. Therefore, a broad-sweeping overview of the frontier mission movement, with its concepts and outcomes, is included in this story. This overview is not intended to be all-inclusive, but enough of an outline to acquaint readers with the gist and breadth of frontier missions. The story of Perspectives, on the other hand, is told in greater detail, serving as a documented history of this incredible movement. Interspersed throughout the narrative are stories of lives transformed through their encounter with Perspectives.

Dr. Ralph Winter, the originator of the Perspectives course, used to say that Perspectives joined a movement of God that was already in progress. This book begins, therefore, with a historical overview of the major trends in American culture and in missions leading up to the mid-1970s. I then document the early development of the Perspectives course, up through 1981, with the publication of the first Perspectives *Reader* and *Study Guide*.

The Perspectives course not only joined a movement of God but itself became a movement, contributing to and accelerating major mission trends. So we will pause in the middle of our story to highlight the developing trends in world missions between 1980 and the year 2000. Those were formative decades in shaping future mission outreach, particularly in the frontiers of mission. Grasping the larger context, the stage is set to continue the story of the expansion and development of the Perspectives course in the final two decades of the twentieth century.

Part 2 ushers us into the twenty-first century, with all its change and chaos but also its increasing fruitfulness for the kingdom of God. Again we will examine the historical and global context impacting how we do mission, noting tectonic shifts in the new millennium. The frontier mission movement matured, continuing its global expansion with new expressions yet at the same time encountering opposition, necessitating consultation and clarification. The mission *field* became the mission *force*, and God surprised everyone with cascading people movements to Christ. With broad strokes of the paint brush, I attempt to capture significant developments in frontier missions during the next two decades.

The Perspectives movement also continued to mature and expand. Rapid momentum of classes and students brought with it struggle, restructuring, and new initiatives to develop tools and people. The transformative paradigm for which Perspectives is renown was more clearly defined, enabling the students to engage in even richer ways. Deepening theological and missiological insight, now not just from the West but from many regions of the world, contributed to further curriculum development. Global growth focused the need for a stronger course identity. Picking back up with the Perspectives story, I trace the developments from 2000 to 2020 in the North American course and organization. A significant section is given to the wonderful spread of Perspectives globally, most of which has occurred in only the past decade.

The three-year period of 2020 to 2022 is forever etched in our memories. The global pandemic impacted Perspectives as it did everything else. During this time Perspectives USA restructured once more to position itself for future growth. Despite national lockdowns, many global programs reported surprising advances. The challenge of recovering from the pandemic is where we conclude our story.

I often encourage my Perspectives students to be history-makers. But it is more than that. As we engage God's global purpose, we are not just making history—we are fulfilling it. The hope for which we labor is that heaven is richer and fuller and God is more glorified because of our praying and giving and going and supporting and living for God's eternal purpose: that all tribes and tongues will know, worship, and adore him.

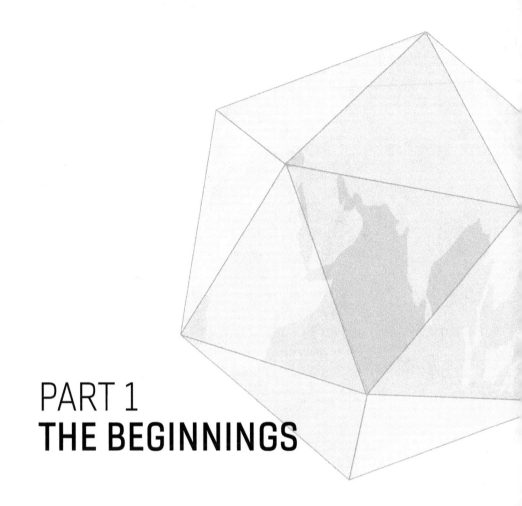

PART 1
THE BEGINNINGS

1

The Historical Context in Which Perspectives Emerged

"The day of the missionary is over. We have completed the missionary task; all that remains is local evangelism by the national church."

Or so went the thinking of much of the Christian church as the 1960s came to a close. The celebrated fact of the time was the recognition of the "younger churches"—those planted by earlier mission efforts—on every continent and in almost every country. This led many to believe that Christ's Great Commission was nearly fulfilled and all that remained was a mop-up job to be done by the national churches within each country.[1] Furthering this popular belief was a call by some in the "younger churches of the Third World," as they were then called, for a moratorium on missions.[2]

Global Realignments

What occasioned this sentiment that the missionary vocation was no longer welcome or appropriate? A principal answer lies in one of the most massive global political realignments in history. In his remarkable book, *The Twenty-Five Unbelievable Years, 1945–1969*, missiologist Ralph Winter recounts how rapidly the world shifted from a colonial-dominated landscape to a

---

1 McGavran, "Crucial Issues in Missions," 169–70.
2 Howard, "A Moratorium on Missions?"

vast array of newly independent nations. By the cessation of World War II in 1945, Europeans had virtual control over 99.5 percent of the non-Western world. In an astonishingly brief twenty-five-year period, Western nations had lost control over all but 5 percent of the non-Western population of the world. In a tide of rising nationalism, missionary presence was often equated with colonial rule; therefore, in the minds of many in both the non-West and the West, as one form of Western dominance was shed, so should the other.

Such rapid change brought with it unrest, resulting in regional conflicts. Many newly independent nations turned to authoritarian governments, often embracing Marxism and coming under the shadow of the Soviet Union. The long war in Vietnam raged as America sought unsuccessfully to push back the communist forces in Southeast Asia. Coming on the heels of the recent harsh repressions of Chairman Mao in China, there was a sense that communism was winning the Cold War.[3]

Not only did communism seem to be gaining ground around the world, but Christianity seemed to be losing ground in the West. In American society the Vietnam War fed the youth revolution of the 1960s, fostering anger and disillusionment with "the establishment." Racial injustice and segregation in church and society betrayed the truth of the gospel. American Christians watched hopelessly as a whole generation dropped out into an alternative culture of drugs, sex, and rock and roll. David Howard, InterVarsity director of the Urbana student mission conventions in the early 1970s commented that

> the student world of the 1960s was marked by activism, violent upheavals, and negative attitudes. The anti-government, anti-establishment, anti-family, anti-church attitudes were also expressed in anti-mission reactions. Seldom have missions been looked upon with less favor by students than during that decade.[4]

Societal Trends

Secularism replaced the Judeo-Christian worldview in American media, government, and educational systems. What could not be proved by science was considered a private belief system and little by little was extracted from the public square. Major denominations and seminaries removed belief in the supernatural, including the resurrection of Jesus, from their

---

3 Crawley, *World Christianity*, 10–12.
4 Howard, "Road to Urbana and Beyond."

interpretation of Scripture, demythologizing the Bible into something "modern man" can accept. Salvation takes on a whole new meaning when the immortal soul is dismissed. Indeed, the very meaning of salvation was the theme of the World Council of Churches' Bangkok assembly in 1973. They defined salvation exclusively in this-worldly terms as a struggle for economic justice and human dignity against exploitation and oppression, solidarity with the marginalized poor, and hope against despair.[5] The purpose and goal of mission accordingly turns upon the definition of salvation. Simultaneously, salvation in Catholic circles began to be equated with socio-political liberation. Arising out of Latin America and emerging from the reforms of Vatican II (1962–65), liberation theology focused the mission efforts of the church on working for political and economic liberation for the oppressed and marginalized masses, even if it meant revolution. Liberation theology overflowed its geographical and ecclesiastical boundaries, becoming both a popular and controversial theological approach to missions in the 1970s.[6]

Alongside secularism, an equally damaging societal trend in the early seventies was the rising tide of religious pluralism (understood in its original sense that all religions contain equal truth and validity). The world was shrinking due to astounding advances in technology. Familiarity with those of other religions made it harder to conceive of an acquaintance going to hell for holding a non-Christian belief system. The plurality of religions and the outworking of secularism produced a relativism of truth.

Religious pluralism and relativism obviously have disastrous consequences for missions and evangelism. Why proclaim the gospel of Jesus Christ to others if it is not ultimate truth and they are "saved" through their own religion anyway?

Negative View of Missions

The combination of these and other factors in the 1960s—a collective guilty conscience over colonialism, rapid moral degeneration, alluring materialism, the struggle for racial equality, shocking political assassinations—permeated the American church at the turn of the decade with a spirit of negativism and despair. With the nightly news showing horrible footage from Vietnam, popular books making dire predictions about global overpopulation, reports on the seriousness of the drug problem in public schools, the ubiquitous fear of communism, and the cataclysmic threat of the arms race, the entire country was in a funk.

---

5 Bosch, *Transforming Mission*, 396–97.
6 Bosch, 432–42.

Ralph Winter reflects on those days:

> I wrote a book in 1969 called *The Twenty-Five Unbelievable Years*. The title of every chapter was negative on the grounds that I did not think it would arouse interest if it took an optimistic approach. That is how bad the negativism was in popular Christian culture at the time. That's why McGavran's famous lecture, "The Sunrise [not the sunset] of Missions," was so shocking to so many people.[7]

A common question was, Is there a future for the missionary enterprise? The seminaries of liberal denominations were terminating their mission programs.[8] The deeper issue for liberal denominations was a questioning of the entire theological basis for mission. Liberal theology and religious pluralism had shifted much of the church away from the conviction of the Christian responsibility to evangelize.

Another momentous issue concerned the tension between the mission and the "younger churches." The hesitation and delay in transferring authority and responsibility from the missionary to national church leaders was causing great consternation on the part of many in the newly independent countries. Some in Africa were calling for a complete withdrawal of all European and American missionaries.[9]

At the close of the 1960s the view of missions among evangelical students was similarly grim. Students on Christian-college campuses seemed to have the most negative view of all! To get a clear picture, I will quote at length from a 1970 article in *Evangelical Missions Quarterly*. As I read this article, I was struck by how well it described my own view of missions as a student in the 1970s … and the view I continued to hold until I took the *Perspectives on the World Christian Movement* course in 1989. The authors of this article catalogue the contemporary student impressions of missions.

> *Missions as "out of it."* Many students consider missions not much more than a dead cause because missions seem so irrelevant to the issues and problems of the day. … Students still accuse *missionaries of being drab.* In emphasizing devotion to God and sacrifice for His work, many evangelical missionaries seem to deny certain essential aspects of personality and beauty. … *Missions as traditional and inflexible.* Students fear that missions strategy and policies have not changed in the last twenty years. Frequently the terminology they hear from the missionary on

---

7 Ralph D. Winter, interview by author, June 20, 2005, audio tape recording.

8 Kane, "Changes in Missiological Studies."

9 Crawley, *World Christianity*, 83.

the campus is very much the same that they heard as children; this gives rise to the suspicion that perhaps the whole enterprise is static and unimaginative. ... *Missions as non-personal.* Youth are desperately scared that they might get involved in an organization where they are just another cog, going around in circles like the next one! ... *Missions as unsuccessful.* ... Because students question the validity of the institutional church here at home, they also question the validity of exporting institutional churches overseas. They also question the need for North American missionaries abroad when there is a national church in existence among all groups. They have nagging suspicions that missionaries have exported more Americanism than Christianity. ... *The whole concept of the missionary has become "foreign" to the students.* They see the missionary as having a totally different life orientation and style. *They can hardly imagine themselves in a similar role; far be it from them!*[10]

This, then, is the negative environment preceding the 1974 launch of the *Perspectives on the World Christian Movement* course. However, to borrow a phrase from a popular song of the decade, a change was "blowin' in the wind."[11]

A New Spiritual Vitality

Emerging from the turbulent 60s, the "Jesus Movement" erupted on the national youth scene. Beginning on the West Coast, hippies turned from drugs to Jesus and found in him the love, freedom, and purpose for which they were searching. Christianity began to take on a radically different appearance as they melded their music and youth culture with their newfound faith. The radical activism that ignited protests in the 60s now found expression in bold and passionate witness to their faith.

EXPLO '72, sponsored by Campus Crusade for Christ, attracted an unprecedented eighty thousand students, capturing the attention of national media. The magnitude of the event signaled a shifting in the youth culture. It was obvious that the Holy Spirit was at work among American youth.

This change was noticed at the Urbana '70 Student Missions Conference, which recorded an upsurge in attendance. Although still not enamored with the institutional church, "This generation of students," observed James Reapsome, was "looking for and finding spiritual vitality centered around the person of Jesus Christ."[12]

---

10 Schwas and Melick, "How to Close the Gap between Students and Missionaries," italics mine.
11 From the song, *Blowin' in the Wind*, written by Bob Dylan in 1962 and released in 1963.
12 Reapsome, "Urbana '70."

The Urbana Student Missions Conference is held every three years by InterVarsity Christian Fellowship/USA. The planners of Urbana '73 decided they had had enough of negativism.

> Students have heard much about colonialism, paternalism, western imperialism (religious as well as political), failures of mission policies, racism in missions, superiority attitudes of missionaries, ad infinitum. However, although a critical analysis of past failures is necessary for future progress, there comes a time when negativism can no longer produce positive results. In my opinion, we have reached that point in missions. … Therefore, the planners for Urbana 73 … have decided to take a positive approach. … We want to sound a forward-looking note of hope based on the sovereignty of God as the Lord of history who will fulfill all of his purposes.[13]

The call for a positive outlook hit a chord. The following year an entire issue of the *Evangelical Missions Quarterly* was devoted to the "remarkable expansion" of the "evangelical missionary enterprise." Editor Jim Reapsome proclaimed, "There is no sign we can detect that missions are going out of business."[14] Several Bible schools had added a year of missions to their programs. Many seminaries, including Wheaton, Fuller, Concordia, and Trinity had established a school of world mission within the past decade.

Missiology, a fairly new discipline, was maturing. The American Society for Missiology—with its new publication, *Missiology: An International Review*—was founded in 1973. Other journals and publications were founded to feed and inform the growing evangelical interest in missions. The William Carey Library publishing house was established to enable mission titles to be printed and distributed economically. Missiologist Herbert Kane commented in 1974, "Thirty years ago a new book on missions was an event. Not so today. Mission books are coming off the press so rapidly that one hardly has the time to read them, much less the money to buy them."[15]

But it is what happened at Urbana '73 that sounded a trumpet call proclaiming that a new day in missions had indeed arrived.

Billy Graham frequently gave the keynote address at Urbana conventions, in which he would challenge students to sign a commitment card to pursue God's call on their lives regarding missions. In those days, being a missionary almost exclusively meant leaving home and going

---

13 Howard, "Urbana '73 Theme."

14 Reapsome, "A Positive Outlook."

15 Kane, "Changes in Missiological Studies."

to live overseas. Attendance at the conferences gradually rose over the years, but the number of students signing commitment cards declined. Then suddenly, and quite unexpectedly, there was a sharp turnaround. At Urbana '73, when the challenge was issued for students to commit themselves to whatever course God had for them in world missions, the Urbana leaders were surprised at how many stood up and responded. Thinking that the students didn't understand the challenge, the leaders instructed the students to sit down and the challenge was repeated, this time making it harder. But even more students stood up in response! It was the largest response in Urbana history. Within weeks, 38 percent of the 14,158 students signed a commitment card. At the next conference, in 1976, the percentage of students signing commitment cards grew to 50 percent![16] Students had left the negativism of the 1960s behind; God was stirring a new generation of students for his global purpose.

It is at this point, with the great and unexpected student response at Urbana '73, that the story of the *Perspectives on the World Christian Movement* course begins.

---

16 Howard, "What Happened at Urbana."

2

Responding to the Move of the Holy Spirit

Fuller Foundation

Ralph Winter heard the report of the amazing student response at Urbana '73. Could this be the beginnings of another Student Volunteer Movement, he wondered.

Early in the twentieth century, the Holy Spirit moved upon a whole generation of students, calling them into the mission fields of the world. Motivated by the motto "The evangelization of the world in this generation," they began what came to be referred to as the "Student Volunteer Movement." The Student Volunteer Movement (SVM) made possible great progress in world evangelization during the twentieth century. Yet now in the last quarter of the century, most of those SVM missionaries were retiring. A new wave of recruits was needed to replace them.

Ralph Winter was a professor at the relatively new School of World Mission at Fuller Theological Seminary in Pasadena, California. Holding numerous degrees, including a degree in engineering from the California Institute of Technology and a PhD in linguistics and anthropology from Cornell University, Winter and his family had spent ten years working as missionaries among the Mayan Indians of Guatemala. During Winter's furlough in Pasadena in 1966, Donald McGavran approached him about

Ralph D. Winter in 1974.

teaching at the newly established School of World Mission. The permanent missions faculty at that time consisted of McGavran and Alan Tippett, a well-known missionary anthropologist. Intending at first to split their time between Pasadena and Guatemala, Ralph and Roberta Winter discerned God's leading to accept a full professorship.[1]

Donald McGavran was considered by many to be a leading missiologist of the twentieth century. He raised awareness of cultural (not just linguistic) barriers to evangelism and, through his writings, disseminated the concept of people movements coming to Christ. McGavran wrote a seminal book, *The Bridges of God*, in which he made a case for the spontaneous expansion of the church through Christward movements within every cultural-linguistic ethnic group. This strategy contrasted with the prevalent mission-station approach, persisting from the nineteenth century, of gathering individual converts into compounds or conglomerate churches isolated from the societal mainstream.

McGavran founded the School of World Mission at Fuller Theological Seminary, which quickly became a premiere institution for missionary thinking and education. Working alongside McGavran at Fuller was formative for Winter. His wife, Roberta, elaborated in her book *I Will Do a New Thing*:

> Although in Guatemala we had seen the wonderful changes that the Gospel brought into a community, we were surprised at Fuller by Dr. McGavran's exuberant conviction that we were in the sunrise, not the sunset, of missions. Like others, we had heard plenty of the bad news of the world, as reported in the newspapers. At the School of World Mission we were privileged like few others to have access to the good news, the wonderful news that God was no liar: that as He promised, His gospel was spreading and growing, often out of control, all around the world.[2]

---

1 Roberta H. Winter, *I Will Do a New Thing*, 16–19, 302.
2 Roberta Winter, 18.

McGavran's thinking about people movements also deeply influenced Winter. Through his own study of how the gospel flowed throughout history from one cultural basin into another, Winter became convinced that a distinct church planting movement was needed for every people group on earth in order for the church to complete the Great Commission. This would require a massive change in strategy among mission agencies. It would also require multitudes of new missionaries.

Suddenly, in 1973, a new surge of mission interest appears among Urbana students. Could the Holy Spirit be moving again among another student generation?

Zechariah 4:10

Ralph Winter witnessed this response at Urbana '73. Fuller student T. V. Thomas recalls Winter turning to him repeatedly as they exited the auditorium, exclaiming with great intensity,

> Thomas, what are we going to do with all these students who are responding to the Great Commission? In two years, their commitment could wither before they can actually go overseas. We need to equip them *now* to keep that commitment aflame.[3]

Winter immediately contacted his long-time friend David Howard, InterVarsity's Urbana director. He challenged InterVarsity to offer a follow-up course for the students who had indicated mission interest. Considering his overwhelmed staff, Howard's response was that they could not do it. Winter then offered to conduct a follow-up course himself if InterVarsity would release the students' contact information. Howard responded to Winter with his own challenge:

> You need to answer five questions before we will consider giving out our address list: (1) Who will teach? (2) What will you teach? (3) Where will you hold the class? (4) Who will sponsor it? And (5) Who will hold the bag financially?

If the questions were intended to dissuade Winter, they did not. Over the course of the next two weeks, Winter made about two hundred phone calls, attaining answers to all five questions, much to Howard's surprise.[4]

Amid an already busy schedule, Winter set about organizing and promoting a summer follow-up mission course for the Urbana students. He wanted to challenge students not simply to a missionary career, but to lay hold of the total task of world evangelization. An early oft-repeated motto in

3 T. V. Thomas, interview by author, January 8, 2019, email.
4 Winter, interview.

the Perspectives course was "Every major decision you make will be faulty unless you see it from God's perspective."[5]

Winter also had four daughters and was looking at the college generation through their eyes. He recalls,

> My own kids didn't have a knowledge of missions. My oldest, who is very sharp, asked me one day, "Dad, who is William Carey?" I was shocked. I could see through their eyes that something foundational was needed.[6]

Winter first addressed the task of establishing a board of directors. He formed a small five-man board of prominent mission executives.

T. V. Thomas became a global mission leader and Perspectives Canada leader.

The original board consisted of himself, Ted Ward, Charlie Mellis, Jack Frizen, and Warren Webster. Winter recruited Malaysian seminary student T. V. Thomas to help facilitate the class, telling him to bring with him all the mission books he owned. Thomas thought he would just be helping with the logistics of setting up chairs and running errands. Hardly! It turns out that Winter invited him to teach parts of the class. "Those mission books that I brought with me came in very handy to prepare my lectures!"[7]

The course was planned for the summer of 1974 and named the *Summer Institute of International Studies* (SIIS). The name and nature of the course was patterned after Wycliffe Bible Translators' *Summer Institute of Linguistics* (SIL), which Winter had taken as a student. SIIS became the forerunner of the Perspectives course.

When Winter saw that InterVarsity was not going to do very much to promote the course, he was able to get Billy Graham to mention it twice on his "Hour of Decision" radio program. He also succeeded in convincing Harold Lindsell, editor of *Christianity Today* and one of Winter's former professors, to allow Winter to write a full-page ad/article in *Christianity Today*. The article questioned if another "Student Volunteer Movement" might be emerging and announced the upcoming SIIS course.[8] For a more

---

5 Hawthorne, "History of the Perspectives Course."

6 Winter, interview.

7 Thomas, interview.

8 Ralph D. Winter, "Big New Student Mission Movement?"

direct approach, Winter enlisted his college-age daughters to call Urbana students and invite them to the class. Twenty-nine students enrolled in the first semester of the *Summer Institute of International Studies.*[9]

Winter asked an old friend, Herbert Kane, to be the dean. As he contacted other mission professors, he realized that most of them already had their summer schedules in place and could, at best, give only one week to the program. As a last resort they decided to have a different professor come in each week to teach. Fretting that such a structure would be way too confusing and messy, Kane dropped out from serving as dean. Instead, it turned out to be a smashing success and Perspectives has continued the multi-instructor practice to this day. The only downside, Winter recalls, was during that first summer each visiting professor wanted to assign a term paper for their week of teaching, thereby overloading the students.[10]

Winter developed a ten-week curriculum, divided into two sessions. The four-section structure of the course—biblical, historical, cultural, and strategic—came from the structure of the Fuller School of World Mission curriculum. Excited students recruited friends to join them for the second session, boosting enrollment to forty. SIIS was held at Wheaton College, where the students lived and studied for the entire summer session. The visiting professors would also live in the dorms, eat with the students, and share their life stories during their week of teaching. Having so much access to the professors, most of whom were also former missionaries, was a rich experience for the students. They were not only acquiring knowledge; they were being mentored by some of the brightest and most experienced mission leaders of the day.[11]

The historic first SIIS class in 1974. Students with professors pictured.

---

9   Ralph D. Winter, "Personal Recollections."
10 Winter interview.
11 Bruce Graham, interview by author, July 13, 2005, email.

Another photo of the students and professors of the1974 SIIS class.

The roster of the original SIIS professors reads like a Who's Who in Missions: Harvie M. Conn, Elisabeth Elliot, Arthur F. Glasser, Paul Hiebert, David M. Howard, J. Herbert Kane, C. Peter Wagner, Ted Ward, and Ralph D. Winter. The class was coordinated by Alvin Martin, the extension director at Fuller at the time. College credit was extended through Whitworth College (now Whitworth University) in Spokane, Washington.[12]

During the first week of the first-ever SIIS course, Dr. Arthur Glasser stood up and paraphrased the first part of Zechariah 4:10 to the small group of twenty-nine students: "Do not despise the day of small beginnings."[13] What a prophetic word that was as the global *Perspectives on the World Christian Movement* was launched!

Lausanne '74

In the middle of the first SIIS session, Ralph Winter stopped by on his way to Lausanne, Switzerland, for the First International Congress on World Evangelization, sponsored by the Billy Graham Evangelistic Association. The Lausanne Congress gathered close to 2,500 participants from around the world for study and discussion of the church's evangelistic and missionary mandate.

Winter was on the program to deliver a plenary address on the fifth day of the congress. Still working on his presentation, he shared with the SIIS students the groundbreaking challenge he was going to deliver at Lausanne. Bruce Graham, an engineering student, recalls Winter, a fellow engineer, asking him to help draw up pie charts to illustrate the present state of the world in terms of evangelization. According to Graham, the impact of looking at those pie charts, clearly displaying the facts regarding unreached people groups, "captured the SIIS students for life."[14]

---

12 Winter, interview.

13 Graham, interview.

14 Graham, "Personal Recollections."

It is not an overstatement to say that Winter's address at Lausanne '74 so radically altered the focus and strategy of global mission efforts that a line of demarcation can be drawn between pre-Lausanne '74 understanding and efforts and post-Lausanne '74 understanding and efforts. In a day when so much contemporary thought asserted that the day of the missionary is over, the church is planted in every country of the world, and the remaining non-Christians in the world can be reached by the ongoing evangelism of the national church, Winter's address came as a bombshell.[15]

Building on McGavran's missiology, Winter introduced the concept of unreached people groups, referring to them as "hidden people groups." The term "unreached people groups" came a few years later. Using examples from India and Indonesia, Winter demonstrated how the existing church within each of those countries was not and could not evangelize all of their fellow countrymen without crossing significant barriers of both language and culture—a truly *missionary* task. He supported his research biblically, noting that when Scripture speaks of "nations," it is usually referring to cultural-linguistic ethnic groups, not geopolitical countries.

Winter then drove the point home, asserting that

> cross-cultural evangelism must still be the highest priority. Far from being a task that is now out-of-date, the shattering truth is that at least four out of five non-Christians in the world today are beyond the reach of any Christian's E-1 (same culture) evangelism.[16]

Winter called attention to the huge Muslim and Hindu spheres as examples of millions of non-Christians lacking any gospel witness within their language and culture. "Why is this fact not more widely known?" Winter asked. "I'm afraid that all our exultation about the fact that every *country* of the world has been penetrated has allowed many to suppose that every *culture* has by now been penetrated."[17] Winter called this "people blindness."

Winter's controversial address at Lausanne '74 caused quite a stir. As the implications of his challenge sank in over the next few years, they prompted widespread discussion and eventual changes in mission goals and strategies. In an interview with *Evangelical Missions Quarterly*, the leaders of the two largest evangelical missions associations—Wade Coggins of the EFMA[18]

---

15 The text of this address, "The New Macedonia: A Revolutionary New Era in Mission Begins," can be found in *Perspectives on the World Christian Movement: A Reader*, 4th ed., 347–60.

16 Winter, "New Macedonia," 353.

17 Winter, 353.

18 The Evangelical Fellowship of Mission Agencies (EFMA) was renamed The Mission Exchange in 2007. It joined with the IFMA in 2012 to become Missio Nexus.

and Edwin (Jack) Frizen Jr. of the IFMA[19]—pointed back to the significance of this historic crossroads.

The interviewer asked, "If you could pick out only one thing, what would be the most significant thing that has happened in world missions since 1964?" Both selected "the new way of viewing the unfinished task" and the focus on unreached people groups, attesting that these had influenced and invigorated mission agencies, churches, missionaries, and training schools.[20]

Through his writing and speaking over the next months and years, Winter continued to call attention to the unfinished task of world evangelization, advocating for efforts to reach the unreached people groups. Through statistics, charts, and graphs he visually portrayed the grossly disparate distribution of the world's missionary force.

In September 1976 Winter addressed a joint conference of mission executives and mission professors. Using carefully drafted graphical charts drawn precisely to scale, Winter helped his audience visualize the extent of the remaining task (see appendix A). The size of believing communities within Muslim peoples, whether in Asia or Africa, was so small that it could not even be shown graphically on the chart! And the size of the missionary force working among the vast Muslim sphere was graphically illustrated as barely more than a dot on the page.

Winter sought to shock his esteemed audience into action with comments like these:

> It is not difficult to understand how it may be claimed that the average missionary today is no more likely to be fulfilling a ministry directly among non-Christians than are his supporters back home. … As a result, the front-line evangelical missionary today may not be as extinct as the dodo, but is far less visible than the general practitioner in medicine. It is eminently fair to say that most present-day missionaries are specialists working in tasks other than cross-cultural evangelism among totally non-Christian people. …
>
> This may be the welcome "new day" in relation to national churches, but it represents a massive, mainly tragic swerving away from the straightforward requirements of the unfulfilled task in regard to the 2.8 billion non-Christians.[21]

---

19 The Interdenominational Foreign Mission Association (IFMA) was renamed CrossGlobal Link in 2007. It joined with the EFMA in 2012 to become Misso Nexus.

20 Merrill, "It's Our 20th Birthday."

21 Winter, "Grounds for a New Thrust," 479–80.

At this same mission leaders' meeting, Winter proposed the establishment of a major mission center that would focus attention on the Chinese, Hindu, and Muslim blocks of unreached peoples. The emergence of the U.S. Center for World Mission was on the horizon.

In the Gap

The students of the first *Summer Institute of International Studies*, held at Wheaton College in 1974, returned home to share enthusiastically with their churches, families, and friends, seeking to mobilize them also to mission among unreached peoples. Two of those students, Bruce and Christy Graham, were to play a large role in the future development of SIIS.

Upon completion of a master's degree from the Massachusetts Institute in Technology in aeronautics and astronautics, Bruce decided to study for a year at Gordon-Conwell Theological Seminary before seeking employment. It just so happened that Ralph Winter was teaching as a visiting professor that year. On one of Bruce's graded papers, Winter wrote a note asking him to consider coming to that first SIIS—a decision that would change the trajectory of their lives.

Bruce and Christy returned to Park Street Church in Boston and started a missions fellowship, where they shared many of the concepts they had learned in SIIS. The following summer they returned to attend the second SIIS, mobilizing twenty-two students to join them. They piled in a caravan of cars to travel from Boston to Wheaton, stopping en route to visit the famous "Haystack Prayer Meeting" monument in Williamstown, Massachusetts. This was where the first small group of American students, in 1806, consecrated themselves to foreign missions, leading to an active recruitment of students into missionary service and the establishment of the first-ever American mission society.[22] The sense that another Student Volunteer Movement might be igniting, and that they were part of it, powerfully captured and motivated the SIIS students.

Bruce and Christy Graham, circa 1978.

---

22 Wallstrom, *Creation of a Student Movement*, 24–29.

The alumni out of these earlier classes felt like we were becoming part of a student movement for missions after earlier student mission movements. This was not a course or a program for us, but a cause to live for. Many alumni stayed connected and recruited others into the movement. We just wanted to be together and work together toward a world-size cause that had eternal significance.[23]

The 1975 SIIS, held again at Wheaton College, was similar to the first, however a few extra weeks were added at the end so that returning alumni could obtain further scholastic credit. Charlie Mellis, who was the former president of Mission Aviation Fellowship and on the SIIS board of directors, coordinated the class.

The second SIIS course concluded with a field trip to Guatemala. Ralph and Roberta Winter, along with their four daughters, joined the students, returning to the country they had served as missionaries. They traveled in a caravan of seven cars driving nonstop from Chicago to Guatemala. Winter recalls that twice they were lost, and the caravan became separated in the huge metropolis of Mexico City. Only by a miracle (in the days before GPS and mobile phones) did they ever find each other again! In Guatemala they visited several mission stations during the day and gathered in the evening to learn from and critique both the good and the bad of the mission-station strategies.[24]

A challenge for the students was how to maintain this mission movement between summer courses. They decided to organize Student Conferences on World Evangelization (SCOWE) and begin study groups on various campuses to mobilize others and nurture their own mission commitment. Ralph and Roberta's daughter, Rebecca, mobilized her friends to hold a SCOWE at Caltech every year, drawing over eight hundred students from southern California universities in the first year. All of this was modeled after the historic Student Volunteer Movement. The SCOWE, an outflow of SIIS, became a very influential tool of recruitment of students into frontier missions.[25]

One of the participants in the 1975 SIIS class was David Bryant, now known internationally for promoting concerts of prayer, for serving as chairman of America's National Prayer Committee, and through the many books he has authored. In 1974, Bryant noticed Winter's article in *Christianity Today* questioning whether another Student Volunteer

---

23 Graham, interview.

24 Winter, interview.

25 Rebecca Winter Lewis, October 31, 2016, email to author.

Robyn (L) and David (R) Bryant promoting SIIS at a mission booth.

Movement might be in the making and was filled with wonder that maybe God would do it again. Bryant also noticed that the author, Ralph Winter, was a professor at the Fuller School of World Mission (SWM). He was unaware that such a school existed. By the fall of that year, he had moved from his pastorate in Ohio to Pasadena to enroll in Fuller. One of the first things he wanted to do was meet Professor Winter. As he stood knocking on the door of Winter's office, he was confronted by a sign on the door: "God cannot lead you on the basis of facts you do not know." That sign and Winter's influence led to his long-term involvement with SIIS and what would later become the Perspectives course.[26]

After Bryant completed a master's degree in missiology at Fuller SWM, he raised support and joined the staff of SIIS in 1975 as national coordinator of the program. In this capacity he developed curriculum, recruited students from coast to coast, designed field trips, and wrote a songbook and an inductive Bible study series with a world missions focus. SIIS opened an official office in Pasadena in the fall of 1975. In January of 1976, Bryant conducted a one-month intensive course on the campus of Erskine College, a Christian college in Due West, South Carolina. Around forty enrolled in that class, coming from all over the nation. The summer of 1976 saw SIIS back on the Wheaton College campus, with Bryant coordinating a class of around eighty, all students in-residence, as previously.

---

26 Bryant, "Personal Recollections."

SIIS class in 1976 at Wheaton College.

Bryant taught the students about "World Christian discipleship," referring to "what it means to live a life that is fully wrapped around Christ and his global cause on every level of practical daily discipleship."[27] He popularized the term "World Christian" through his highly influential book, *In the Gap: What It Means to Be a World Christian*, published in 1979. *In the Gap* was promoted at Urbana '79 and became a well-read book among young people for the next twenty years.

For the 1976 SIIS class, Bryant spent much time negotiating with the leaders of the major student organizations to secure their support and to recruit from among their ranks. The well-attended 1976 course provided specialized modules for those from organizations such as InterVarsity, Navigators, and Campus Crusade for Christ to be able to study and share together. Using Chicago as a cross-cultural laboratory, research teams were sent into a variety of ethnic neighborhoods to spend full days interpreting the cultures and then reporting back to the class what they discovered. The practical application intensified the learning for the SIIS students.

But then a division arose. During the summer of 1976, the SIIS board came to a disagreement over the nature of the course. Some wanted to see it continue to expand in order to mobilize a new wave of World Christians, while others wanted to focus on the academic nature of the class, keeping it small to refine the pedagogy. It was at this point that David Bryant resigned from SIIS, taking a position with InterVarsity Christian Fellowship, where for the next twelve years he continued mobilizing students into World Christian discipleship. Bryant credits Fuller's School of World Mission and SIIS for having had a profound influence on his life and ministry.

---

27 David Bryant, interview by author, August 15, 2005, email.

Above everything else, SWM, SIIS, and Perspectives have each provided the same fundamental overhaul of my whole worldview, and they have done so in two major directions: (1) a massively enlarged Christology; and (2) an abounding, unrelenting hope about the task before us and its ultimate outcome among the nations.[28]

Laying Foundation Stones

Up until this time the SIIS courses did not have a codified curriculum. The four-section structure was in place from the beginning, adopted from the structure of the Fuller School of World Mission. The initial academic core courses of the Fuller SWM that the Perspectives course was patterned after were (1) biblical theology of mission; (2) history of the advance of the world Christian movement; (3) cultural anthropology; and (4) church-growth strategy. The SIIS curriculum consisted of various readings—often photocopied—from multiple sources. The Lausanne Occasional Papers, which came out after the 1974 Congress, provided an abundant resource on current mission issues.

With rising student interest in missions, Moody Bible Institute asked Peter Wagner to develop a curriculum for an introductory missions course in their extension program. Wagner, in turn, asked Arthur Glasser to write the theological dimension of the curriculum and Ralph Winter to write the historical dimension, while he set about writing on the strategic dimension of missions. Paul Hiebert was chosen to write the cultural and anthropological dimension.[29] These four missiologists worked together to produce a highly relevant, insightful text for the day: *Crucial Dimensions in World Evangelization*, published in 1976. Contributing authors to the text were well-known mission professionals Donald McGavran, Alan R. Tippett, Roger Greenway, Edward Murphy, Warren Webster, J. Robertson McQuilkin, and Ralph R. Covell. For some reason, Moody Bible Institute never used the curriculum. However, it became a foundational text for the next several years for the *Institute of International Studies*. It was, in fact, in structure and format, a forerunner to *Perspectives on the World Christian Movement: A Reader*.

Another critical foundation stone was laid in 1976. Ralph Winter was increasingly burdened that there needed to be a world missions center focused on unreached people groups. Momentum was picking up in terms of awareness and interest in the unfinished task of world evangelization, but so much more needed to be done to push it front and center in the

---

28 David Bryant, from an email reflection written at the author's request, September 4, 2008.
29 Winter, "Personal Recollections."

thinking of mission agencies and the church. A massive amount of research was needed to uncover who are and where are the unreached people groups, develop strategies concerning the best way to reach them, and create tools to educate and mobilize the church. It would also provide a nonproprietary place where a mosaic of agencies and organizations could network and collaborate toward a single purpose. For months Winter struggled over a decision of whether to resign from Fuller and focus on starting such a center.

> "I must admit," he told others, "that this project may very well fail. But I am overwhelmingly convinced that God wants someone to try it. No one else seems willing, so I guess I'll have to."[30]

Such a sentiment was characteristic of Winter. He had been known over the years for saying, "Do not do things others can do; do things others cannot or will not do."

Ralph and Roberta Winter on the campus of the U.S. Center for World Mission.

Letting go of financial security and a prestigious career, Ralph and Roberta Winter launched out on the riskiest venture of their lifetime, confident in faith that God was calling them. The U.S. Center for World Mission (USCWM) was formally founded in November of 1976. Most of the original staff were SIIS alumni. The worldview and lives of the SIIS students had been dramatically changed; they felt strongly that they were part of a new movement of God

Outdoor signage for USCWM
1605 Elizabeth Street, Pasadena, California.

---

30 Roberta H. Winter, *I Will Do a New Thing*, 32.

stirring up the church to finish the task of world evangelization. Winter had taught them to work for a cause rather than a career. It was a natural next step to follow their passion to Pasadena to staff this exciting new world mission center.

The Living God Is a Missionary God

In a year of laying critical foundations, 1976 yielded yet another advance in the development of the Perspectives course. Once again it came about through the Urbana student missionary conference.

Student interest in missions was continuing to swell, evidenced by the increased attendance and response at Urbana '76. When, on the fourth night of the convention, Billy Graham once again issued his customary call for students to commit themselves to God and his global purposes, several thousand stood. Fifty percent of the students signed mission-commitment cards.[31]

Summer mission projects for college students were fueling missionary interest, and increased ease of travel made it possible. The mission boards were also beginning to change their perception of students.

> What is interesting is that no one adopted a deliberate plan to change the student mood toward missions. ... Sociologists are still trying to figure out what happened to the widely-heralded youth rebellion, the youth culture of the late '60s and early '70s.
>
> This sudden turnaround should perhaps tell us ... that after all there is a Lord of the harvest who sends out his workers. We have at times preached this without the faintest hope that the Lord of the harvest would indeed change things so drastically that rebellious kids would be applying for missionary service.[32]

Once again Ralph and Roberta Winter designed a follow-up curriculum for Urbana students wanting to pursue a mission interest. They came to Urbana to introduce their new curriculum, *Understanding World Evangelization* (UWE). Developed by the same four missiologists who produced the *Crucial Dimensions* text, it consisted of a study guide tied to four books, along with a cassette-tape introduction.[33] Credit was available through Westmont College.

---

31 Howard, "What Happened at Urbana."

32 Reapsome, "Unexpected Turnaround."

33 The four study texts were *Crucial Dimensions in World Evangelization*; *The Twenty-Five Unbelievable Years: 1945–1969*, by Ralph D. Winter; *Frontiers in Missionary Strategy*, by C. Peter Wagner; and *Stop the World, I Want to Get On*, also by Wagner.

John R. W. Stott, the famous British evangelical Bible expositor, was scheduled to deliver the opening Bible lecture at Urbana '76. Sitting in the large assembly hall was a student with only a mild interest in missions but a profound eagerness to hear Dr. Stott—a student by the name of Steve Hawthorne. He recalls that morning vividly:

> It was about 10:15 on the morning of December 28, 1976, when Stott took the stage. With his grand British accent, Stott announced the title of his address: "The Living God Is a Missionary God." I expected good exposition, but I did not expect an integrated focal point. Stott presented the entire Bible as a single escalating story of God accomplishing his purpose among all the peoples of the earth. The first chapter of the Perspectives *Reader* is the transcript of that very address by Stott.[34]

Three days later, Hawthorne attended an Urbana seminar taught by Ralph and Roberta Winter. The classroom was packed with students. When Dr. Winter entered wearing his trademark bowtie, Hawthorne, unimpressed, wanted to exit. But he was sitting on the front row and there was no way out. Armed with graphs and statistics, Winter spoke on the concept of actually completing the Great Commission. Hawthorne recalls that what caught his attention the most was the "doughnut chart," contrasting where the gospel had gone and had yet to go, and highlighting the gross imbalance of missionary deployment at that time (see appendix A). At the end of the seminar, Winter excitedly announced the *Understanding World Evangelization* correspondence course.

Steve Hawthorne returned from Urbana and told his fiancée Barbara that he thought "missions" might be in their future. That came as a shock to Barbara! Hawthorne had not been antagonistic toward missions; he just felt it was for other believers.

Steve and Barbara Hawthorne in the early years.

Hawthorne completed the UWE correspondence course in the spring of 1977. His mission understanding and commitment began to grow, at variance with the California Christian youth culture

---

34 Steven C. Hawthorne, interview by author, June 11, 2005, tape recording.

of which he was a part. Through his local church, Hawthorne set about educating and mobilizing his contemporaries with what he was learning.

At the conclusion of the school year in 1978, Hawthorne—eager to implement what he was learning—led a team of twelve on a three-month outreach to Thailand. When it became painfully clear that the sponsoring church leadership had different goals than Hawthorne, there came a parting of ways. That point of difficulty became a step forward in Hawthorne's work in mission education. He recalls,

> Upon leaving the church office for the last time, one of the leaders approached me and asked, "Steve, what are you going to do?"
>
> I responded, "I think I'm going to go to Pasadena and enroll in the Fuller School of World Mission." And then I paused and for some reason I blurted out, "I'm going to write a book. Yes, I see it as a big book that will change how people think of the world."
>
> I don't know where that came from. It didn't make any sense at all. I didn't have any ambitions to write a book. Something just came over me.[35]

On December 31, 1978, Hawthorne and his young bride Barbara moved onto the campus of the U.S. Center for World Mission. A mere two years after being transformed by Stott's bold declaration that "the living God is a missionary God" and Winter's "doughnut charts," Hawthorne was embarking upon what would become a defining life calling.

Decline, Reorganization, and Expansion

Even though many of the SIIS alumni, the key to new student recruitment, were now living and working in Pasadena at the USCWM, the SIIS board wanted to continue to hold the *Summer Institute of International Studies* at Wheaton College. Due to disagreement on the board over the direction SIIS should take, enrollment plummeted and the 1977 class had to be cancelled. A second class in Boulder, Colorado, enrolled only fifteen students. Charlie Mellis, the administrator of SIIS at the time, wanted to dissolve the course.

Winter intervened, convincing the board to transfer it to the Center staff at Pasadena. The U.S. Center would take all the financial responsibility for the course. Bruce and Christy Graham assumed administrative oversight. Looking back, Winter reflects that the failure of the 1977 classes was actually a good thing, for it allowed them to relieve a divided board of responsibility and bring SIIS under the auspices of the USCWM.[36]

---

35 Hawthorne, interview.
36 Winter, interview.

A major change came in 1979, when the course was expanded to a full semester—conducted in the fall, spring, and summer—granting sixteen credit hours. Consequently, *Summer* was dropped out of the name; it was now called the *Institute of International Studies* (IIS). The frontier mission vision had matured to such a level that now four fully developed courses could be offered.

The format for the semester-long IIS course was the same as it had been for the SIIS courses at Wheaton. The students lived in residence and the instructors would spend an entire week with the students. Hawthorne fondly recalls how the teachers didn't simply teach the material; they also poured out their hearts, along with their fascinating life stories. Some of the instructors during that time were Donald A. McGavran, J. Christy Wilson Jr., Elisabeth Elliot, Harvie M. Conn, David J. Hesselgrave, Don M. McCurry Jr., Sam Wilson of the Zwemer Institute, and many other respected leaders in the mission world.[37] Bruce and Christy Graham led IIS alumni on short-term outreaches to India, solidifying commitment to world mission. Many of those early students became active in career missions in various parts of the world.[38] The impact of the IIS course and the motivation of the alumni to recruit their friends was so potent that by the end of 1979 the cumulative total of students surpassed five hundred, even though less than a dozen classes were conducted over that six-year period.

The Remarkable Penn State Class

Realizing that only a handful of students would ever be able to come to Pasadena to study, the USCWM staff began to dream of taking IIS to students via extension classes. Enrolled in a 1978 Intensive IIS class were Jay and Olgy Gary, preparing to join the USCWM staff. When they returned to the East Coast to raise ministry support, they ran into Phil Hardin, Campus Crusade staff member at Pennsylvania State University. That visit turned out to be divinely orchestrated for the future of the Perspectives movement. Jay Gary recounts the progression of events.

> We shared with Phil how reaching hidden peoples was key to fulfilling the Great Commission, and how students needed to be awakened to this challenge. He was open to this vision and invited us to bring a SCOWE, a Student Conference on World Evangelization, to his beach project the following summer of 1979. ...
>
> That band of Campus Crusade for Christ students attending the SCOWE in Lake Tahoe was blown away by what

---

37 Hawthorne, interview.
38 Graham, interview.

they learned. Phil then invited me to come back that coming winter to do a SCOWE for Penn State students. At that time, Penn State had the largest concentration of Christian students active in campus ministries out of all the universities in the U.S. I remember telling Phil, "We will come, but only if you let us run an IIS Extension course following the conference." Phil agreed.

During that fall leading up to the conference, I spent time at Penn State, sharing the story of the Student Volunteer Movement, how it began with 100 students banding together to fulfill the Great Commission. It too had started at a conference. I began to ask others, "Could God be raising up a Penn State 100?" The SCOWE conference at Penn State drew some 450 students. Greg Livingstone, Ralph Winter, and I shared the platform. By the end of the first evening, two students had registered for the course.

I remember telling Fran Patt, the conference coordinator, "Those two are Caleb and Joshua." By the end of the conference, sixty-five students had signed up. Sensing that God was still at work, I delayed my trip back to Los Angeles. I set up camp and by week's end we reached our prayer goal of 100 students registered for that Spring term, starting in less than 4 weeks. I returned to Pasadena, took a leave from my job as director of personnel at the Center, and Olgy and I drove back to Penn State—to lead the first "Perspectives" extension class.[39]

Once again, Winter and IIS intersected with a movement of God already in progress among American students. Hundreds were coming to Christ each year on the Penn State campus through the active witness of other students.

Fran Patt, who later opened the first USCWM regional office, was a recent Penn State graduate when approached by Phil Hardin about coordinating the Student Conference of World Evangelization (SCOWE) on the Penn State campus. Patt worked with Jay Gary to set up the SCOWE the first week of February, 1980. Gary, however, never mentioned to Patt that the SCOWE was intended to be a forerunner to a follow-up semester-long course.[40]

Speaking at the conference, Ralph Winter laid out the challenge of unreached people groups. Greg Livingstone, then a director of North Africa Mission, laid out the challenge of North Africa—once the heartland of Christianity, now almost completely devoid of Christians. Livingstone really captured the imagination of the students, stirring their passions.

---

39 Gary, "Perspectives Marks 30th Anniversary."
40 Fran Patt, interview by author, August 7, 2005, transcript.

One of the students called out to Livingstone, "What's happening in Libya?" At the time, Libya was considered one of the most difficult countries to get into in the world. Livingstone replied,

> We don't have anybody in Libya. The last missionaries who were there were arrested and sentenced to eight years in prison. We are, however, looking for four men to go to Libya to see if they can get in and stay in.[41]

Such a challenge would not slip by unnoticed. Four Penn State students subsequently volunteered to go to Libya: Al Stahl, Harry Gray, Greg Fritz, and Bob Sjogren. Fran Patt recollects, "I remember sitting down specifically with Stahl, Sjogren, and Fritz to challenge them to attend the SCOWE, telling them that it would change their lives."[42] It certainly did.

Within a week after the SCOWE, Jay Gary gave another project to Fran Patt: Prepare to run a semester-long follow-up course—beginning in two weeks! Patt was listed as co-coordinator with Gary for the IIS course, even though he had never heard of it before.

The first IIS class meeting began unusually, Patt recalls. A blizzard arose the day that Ralph Winter was flying in to speak, leaving him stuck in Pittsburg due to the snow. The airline told Winter that there was no way he was going to get to Penn State that night. Back at the university, they began to pray. The blizzard stopped for about one hour—just enough time to get Winter's small commuter plane airborne. As the plane landed, the snow began in earnest, shutting down the airport.

When Winter arrived to teach, he shared his adventure with the students, who had been praying all day. "You could have heard a pin drop," Patt remembers, "as the students realized God's intervention in answer to their prayers. Dr. Winter was powerful that night. He spoke for two hours, and the students stayed another hour-and-a-half asking him questions."[43]

The Penn State IIS class met for ninety minutes twice a week, on Tuesdays and Thursdays. On one of those days, a guest instructor taught the lesson; on the other day, Gary reviewed the lesson and the students met for discussion in small groups. They used the *Understanding World Evangelization* curriculum and added David Bryant's new book, *In the Gap*. By this time the course consisted of twenty lessons. Seventy-seven excited students were enrolled in this first-ever IIS extension class. A student intern named Bob Sjogren ran errands for the class. In addition to Winter, some

---

41 Bob Sjogren, interview by author, August 5, 2005, transcript.
42 Patt, interview.
43 Patt.

First IIS extension class at Penn State in 1980.

of the visiting professors for the Penn State class were Roberta Winter, Greg Livingstone, Walter Hannum, George Patterson, and William Miller.[44]

The four men who had volunteered to go to Libya were in the IIS class. That summer they went for training at the Zwemer Institute for Muslim Studies on the USCWM campus before going on to Libya. They called themselves the "Caleb Project," and, like the historic Student Volunteer Movement, they developed a declaration of commitment to be signed by their student support team. This pledge became known as the "Caleb Declaration."

In September of 1980 the Caleb Project team headed to Libya with a plan to stay one year. The strong-arm dictator, Colonel Moammar al-Qadhafi (Gadhafi), was ruling the country. Even though Americans were quite unwelcome in Libya, the team was full of faith that God would make a way. Through a series of miracles, they were issued a government invitation into the country to teach English.[45]

Edinburgh 1980, a global missionary consultation focused exclusively on frontier mission, occurred only months after the conclusion of the Penn State IIS. Caleb Project influenced the student track of this consultation. In fact, Sjogren left Malta, where he was waiting for entrance into Libya,

---

44 Jay Gary, interview by author, June 26, 2005, email.
45 Caleb Project, "Libya To Libya."

to go up to Edinburgh, Scotland, to promote Caleb Project.[46] The students at this International Student Consultation on Frontier Mission, many from Penn State, officially composed the "Caleb Declaration" to mobilize their generation. By signing it, students committed their lives to make God's purpose their purpose in life. It reads,

> By the grace of God and for his glory, I commit my entire life to obeying his commission of Matthew 28, wherever and however he leads me, giving priority to the peoples currently beyond the reach of the gospel. I will also endeavor to pass this vision on to others.[47]

Over the years, thousands signed the Caleb Declaration.

Greg Fritz returned from Libya with a passion to mobilize his generation to reach those with no access to the gospel. He formalized Caleb Project as a mission mobilization organization, conducting research and creating resources to aid and challenge the church in reaching the unreached. Caleb Project became a widely respected organization as it fulfilled a major role in mission mobilization. In July of 2006, Caleb Project merged with ACMC (Advancing Churches in Mission Commitment). Later many of the ministries of both organizations were absorbed by Pioneers, a mission agency focused upon the unreached.

Bob Sjogren left Libya for a tour around the world in order, as he recalled, to have the peoples of the world in his heart, not just in his head. Greg Livingstone asked him to join North Africa Mission (NAM) for the purpose of recruiting many more students to the mission. The mission board, however, did not feel they could handle the large number of new candidates that Livingstone and Sjogren were recruiting, so Livingstone launched a new agency that was focused specifically on Muslims and had a team approach. We know that agency today as Frontiers.[48]

Sjogren eventually went on to develop his own mission mobilization and teaching ministry, which distills many of the Perspectives concepts. His teaching has shifted paradigms in churches across America in calling Christians to wrap their lives around the purposes of God in world evangelization. He states, "The principles taught in Perspectives of 'blessed to be a blessing' and the understanding that the Abrahamic Covenant is the Great Commission in the Old Testament were foundational to me."[49]

---

46 Sjogren, interview.
47 Caleb Project, "Caleb Declaration."
48 Sjogren, interview.
49 Sjogren.

Jay Gary later worked with Campus Crusade for Christ, helping them launch the Worldwide Student Network, which partnered US campuses with universities in other parts of the world. Through Gary's influence, many of the concepts of IIS were mainstreamed into that movement, including the history of the Student Volunteer Movement, the focus on unreached peoples, and developing campus "sending" structures.[50]

Fran Patt joined the staff of the U.S. Center for World Mission, returning to Pennsylvania to open the first regional office of the USCWM. His first staff members, including his wife Sue, were also out of the Penn State class.[51]

All these students from the Penn State 1980 IIS class went on to influence and mobilize other individuals, who in turn became key church and mission leaders with substantial ministries focused on the unfinished task of world evangelization. This mobilization dynamic has been a hallmark of the Perspectives course from the beginning.

Jay Gary, who planned and coordinated the first IIS extension class.

Fran & Sue Patt are some of the longest-serving members of Frontier Ventures (formerly USCWM).

A Published Text at Last

In preparing for the 1980 Penn State class, the USCWM staff realized that the IIS curriculum needed to be revised into a format more suitable for an extension class. Bruce Graham, director of IIS in Pasadena, began the process through organizing curriculum ideas and researching content. When he and Christy felt led to move to India, Graham recruited Steve Hawthorne to develop curriculum that could be presented as one course in multiple regions. By now it was deemed more strategic to condense the course back down to a single semester to enable more students to access the course. It still covered all four components, but in a less extensive way.

---

50 Gary, interview.
51 Patt, interview.

Hawthorne was living on the USCWM campus serving in a volunteer capacity for IIS while studying at Fuller. It was a rich time for USCWM personnel, learning from and interacting with great missionary teachers like J. Christy Wilson, Jr., Harvie M. Conn, Lloyd Kwast, Charles Kraft, Paul Hiebert, Don Richardson, Phil Elkins, J. Edwin Orr, Larry Poland, J. Robertson McQuilkin, and Donald McGavran—all of whom were instructors in the early IIS classes. The young staff on the USCWM campus had tremendous access to many eminent missiologists, but more importantly, they were regularly exposed to late-breaking reports of what was unfolding in frontier mission situations. Ralph Winter repeatedly offered his analysis and insights.

When the Grahams left for India, Darrell and Linda Dorr (Winters' daughter) took over the administration of the IIS courses in Pasadena. Jay Gary assumed directorship of the total IIS program. The number of courses jumped to seven per year in 1980 and 1981. After the hugely successful Penn State course, Jay Gary attempted two other extension courses, but they did not emulate the success of the 1980 Penn State class. Gary realized that the key to successful extension classes was well-trained coordinators to run them. One successful program was run during that time, however, at a church near Goleta, California, by Rick Love, who later became the international director of Frontiers mission agency.

Jay and Olgy Gary pursued a passion to train IIS alumni to coordinate extension classes all over the country. As a couple, they went back to school so that both of them could earn a master's degree in curriculum development, with the intention of developing a coordinator-training curriculum.[52] In retrospect, the development of trained coordinators was as important to the success of the Perspectives course as the development of curriculum.

Under Gary's leadership, Hawthorne began to design learning objectives and gather articles for the codified text that would become the Perspectives *Reader* and *Study Guide*. By the spring of 1981, Hawthorne was working full-time on curriculum development. Winter sent him out to meet with numerous mission leaders to learn and obtain articles from them. Back at the Center, Hawthorne and Gary would present articles they selected to Winter for his review and approval. The title of the text, *Perspectives on the World Christian Movement*, originated with Gary.

As the curriculum neared completion, Winter directed Hawthorne to enlist well-known missiologists David Hesselgrave, Herbert Kane, Lloyd Kwast, and Donald McGavran to be listed along with Winter, as coeditors. Hawthorne contacted all four of them, and each one responded in like manner. They felt that the text was already well edited, and therefore it would not be appropriate for them to be identified as a coeditor. They

---

52 Gary, interview.

each proposed, however, that they could be listed as a contributing editor. When the curriculum team reported this back to Winter, he asked the team which one of them did the most work on the text. Everyone sat silent. Finally someone said, "Steve did the vast majority of the work." Much to Hawthorne's surprise, Winter replied, "You are the coeditor, then."[53] Darrell Dorr and Bruce Graham were associate editors.

In the summer of 1981, a group of influential mission professors met with Winter and the curriculum team on the USCWM campus. The team had assembled the basic structure and articles, and for several hours they presented their work. To their delight, the professors profusely praised the text. Hawthorne recollects, "I remember David Hesselgrave leaning back and saying, 'This is a book we have all been waiting for! Everyone will use it!'"[54]

To ascertain the extent to which the Perspectives text was forward thinking, Winter relates this revealing episode:

> When we were readying the 1981 curriculum to be published, Steve Hawthorne and Jay Gary came to my house seeking my approval on the complete curriculum. I said, "We've got to put in there that the Great Commission is found in the Abrahamic Covenant."
>
> They responded, "Nobody else believes this; we can't put that in there."
>
> We were at an impasse. Then I was asked to speak at the dedication of the Billy Graham Center at Wheaton College. Walter Kaiser was there also. I had recently seen his book on the Old Testament. In it he regularly mentioned "the Promise" referring to the Abrahamic Covenant. I approached him and said, "You know, the Abrahamic Covenant is not only a promise; it is a mandate, a commission."
>
> He said, "Well, you can call it a Great Commission if you want." I was really quite surprised. I told him, "I can't go around saying that. I need someone like you to say that. Do you have that in print?" He replied, "You quote me, and I'll put it in print."
>
> A few days later I received a cassette tape of a chapel talk, which he had given at Trinity Seminary, called "Israel's Missionary Call." We put that address by Kaiser in the Perspectives *Reader*. That was the single most provocative thing in the book in those days. That's what shocked a lot of seminary students, and is what gives people a totally new view of the Bible.[55]

---

53 Hawthorne, interview.
54 Hawthorne.
55 Winter, interview.

The next hurdle was deciding whether they would actually typeset and print the book. The common approach for USCWM materials at the time was to photocopy and spiral-bind the pages. The age of desktop publishing had not yet arrived. Indeed, inputting the text into a computer instead of typing it on a typewriter was a major invention at the time! The typeset machine had the ability to convert the original documents to typeset. Unfortunately, there were many typos in the original manuscripts, which meant that they were reproduced in the typeset copy.

A team of sixteen people with X-Acto knives worked day and night correcting typos. Moreover, the galleys would come to them on large rolls; they had to cut and paste the galleys into book-size format. The goal was to have the text ready for release in December at Urbana '81. Many days stretched into evenings and then into all-night "paste-up parties," which even Ralph Winter joined. A careful inspection of the first edition will reveal that some pages are a little crooked or a letter is cut off here and there because of a slip of the X-Acto knife![56]

Through the long and tedious labor of the entire team the deadline was met, and the *Perspectives Reader* and *Study Guide* were introduced at Urbana '81. With the introduction of the new textbook, the course ceased to be called *Institute of International Studies* and became *Perspectives on the World Christian Movement*.

Given the comprehensive and outstanding quality of the text, it is amazing that it was produced with so few financial resources. The publication of the *Perspectives Reader* and *Study Guide* was financed by IIS tuition. The personnel working on the project all raised their own support. Hawthorne worked in a volunteer capacity, with his wife Barbara working to supply the family income during the project. For all involved, it was truly a labor of love and passion for God's purposes to be realized through the evangelization of all peoples.

The stage was now set for the Perspectives course and textbook to expand its reach, mobilizing and educating increasing numbers of students for world evangelization. Laying the foundations of the course, pursuing vision in the face of obstacles, calling out as a seemingly lonely voice in the wilderness to recognize and do something about the overlooked and unreached people groups of the world had been a challenging eight years.

---

56 Winter.

We were not simply going upstream. The Holy Spirit produced a change, which affected us. We didn't effect the change; we were affected by that change, and we simply responded to it.[57]

As the Perspectives course responded to the move of the Holy Spirit among the student generation in the latter half of the 1970s, so both the U.S. Center for World Mission and Perspectives would continue to respond to and catalyze change in mission thinking and involvement through the remainder of the century and beyond.

A weeklong IIS January 1982 immediately following Urbana '81. Instructors on front row L–R: unidentified man; David Bryant; Steve and Barb Hawthorne; Robert Douglas; Darrell Dorr; Phil Elkins; Olgy and Jay Gary.

---

57 Winter.

3

Developing Trends in World Missions 1980–2000

I was introduced to the *Perspectives on the World Christian Movement* course in 1989 in Austin, Texas. What amazed me was how different missions was than what I had been exposed to as a child. My parents were always interested in missions, so we attended all the mission functions at church. Well, to be honest, we were at church whenever the doors were open.

I well remember the Sunday nights when a missionary family was in town. It was always the same. They dressed in the native costume of their country, they prayed in the native tongue, they showed their interminably long slide show, and they seemed completely out of touch with American society. Just one look at their out-of-date hairstyles told you that. I was sure that missions was somehow important, but it sure was not for me. I was part of the "hip" generation; and missions was definitely not hip!

As I grew older, my passion for the Lord grew, as did my interest in the world. At the age of nineteen, God placed a calling on my heart for global ministry. I didn't know what that would look like. But I told the Lord, "I'll be happy to serve you anywhere in the world; just please don't make me a missionary!" *Missions*, to me, was still quite boring. Later I discovered that many of my peers in the Boomer generation carried this same perception.

I walked into the Austin Perspectives class in 1989 unaware of the rapid changes that were occurring in "the mission industry." I was employed in the high-tech industry, accustomed to market research and strategic business plans—a world away in mindset from missions as I knew it. Working for a start-up company, I certainly did not have time to take the Perspectives course, yet I had seen something unusual in my new church that intrigued me.

On my very first visit to Hope Chapel, they were praying as they sent off a team headed to Turkey. This team was raised up out of the church, trained together, and sent out by the church. As I met the people sitting around me, I discovered that a few of them had visited Turkey; others were taking language classes at the university. Clearly the church members felt an ownership not only of the team, but of a church being planted in that Muslim land. They were well informed, engaged, praying, *ordinary lay people*! I had never seen anything like it.

I inquired how this came to be. I was told that the senior pastor, Dan Davis, had taken a course called *Perspectives on the World Christian Movement*. He became so excited about it that he had all his senior leadership take Perspectives. Subsequently they took a vision journey to Turkey to pray about God's role for their church in this land. They returned, adopting the Turks as an unreached people group whom they felt God was calling the entire congregation to engage. Now, a few years later, a trained team was being released. I had never heard of this Perspectives course before; but whatever it was, I had to check it out!

Sitting in the Perspectives class, I was first shocked to discover that the Abrahamic Covenant was God's Great Commission to Israel in the Old Testament. I had a Master of Divinity degree, and I was never taught that! I was startled to see that the Old Testament was not just about God's dealings with the Jews; God cared for the Gentiles and intended for Israel to display his glory to the rest of the world. The concept that God pours out his blessings upon us so that we might be a blessing to the peoples of the earth was convicting. I was part of the "me" generation of the eighties; so much teaching in the church was about how to *be blessed*, not about how to *be a blessing*. But the teaching that captured me the most was a new understanding of God's purpose that people from every tribe and tongue know and worship him. Due to computer technology, the industry in which I worked, we could now make substantial progress in cataloguing the people groups on earth. We could discover if the church has been planted among them or if anyone has even preached the gospel to them. Missions to me had been about an endless cycle of meeting needs and trying to get the gospel to billions of individuals. The idea that missions could be strategic, that we could approach the missionary task with serious planning in the hope of completing it, was exciting.

Furthermore, I was astounded and highly encouraged to discover that mission agencies and denominations were *intentionally* working with each other. In reality, missionaries on the field had a long history of working together, but the new level of strategic networking and cooperation by agencies and denominations was refreshing. Suddenly missions no longer seemed boring, but exciting. And the mission presenters, I might add, no longer seemed strange and "out of touch." *I* had changed, as I understood more about missions; but *missions* had certainly changed since the 1960s!

Paradigm Shifts

In addition to highlighting the growing change in missions, the Perspectives course *fostered* change. Perspectives reflected some major missiological paradigm shifts, popularizing them and sometimes pushing them further. For example, Donald McGavran highlighted the reality of distinct ethnic groups within geopolitical nations and the importance of these groupings to the advance of the gospel. Instead of asking how individuals become Christian, he asked how *peoples* become Christian. He advocated exploring what it takes to see people movements to Christ happen. This was a missiological turning point.

Ralph Winter propagated McGavran's teachings, extrapolating them further. He traced the advance of the Christian movement throughout history, demonstrating that it has occurred via people movements to Christ within cultural basins.

Winter also advocated for the flipside of McGavran's teaching. McGavran taught to look for "bridges of God"—converts from an unreached people group—to see a people movement to Christ begin. Winter asked, "What if there is no bridge of God? How do you reach a people group where there has never been a mission encounter?"

> I said to myself, we have to find out how many groups there are that don't have bridges, which are completely without a witness or church. The whole idea of quantifying the remaining task in terms of peoples that have not yet been penetrated was not yet in McGavran's thinking. His idea was if you do have a bridge, follow it; my idea was if you don't have a bridge, build it.[1]

Winter portrayed the continuity of God's purposes throughout history and how, instead of being in decline as popular thought asserted, the world was being increasingly evangelized. He reflects, "I had been thinking for

1 Winter, interview.

years, Is anything coherently unfolding? I began to realize that there is a story here—an unfolding, increasing influence that can be described."[2]

Combining these two concepts—(1) continuity of God's purposes being fulfilled throughout history through increasing numbers of people groups embracing Christ, and (2) quantifying the number of people groups still lacking a church or movement to Christ—led to the radical idea of *closure*. The idea of completing the Great Commission was not novel; such a call had been issued at various times throughout history. However, the concept that the missionary task can be completed *by establishing a church planting movement among every people group* was fundamentally new.

The closure concept became a mobilization challenge. The idea of closure calls one to think in terms of the *total task*, not just the area in which one has an interest. Yet even Winter noticed evolution in his own thinking in terms of closure. At Lausanne he pictured the large size of the remaining task, postulating that possibly 16,750 cultural-linguistic groups have yet to be penetrated. Later he reevaluated the immensity of the task; it dramatically shrinks when seen in proportion to the vast number of churches in the world. He calculated that in 1980 there were about 162 churches for every unreached people group. "Instead of talking about the unfinished task, I started talking about the finish-able task."[3]

The Perspectives course was founded on these major missiological paradigm shifts:

- missions focused on ethnolinguistic people groups rather than geopolitical countries
- the goal of a church planting movement within every people group
- the continuity of God's purpose being fulfilled down through history
- understanding the missionary task in terms of the total task that can be completed
- mobilization to complete the Great Commission through identifying and engaging the unreached people groups.

Perspectives also raised the bar of expectation for the average Christian. All Christians can be "World Christians," as David Bryant asserted. Every Christian, not just those in "full-time Christian service," has a valuable and strategic role to play in completion of the missionary task.[4]

These key concepts were not being promoted solely through the Perspectives course. They were infused into the Lausanne Movement and

---

2 Winter.
3 Winter.
4 Hawthorne, "History of the Perspectives Course."

were taught in the Fuller School of World Mission. However, Perspectives was unique in that it pulled all these concepts together as a package. Yet neither Winter nor Hawthorne anticipated that the Perspectives course would become so influential, nor that the Perspectives *Reader* would become such a landmark text.

New Strategies

Other trends emerged and matured during the last two decades of the twentieth century, which Perspectives both incorporated and contributed to in their development. The focus on unreached people groups highlighted the need for greater research and new strategies to reach the Hindu, Muslim, Buddhist, and Chinese worlds. This became a major focus of the U.S. Center for World Mission. The Perspectives course, as early as the first edition, educated churches and new missionaries concerning the need to discover new strategies if we are going to be successful in the huge spheres of the major non-Christian religions.

In the 1970s the role of pioneer church planting had dwindled on the mission field, as the vast majority of missionaries were serving in already reached areas where the church was established. The USCWM and the Perspectives course emphasized the urgency of training missionaries to be pioneer church planters. With the increased emphasis on the unreached, seminaries and missionary training schools gradually began to add church planting courses to their curricula.[5]

The red-hot controversy of evangelism versus social action began to subside somewhat in the latter part of the century. While evangelism was still considered primary among most evangelicals, the work of relief, community development, and sustainable microenterprise gained a new respectability. Mission agencies began to view both elements as part of taking the whole gospel to the whole world. Once again, from the first edition of the Perspectives text in 1981 these developing trends were highlighted and became a means of educating both prospective missionaries and the church at large.

At the beginning of the 1980s, the utilization of businessmen and businesswomen as missionaries was an unexplored strategy. Apart from those serving in medicine and education, evangelicals generally expected a missionary to have a theological degree and pastoral experience. A 1984 article on mission trends published in *Evangelical Missions Quarterly* mentions early excitement about the "new" role of tentmakers, but also adds that it does not yet seem to have generated enough interest to be a trend.[6] Yet as early as 1981, the Perspectives text was advocating for business missionaries. Today, of

5 Merrill, "It's Our 20th Birthday."
6 Merrill, "It's Our 20th Birthday."

course, a person with a degree in just about any area can find a place to serve using their skills on the mission field, and Christians employed overseas are also being encouraged to serve intentionally in a mission capacity.

Activisim

Changing technological and sociological trends in America also greatly impacted the perception and function of missions. The expanding ease of global travel and communication lit the fuse of the short-term mission boom. The collapse of the Soviet Union and consequent freedom for citizens of the Eastern European nations added fuel to the fire. First university ministries and then churches began to regularly send out short-term mission teams. Such exposure and experience fueled interest in continued mission involvement on the local level. Mission outreach moved from a back-page, small-print announcement to a front-and-center emphasis in many churches.

The explosion of short-term mission trips may have begun in the student world, but it could not be contained there. The huge American demographic of Baby Boomers was entering middle-age. As the former activists of the 1960s, they had not given up their spirit of activism and desire to make a difference in the world. They were not content simply to write checks to support missionaries, as their parents had done; they wanted active involvement. Through their influence and leadership, churches began to assume a greater amount of involvement and decision-making concerning the missionaries they supported. Interestingly, a major organ for educating church pastors and mission committees, ACMC (Association of Church Mission Committees),[7] arose in 1974, the same year as SIIS, the forerunner of Perspectives. Not surprisingly, Ralph Winter also had a hand in its development.[8]

As interest in and involvement of the local church in missions escalated, the role of a mission pastor arose. A mission pastor was unheard of in my growing-up years. Churches did not "do missions"; mission agencies did. Churches gave money and prayed and occasionally supplied a missionary recruit. That was generally the extent of their involvement. Even as late as 1995, when I began a mission mobilization ministry in Nashville, Tennessee—a city chock-full of churches—I was only aware of two churches in the entire city that staffed a pastor dedicated exclusively (or even primarily) to missions. But that changed rapidly over the next decade.

Increasing numbers of churches and mission agencies seeking to reach the same unreached people group, or a cluster of similar peoples,

---

7 ACMC later changed their name to Advancing Churches in Missions Commitment.
8 Winter, interview.

highlighted the need for partnership and collaboration. Phill Butler created a mechanism to meet that need by founding InterDev, a pioneer in multi-agency, multi-denominational networks. This one organizational development facilitated synergistic outcomes beyond anything previously operative. Starting in 1986 with one partnership of eight ministries, by 2002 InterDev was facilitating 157 partnerships of more than three thousand organizations in fifty-five countries.[9] It was a precursor to the explosion of networks yet to come.

Baby Boomers not only pushed their churches into greater active involvement in missions, but they also began to volunteer for the mission field themselves. At the end of the century a significant new movement arose, as those in their forties, fifties, and sixties left their careers and headed to the mission field as a second career. Recognizing this huge potential of mature adults with developed skills, mission agencies partnered with the newly established Finishers Project[10] to help prepare and steer this wave of a new breed of missionary.

Although the Perspectives course encouraged professional excellence in carrying out the missionary task, it set forth the then-radical idea that every Christian can fulfill a strategic role in the completion of the Great Commission. And while the Perspectives course called for renewed honor for mission structures, it also encouraged local church engagement. The Perspectives course, as it expanded into multiple cities, multiple churches, and multiple denominations in the last two decades of the twentieth century, became a prime catalyst of mission awareness, education, and mobilization in North America.

From Mission Field to Mission Force

One of the most significant trends of the late twentieth century, however, did not occur in North America. Practically unnoticed by the American church, the global Christian movement shifted from the north and the west to the south and the east of our globe. An explosion of new believers in Asia and the southern hemisphere, and a corresponding decline of Christian faith in the West, suddenly shifted the bulk of Christianity out of its traditional heartlands.

Along with this enormous growth of Southern Christianity came the emergence of non-Western mission agencies and missionaries. Not only was the church becoming truly global, but the mission of the church was also budding into a truly global enterprise at the close of the century. The development of non-Western mission agencies, along with the renewed

---

9   InterDev is now visionSynergy (www.visionsynergy.net).

10 The Finishers Project evolved into MissionNext (www.missionnext.org).

focus on the frontiers, eased the contentious church/mission controversy that had been raging since the 1960s. As both the non-Western church and the Western missionary shifted their focus to the yet unreached, the tension over competing roles of the missionary and the national pastor began to subside. A greater sense of cooperation and networking developed, not only between the West and the non-West, but between denominations and mission agencies as well.[11]

In terms of mission strategy, however, no development in the latter half of the twentieth century was as significant as the focus on unreached people groups. In a 1984 EMQ article, editor Jim Reapsome revealed how powerfully the concept had caught on within only a short decade.

> No innovation in missionary thinking has so profoundly affected the basic concept of missions since theological education by extension burst on the scene in the 1960's. But in the last decade what might be called the "unreached people groups" strategy has shaken the missions community to the core. ... After the first tentative "baby steps" at Lausanne, this new missions concept soon became a walking youngster, and then a full grown Olympic runner.
>
> There is no sign of diminishing influence. Local churches and young people interested in missionary careers eagerly follow the "unreached peoples" theme. Sending agencies face hard questions from constituents about whether or not they are indeed aiming at unreached peoples. Ralph Winter's "Unreached Peoples of the World" chart became the yardstick by which recruiting, planning and sending are measured.
>
> Mission agencies and missionaries have been forced to look at the world's peoples in a wholly new perspective. This has stimulated an enormous amount of rethinking about basic strategies. Some missions are moving away from the traditional "station" approach to a "people team" approach. Some are subordinating all ministries to that of planting churches within specific cultures. The new approach serves to motivate and mobilize both national churches and new missionaries.
>
> The "unreached people groups" movement has helped to sensitize the church not only to the need of completing the Great Commission, but also to the possibility of doing it.[12]

---

11 Merrill, "It's Our 20th Birthday."
12 Reapsome, "People Groups."

Momentum to Finish the Task

By 1980, the focus on unreached people groups had gained such momentum that two global-level mission convocations were dedicated to the matter. To mark the seventieth anniversary of the historic Edinburgh 1910 Conference (the first global mission congress), the Lausanne Committee for World Evangelization held a world mission congress of invited evangelical leaders in Pattaya, Thailand, in June of 1980. The focus was to build upon the events of Lausanne '74, assess the state of world evangelization, and develop strategies for reaching the unreached peoples of the world. Although the 1980 Pattaya Consultation on World Evangelization Congress ended without any concrete plans of how to do the job, the concept of reaching the world's unreached people groups was furthered among global church leaders.[13]

Ralph Winter issued a call for a gathering of global mission agencies to meet in Edinburgh, Scotland, in October of 1980 to grapple with strategies and implement plans to reach the unreached. Unlike the 1910 meeting being commemorated, the Edinburgh 1980 meeting included dozens of non-Western mission agencies. That marked a significant step forward for truly global mission-agency cooperation. Over the next two decades several more global-level meetings, both large and small, were convened to assess progress, facilitate cooperation, and develop strategies for the unreached people groups of the world.

Much progress was achieved because of this level of global cooperation and focus. One of the driving forces was the slogan that originated in part at Edinburgh 1980: "A Church for Every People and the Gospel for Every Person by the Year 2000." As the movement gained steam, a networking organization sprang into being: the AD2000 and Beyond Movement. The AD2000 Movement became an umbrella organization through which global mission agencies and churches networked and partnered toward the goal of completing the Great Commission by establishing church planting movements within all the remaining unreached people groups. Cochaired by non-Westerners—Luis Bush from Argentina and Thomas Wang from China—the AD2000 and Beyond Movement spawned many regional and global working meetings, the largest being the significant Global Consultation on World Evangelization (GCOWE) held in Korea in 1995 and again in 1997 in South Africa.

Under the AD2000 umbrella, the Joshua Project was established to collect and distribute research on the 1,739 people groups most needing a church planting effort in order to encourage cooperative church planting efforts among every ethnolinguistic people group of more than ten thousand individuals.

---

13 Coggins, "COWE: An Assessment."

Global prayer efforts arose to undergird this accelerating momentum. One of the most widely used prayer tools was the comprehensive *Operation World* prayer guide. Patrick Johnstone researched the nations, peoples, and religions of the entire world, collected data on the Christian ministries at work within each country, and produced this amazing book enabling Christians to pray specifically and knowledgably over every nation. By the fifth edition in 1993, hundreds of thousands of Christians were praying through *Operation World*. A local church in Louisiana, Bethany World Prayer Center, took it upon itself to produce prayer profiles of the unreached people groups to mobilize widespread prayer.

As the century and millennium came to a close, it became obvious that the goal of establishing a mission beachhead in every people group had not been accomplished. The AD2000 Movement felt a need to disband as a formal organization; however, the impetus that had been generated continued on in numerous regions as increased efforts were made to plant Christ-worshipping communities within every people group.

Key Mission Entities and Events with Frontier Mission Focus, 1975-99[14]

Not all-inclusive. Sample representation.

Global Gatherings and Consultations

- Chinese Congress on World Evangelization, Hong Kong, August 1976
- Pattaya Consultation on World Evangelization, Pattaya, Thailand, June 1980
- Edinburgh 1980 World Consultation on Frontier Missions, Edinburgh, Scotland, October 1980
- International Student Consultation on Frontier Missions, Edinburgh, Scotland, October 1980
- COMIBAM '87 (Congress on Ibero American Missions), São Paulo, Brazil, November 1987
- Lausanne Congress on World Evangelization (Lausanne II), Manila, Philippines, 1989
- "March for Jesus" worship/prayer events involving millions globally, 1988–2000, with some Marches still being held. Estimates of 2–3 million in Brazil's March in 2019.

---

14 *Mission Frontiers*, "MF Celebrates 20 Years of Charting the Growth of the Frontier Mission Movement, 1979–1999."

- "Praying Through the Window," a month of dedicated prayer for the least-reached, involving thousands of churches and millions of believers, 1993–97

- "Day that Changed the World," June 25, 1994. The largest prayer gathering in church history. 700,000 gathered in Seoul, Korea, to pray for the peninsula, unreached peoples, and for 100,000 Koreans to be raised up as missionaries. On the same day, 12 million in 177 countries were praying and praising in the global "March for Jesus."

- Global Consultation on World Evangelization I, Seoul, Korea, 1995

- Global Consultation on World Evangelization II, Pretoria, South Africa, 1997

New Mission Agencies and Associations (Year Founded)

- Asia Missions Association, 1975

- Lausanne Committee for World Evangelization, 1976

- Chinese Coordination Centre of World Evangelism (CCCWE), 1976

- Association of Transcultural Missions Agencies of Brazil (AMTB), 1976

- India Missions Association, 1977

- Pioneers, 1979

- Singapore Center for Evangelism and Missions (now Singapore Center for Global Missions), 1980

- Mission to Unreached Peoples (now Beyond), 1981

- Presbyterian Frontier Fellowship (now Frontier Fellowship), 1981

- Frontiers, 1982

- Nigeria Evangelical Mission Association (NEMA), 1982

- Caleb Project, 1983

- Philippine Mission Association, 1983

- Theological Students for Frontier Missions, 1984

- FEDEMEC (Evangelical Mission Association of Costa Rica), 1985

- International Society for Frontier Missiology (ISFM), 1986

- InterDev (now visionSynergy), 1986

- COMIBAM (Ibero-American Missionary Cooperation), 1987

- COMIMEX (Missionary Cooperation of Mexico), 1987

- Mission Korea, 1988
- Adopt-a-People Clearinghouse, 1989
- AD2000 and Beyond, 1989
- Ghana Evangelical Missions Association (GEMA), 1989
- Third World Missions Association (now World Link Missions Association), 1989
- Evangelical Missiological Society (EMS), 1990
- Korean World Mission Association (KWMA), 1992
- Anglican Frontier Missions, 1993
- CRAF (Francophone Africa Regional Consultation), 1998
- SEANET (South, East, Southeast and North Asian Network), 1999

Traditional Missions Focus on Frontier Mission

- The two largest North American mission associations—Interdenominational Foreign Mission Association (IFMA) and Evangelical Fellowship of Mission Agencies (EFMA)—representing hundreds of churches and mission agencies, confirmed their commitment to unreached people groups at a joint meeting in 1984.

Research and Publications—New or Noteworthy Focus on Frontier Mission

- Mission Frontiers, 1979
- *Perspectives on the World Christian Movement: A Reader*, 1981
- *Global Prayer Digest*, 1981
- *World Christian Encyclopedia*, 1982
- *International Journal of Frontier Missiology* (IJFM), 1984
- *Christianity Today* feature article on Ralph Winter and "Hidden Peoples," 1984
- *Operation World*, 5th edition, 1993
- Joshua Project research initiative on all unreached people groups, 1995
- *Brigada Today* email journal promoting resources for frontier mission, 1995
- Bethany World Prayer Center completes Prayer Profiles on 1,739 Joshua Project list of unreached people groups for major church prayer mobilization, 1998

4

Growing Influence, Growing Pains

"Get up and make that phone call right now."

I knew it was God speaking to me; my natural inclination would have been to file the thought away and stick it on a "to do" list, in the low-priority category. I had moved from Austin, Texas, back to my hometown of Nashville, Tennessee, and was not yet employed. In the two years since I took the Perspectives course I had continued to read about missions. As I reclined on the sofa reading the latest issue of *Mission Frontiers* magazine, I noticed that a Perspectives course was scheduled for Nashville.

I casually mused, "I was so busy with my job when I took the class in Austin that I really didn't invest much in it and therefore didn't take away as much as I could have. I should take this class again. Besides that, I am new in the city and have time to volunteer."

A nice thought, until God spoke so clearly to me to phone the course coordinator immediately and offer my services. That phone call initiated what became a twelve-year ministry of coordinating Perspectives classes in the city and joining the staff of the U.S. Center for World Mission to open a Nashville office. Through leading Perspectives classes I discovered my calling as a mission mobilizer and educator. What I did not realize at the time was that despite my lackluster effort, God's purposes had been deeply sown into my spirit from that first Perspectives class I took in Austin.

The Perspectives course became a galvanizing force for missions from Nashville to the nations. During the decade I served in Nashville, the number of individuals taking the course approached one thousand, coming from approximately a hundred churches of multiple denominations and five major universities. One college required the course for their mission majors. Several churches required their mission committees and prospective missionaries to take the course. Some of our alumni were even influential in a strategy change at the mission board of a major denomination; they began to engage unreached people groups and to send teams rather than individuals. We saw well over one hundred new missionaries emerge for long-term service, scores of current missionaries encouraged and enlightened to new paradigms, dozens of churches develop intentional mission efforts aimed at unreached people groups, and hundreds of ordinary lay people begin to take an active role in praying for and serving God's global purposes.

Perspectives coordinators have the supreme joy of watching the lives of their students transform as paradigms shift and they discover that they can have a strategic role in the completion of the Great Commission. Comments I heard repeatedly were "My eyes were opened!" and "My view of God was greatly enlarged!"

One of the aspects of Perspectives that excited me the most is really a wonderful side benefit. Through the interaction between Perspectives students of varying denominations and churches, the unity and cooperation of the church in Nashville increased. Unified citywide efforts emerged in both global and local outreach through the relationships formed in Perspectives. For example, an annual Festival of the Nations, celebrating Nashville's fast-growing ethnic diversity, arose through church mission leaders who met in Perspectives. Leaders from denominations who would not normally work together partnered with one another. In one memorable year, the pastors of churches as diverse as Baptist, Presbyterian, and Episcopalian partnered closely together to conduct a very successful Perspectives class. God was already at work in the city through the efforts of many church leaders to foster unity; Perspectives was privileged to be a strategic part of that effort.

My experience provides a glimpse of what so many Perspectives coordinators and their teams encounter in cities across North America, and now also around the world. Unseen by most, they donate untold hours of prayer and planning and hard work to pulling off a successful class. Why? Not for monetary reward; almost all Perspectives coordinators and their teams serve in a volunteer capacity. Not for glory—it is an uphill battle to catch the attention of most churches. They do it because of their passion to see Jesus receive the reward of his sufferings: the worship of all peoples. They do it for the joy of multiplying their lives into other kingdom-seekers.

They do it because they themselves have been radically changed and they want to "open the eyes" of others also.

Course coordinators are the energy and the backbone of the Perspectives course. Without them, the course would still be stuck in Pasadena, limited to the few individuals who could afford to take a semester off to live and study at the USCWM. The amazing success of the Penn State class in 1980 galvanized the U.S. Center staff to create a mechanism whereby Perspectives could be conducted nationally as an extension class. As we continue our story of recounting the history of the Perspectives movement, we will discover how crafting such a mechanism catapulted Perspectives to new heights.

Extension and Expansion

While both were completing a master's degree in curriculum development, Jay and Olgy Gary designed an in-depth coordinator training curriculum for the Perspectives course. It systematized the process of conducting a Perspectives program and trained alumni to function as adult educators in a coordinating role. In the winter of 1983, they trained eleven alumni in the first Coordinator Training Workshop. For the next three years, Jay Gary conducted biannual, weeklong coordinator-training workshops at the USCWM, training the first two hundred Perspectives coordinators. Some significant ministry leaders were early trainees, such as Steve Shadrach, founder of the international Center for Mission Mobilization (recently renamed Via), and Ron Luce, founder of Teen Mania, a hugely successful youth ministry that mobilized millions of teenagers to mission involvement.[1]

First Perspectives Coordinator Training Workshop 1983.

Training coordinators to conduct extension classes revolutionized the Perspectives program. The evidence can be seen in the statistics. Up until

---

1 Gary, interview.

1983, the largest number of classes conducted in a single year was seven—mostly on the USCWM campus. With the introduction of coordinator training, thirteen classes were held in 1983. As trained coordinators fanned out across the country, the number of annual classes swelled. Thirty-three courses were conducted in 1984, with an increase again to fifty-nine in 1985.

On its ten-year anniversary in 1984, the Perspectives program recorded 3,500 alumni in a cumulative total of seventy-seven classes. Of those alumni, one thousand were garnered in the 1984 classes alone! Additionally, more than one hundred schools were using the Perspectives *Reader* as a textbook, in just the four short years since its publication.[2]

Around 1986, coordinator training expanded beyond Pasadena into regions of the United States and Canada. Recognizing that many of the people who were well suited to be coordinators were not free to take a week off for training, the coordinator training was condensed into a weekend format in 1987. These two strategic decisions—to shorten the training and to expand it regionally—triggered the future growth of Perspectives.[3]

Changing Audience

The Garys left the USCWM to work with the Lausanne Committee for World Evangelization, launching an emerging leaders program in the United States.[4] Jay Gary passed the leadership of the national Perspectives program off to Steve and Kitty Holloway, who were introduced to Perspectives while they were students at the University of California at Santa Barbara and active in InterVarsity. Kitty had taken the semester-long IIS course at the USCWM in 1979. She returned to the college, with great enthusiasm, to host a class on campus. Steve comments that that one class "changed the trajectory of our lives. … We were challenged for the Maldives through a student prayer group during Perspectives, and we eventually spent twelve years there."[5]

As the Holloways headed to the mission field, Wes Tullis assumed responsibility for the national Perspectives program from 1984 through 1986. Under his leadership the course underwent another strategic development. As coordinator training expanded regionally, Tullis actively promoted the idea of hosting Perspectives classes in local churches. Up until this time Perspectives had been designed for and focused upon college students, generally hosted on or near a campus.

As Ralph Winter turned over the administration of the program to young, inexperienced staff who were not as adept in contacting professors

2 *Mission Frontiers*, "IIS Builds Momentum!"
3 Lee Purgason, interview by author, June 21, 2005, email and tape recording.
4 Gary, interview.
5 Holloway, "Personal Recollections."

and acquiring credit, gradually less and less schools extended credit. Winter regretted that the strong focus on students and the acceptance of credit within secular universities was lost. Fran Patt explains,

> Many of those involved in the early days were in campus ministries on secular campuses. But everyone got older and no longer had connections to the campuses. Instead, they had connections to the churches. The USCWM never recruited someone committed to staying in the student world.[6]

To accommodate multiple extension courses, the Perspectives course was shortened to fifteen weeks, granting only three semester units of credit. Colombia Bible College, Denver Seminary, and William Carey International University extended credit. "It was an agonizing decision to collapse a sixteen-unit curriculum down to three units," commented Winter. "We had to decide whether to teach a few students a lot or a lot of students a little."[7]

The intentional outreach to local churches had immediate high-profile results. Three of the most influential churches in America, all in the Los Angeles area, hosted Perspectives classes in 1985: Grace Community Church, pastored by John McArthur; First Evangelical Free Church of Fullerton, pastored by Chuck Swindoll; and the First Foursquare Church of Van Nuys ("Church on the Way"), pastored by Jack Hayford.[8] The visibility and credibility of the Perspectives course was suddenly elevated, while stimulating a mission commitment to unreached peoples within the churches. In the case of the church Swindoll pastored, the vision spread to the entire denomination via an "Adopt-A-People" strategy.[9]

While recognizing the multiplication factor of today's Perspectives classes held in churches across the country, David Bryant laments what was lost when classes ceased being residential in format. He maintains that students living, eating, studying, praying, and worshipping together produced a much deeper and sustained transformation of worldview and commitment.[10] Bruce Graham concurs: "The efforts at solidifying the course curriculum and the training of coordinators began to help spread the course content, but I believe it took something away from the movement mentality."[11]

The early SIIS / Perspectives classes had an electrifying sense of being part of another Student Volunteer Movement for their generation. They were in league, working together for a cause bigger than their own lives.

---

6   Patt, interview.

7   Winter, interview.

8   *Mission Frontiers*, "1985 at the USCWM."

9   Camp, "Evangelical Free Church."

10 Bryant, interview.

11 Graham, interview.

The semester-long, in-residence course with weeklong exposure to the lives of the teaching professors, followed by an experiential cross-cultural ministry trip, was a powerful format indeed. What was lost in depth was replaced with accessibility and breadth. One can argue which pattern is more worthwhile; however, thousands of pastors and church members are grateful that the rich, life-changing education they received in Perspectives was made accessible to them.

First Forays into Other Lands

Barely a decade after its founding, the content of the Perspectives course moved southward, crossing the border into the Spanish-speaking world. Jonathan Lewis, serving with the World Evangelical Association (WEA) Mission Commission, redesigned and condensed Perspectives content into a three-volume workbook entitled *Misión Mundial* (*World Mission*, in English). *Misión Mundial* integrated selected articles from the Perspectives *Reader* with guide notes and questions into a workbook format. Yet, unlike Perspectives, a specific course based on the text was not developed and marketed.

Misión Mundial was first published in Argentina in 1986. Luis Bush, international director of the AD2000 and Beyond Movement, reprinted the first volume, covering the biblical and historical basis of mission, to distribute as pre-congress reading to the three thousand participants of the inaugural COMIBAM Congress in 1987 in Brazil. The COMIBAM Congress gathers leaders from every Ibero-American country to mobilize and strategize for missionary outreach from Latin America into unreached peoples and regions. *Misión Mundial* has been widely used in the Spanish-speaking world, stirring mission vision and helping lay a foundation for the surge of missionary deployment that followed.[12]

Meanwhile, on the other side of the globe, a retired architect named Don Cowey launched the Perspectives course in New Zealand. His pastor, who had taken the course in the United States, persuaded Don to travel to Pasadena for coordinator training. The first Kiwi course was held in 1987 with forty-five students; it created an immediate explosion of interest. The next year recorded two hundred students in six classes, and by 1989 twenty classes enrolled six hundred students—this from a total national population of only three million.[13]

The course had such an impact on the country that Patrick Johnstone made this comment in the "New Zealand" entry of the 1993 version of *Operation World*:

---

12 Jonathan Lewis, interview by author, August 1, 2005, email.

13 Hall, "Global Perspective Grabs New Zealand."

The missions vision of the New Zealand church is an example to many other lands. A new surge of interest has followed the *Perspectives on the World Christian Movement* courses, and many new candidates for missions are coming forward.[14]

These early forays into other cultures were forerunners of the international expansion that was to come.

Stabilization and Growth

Lee and Kitty Purgason. Lee was the longest-serving Perspectives national director, 1986–2000, and served the USCWM for 40 years before passing away in 2020.

In 1986, as the Perspectives course was experiencing substantial growth due to the surging cadre of trained coordinators, Lee Purgason assumed the directorship of the national Perspectives office. Purgason joined the USCWM staff in 1980 at the age of twenty-three. Like so many before him, he was involved in InterVarsity as a college student and went to Urbana, where he heard about the USCWM. IIS was part of his required orientation for joining staff. He recalled the profound impact the teachers and his small group leader, Darrell Dorr, had on his life and those of his classmates, over 20 percent of whom ended up on the mission field.[15]

Under Lee Purgason's fourteen-year leadership (1986–2000) the Perspectives Study Program was established, averaging 15 percent growth in the number of classes held each year. The curriculum also underwent two revisions during his watch.

Purgason oversaw the development of large numbers of new coordinators and instructors. As Perspectives coordinator training was condensed and regionalized in the 1986–88 timeframe, the number of classes held annually began taking off: from forty-four classes in 1986 to seventy classes in 1990. Coordinators generally emerge out of Perspectives classes, identified and mentored by existing coordinators and formally trained by the Perspectives program staff. Gradually a growing corps of veteran coordinators committed to coordinating classes year after year arose. They have discovered the strategic calling of mission mobilization. It is not unusual, though, to lose

---

14 Johnstone, *Operation World*, 415.
15 Purgason, "Personal Recollections."

a good coordinator to the mission field! In that case, the mission recruit is following in the footsteps of so many Student Volunteer Movement leaders of the past who replicated themselves by mobilizing their peers for mission before leaving for the field themselves.

Coordinators are one leg of a three-legged Perspectives stool. The curriculum is a second leg. And the instructors are the third leg necessary for the Perspectives class to stand. Perspectives instructors were originally recruited by personal referral of the USCWM staff, especially Ralph Winter. The Association of Evangelical Professors of Mission also provided several highly qualified teachers. As the ranks of coordinators grew, instructors were increasingly obtained via coordinator referral. And as the coordinators were regionalized, so increasingly were the instructors. Eventually an extensive list of qualified Perspectives instructors was developed.[16]

A stool is only as good as its three legs; over the years it became apparent that the curriculum leg needed some work. After completing the introductory edition of the Perspectives *Reader* and *Study Guide* in 1981, Steve Hawthorne remained in Pasadena and became part of the editorial team of *World Christian Magazine.* As managing editor, Hawthorne needed to acquire photographs of unreached people groups, so he created the Joshua Project—short-term teams who researched and photographed unreached people groups. The Joshua Project was eventually folded into the Caleb Project organization, in which Hawthorne worked for four years. In the spring of 1989, Hawthorne realized that the Perspectives text which he had given his life to eight years earlier needed revision. So much had happened in missions over the last decade. Hawthorne began to lay plans to work on a major revision, lining up forty intercessors to pray for him for forty weeks while he worked.

A surprising turn of events occurred during the first week of those forty weeks of prayer. Hawthorne's friend and colleague at Caleb Project, Greg Fritz, counseled him to step out of active ministry, even the Perspectives revision project, for a season, in order to regain his spiritual equilibrium. Those were the days, Hawthorne recalls, of the downfall of famous Christian leaders. He felt it was God's grace giving him both a warning and the grace to receive it. In a step of obedience, he took a yearlong sabbatical to develop intimacy with God. "It was the turn of the page to the best days of my life. I needed to be revised before I could be a reviser."[17]

During Hawthorne's sabbatical, a theology of worship and the glory of God unfolded. God's utmost desire to be loved and worshipped is the center of a paradigm that Hawthorne began to define. God pursues the

---

16 Purgason, interview.

17 Hawthorne, interview.

redemption of the nations because he desires intimate relationship.[18] Following his sabbatical, Hawthorne wrote the momentous article, "The Story of His Glory," which is now included in the *Reader*.[19] That article expressed Hawthorne's passion and motivation; it also defined the direction in which the Perspectives course was to evolve.

The Perspectives Add-dition

In 1991, in the absence of Hawthorne's involvement, the U.S. Center for World Mission took up the challenge of revising the Perspectives text. Ralph Winter sent out letters to the authors of the articles in the *Reader* asking them if they wanted to add anything to their article to reflect new insights. The *Study Guide* was edited down from twenty to fifteen lessons, yet in reality all the content of the twenty lessons was squeezed into fifteen. Nor were the articles in the *Reader* really edited. Many things were added, but not much was subtracted. As a result, the 1992 revision was bloated with lengthy articles and too heavy a workload for the average Perspectives student.

The 1992 edition is satirically referred to now as the "Perspectives Add-dition"! As Purgason reflected, "We did not have the time, or failed to take the time, to trim back some of the longer articles, nor the time or clout to negotiate shorter versions. We also did not pare back the reading requirement for certificate students."[20]

The result was damaging to the Perspectives course. As Perspectives increasingly attracted a church audience rather than a college audience, a shift occurred in the numbers of students taking the course for credit. Because the workload of the certificate level had become so overwhelming, more and more participants simply audited the class—reading very little, if at all. Those who tried to complete all the assignments were choking on it.

It wasn't long before Perspectives coordinators began to clamor for a lighter educational tool. One possibility was already in print. Jonathan Lewis's *Misión Mundial* was published in English as *World Mission*. This three-volume workbook was derived from the Perspectives course, with heavily condensed articles and an integrated study guide written by Lewis. Intended for a Latin American audience, it was simple and useful, but was not the curriculum Perspectives was designed to be. Several North American Perspectives classes began to use *World Mission* for their audit and certificate students, while continuing to use the Perspectives *Reader* and *Study Guide* as the credit-bearing text. It was sloppy, as the two different texts

---

18 Hawthorne.

19 Hawthorne, "Story of His Glory."

20 Purgason, interview.

didn't match up in lesson format, creating extra work for the coordinator; but it kept the noncredit students engaged.

One of the more entrepreneurial veteran Perspectives coordinators, Meg Crossman, who lived in Phoenix, decided more could and should be done to meet the need of a "lay-friendly" text. She worked with Jonathan Lewis over the next couple of years to reshape his curriculum for a US audience. The result was a curriculum she entitled *Worldwide Perspectives*. Crossman's curriculum quickly caught on in Perspectives classes across America. By the late 1990s, more Perspectives classes were using a curriculum other than the official text, an unfortunate situation. Yet in hindsight, Crossman's curriculum kept the Perspectives course from collapsing under its own weight during those years.

It became painfully clear that a true revision of the Perspectives curriculum was needed. Not only was the 1992 "Add-dition" unwieldy, numerous articles were completely out of date. Ralph Winter also had new articles that he wanted to include in a renewed curriculum. Mission strategies to the least-reached had continued to develop and needed to be included. But a deeper, more underlying purpose would surface in the complete overhaul of the curriculum.

A Shift in Focus

By 1997, Steve Hawthorne was ready to engage a thoroughgoing revision of the Perspectives text. He sat down with Ralph Winter to discuss the changing audience, the changing content, and the need for changing the focal point of the course. That conversation was the first articulation of what became the sixteen Core Ideas of the Perspectives course.[21] (See appendix B.)

Hawthorne's perspective had been radically altered during his sabbatical. In a season of deep intimacy with God, God had sown his passion for his own glory within Hawthorne's soul. Missions is about God receiving the love and worship he so desires from the nations. Perspectives had been so focused on the mandate of the unfinished task that the vision was cast more in anthropocentric terms than in theocentric terms—i.e., what remains for *us* to do rather than what God has determined that *he* is going to accomplish. Our mission is thereby an invitation for us to partner with him. That fresh perspective needed to be infused into all aspects of the revision.

Hawthorne devoted 1998 to working, along with a small revision team, on a third edition of the Perspectives text. They began by identifying sixteen Core Ideas that are the "crown jewels" of the Perspectives course. From the Core Ideas they developed the learning objectives and then

---

21 Hawthorne, interview.

selected the articles.[22] The team was continually contacting global experts and practitioners to review the latest missiological principles and practices. They also solicited editorial input from veteran coordinators and instructors. Although the working team itself was small, they included input from quite a number of people in the revision effort.[23]

Purgason notes the important role USCWM colleague Bruce Koch served as assistant to Steve Hawthorne in this process.

> Bruce spent dozens of hours beyond regular work hours just sitting in the office with Steve at night while he was thinking so that he would have someone to interact with and help shape his thoughts. Bruce knew that Steve worked best that way and just volunteered to be there in that capacity.[24]

Hawthorne adds,

> Few people grasp the heart and soul of this course as well as Bruce Koch. He helped shape and clarify every part of the course. Even today he remains an encouragement to many who are adapting the course for new audiences.[25]

Steve Hawthorne (L), and Bruce Koch (R), two pillars of Perspectives curriculum content.

A change in focus to a more theocentric view demanded a change in structure. Whereas the 1992 edition of Perspectives shortened the biblical section down to just three lessons, the 1999 revision shortened the cultural section instead and extended the biblical section to five lessons in order

---

22 Hawthorne, "History of the Perspectives Course."
23 Purgason, interview.
24 Purgason.
25 Hawthorne, interview.

to develop a full-orbed biblical foundation. Hawthorne contributed his seminal article, "The Story of His Glory," to reveal a story throughout the entire Bible, which is still unfolding today. The focus is on God, not on our compassion or activism. That insight permeated the entire third edition.[26]

An exciting addition to the text reflected a fulfillment of the objectives of the Perspectives course itself. Case studies were included that described church planting movements among previously unreached people groups written by missionaries who were mobilized to the unreached through taking the Perspectives course.[27]

Nearly 60 percent of the material included in the 1999 Perspectives *Reader* was new to the book. There were many new articles, of course, but many of the existing articles were drastically edited. Modular in design, the *Study Guide* became more flexible, allowing three different learning levels (audit, certificate, and credit) to use the same material. The fifteen-lesson format was retained, but each lesson was shortened to about thirty pages of reading for the certificate level.

More than design and content change, the third edition presented the biblical hope of God's purposes being completed in history clearer and brighter than ever before. The seeds of this passion were always there, but it wasn't until the 1999 edition that they came forth in full bloom. It reflected a deep paradigm shift. Oftentimes mission communication focused on the world's vast need and a few isolated Scriptures to challenge people to engage in mission. Mobilization was a response to duty and obligation. The third edition of Perspectives clearly put God's story from Genesis to Revelation and throughout all history before people, calling them to the privilege of joining God on *his* mission, which most certainly will not fail. The difference is in understanding mission principally as God's purpose to be fulfilled, rather than tasks to be achieved; in motivating through Biblical hope rather than by guilt. There is still a holy responsibility to obey the command of God; there is still a duty to fulfill the mandate. But the calling to biblical hope, purpose, and destiny is integrated throughout the third edition as the life-giving power of the commission. This infusion of hope is the most significant development from the preceding editions.

The result was a deep and abiding sense of purpose being sown into the students. Lee Purgason elaborates,

> People came out saying "Now I understand what God is about" rather than "Now I see what remains to be done." Because of

---

26 Hawthorne.

27 *Mission Frontiers*, "Perspectives Course Revision."

that there was more of a grace-infused propelling into service, not because there is work to be done and people are dying but because this is what God is doing and I want to join him.[28]

The third edition (and first true revision) of the Perspectives *Reader* and *Study Guide* was released in 1999. The first semester after its introduction about two-thirds of the Perspectives classes resumed using the *Reader* and *Study Guide* as their curriculum, and by 2001 almost 90 percent of the classes were back to using the official curriculum. Due to confusion over competing textbooks and the continual drifting apart in content and focus, 2002 was the last year that Crossman's *Worldwide Perspectives*[29] was allowed to be used as a text in an official Perspectives course. As it was drawn from Lewis's *World Mission* course rather than directly from the Perspectives course itself, and as it reflected the content and focus of earlier versions of Perspectives, it no longer served the educational objectives of the Perspectives course. Unfortunately, this created a painful rift in the Perspectives movement. Some classes continued to use *Worldwide Perspectives*, but they no longer fell under the jurisdiction of the Perspectives program and were not recognized as official Perspectives classes.

Beginning with the new edition in 1999, the annual number of Perspectives classes increased rapidly—from 75 classes in 1998 to 147 classes in 2002. On the thirtieth anniversary of the Perspectives course in 2004, 179 classes were held across the US and Canada, with more than six thousand participants enrolled.[30]

As the calendar turned the page to a new millennium, Perspectives had become a major mission shaping, education, and mobilization force in global outreach. The Perspectives *Reader* was now in use in a large number of Bible schools and seminaries in the United States and could be found as a core text in many international schools. The number of Perspectives course alumni approached fifty thousand. Graduates had fanned out across the globe, implementing the tools they learned in Perspectives. Many alumni were assuming leadership roles in mission agencies, educational institutions, and churches. Perspectives shaped their thinking and the programs and strategies they implemented.

Standing on the brink of a new millennium, few would have imagined the dramatic developments that would soon unfold in global events, spurring on significant shifts in frontier mission and, as an outgrowth, in the Perspectives movement.

---

28 Purgason, interview.

29 Retitled *Pathways to Global Understanding* in 2008.

30 Bruce Koch, interview by author, September 26, 2005.

Follow the Fruit

God does so much in and through the lives of those who enroll in a Perspectives class. However, that fruit is often not fully manifested for years. Unless a class coordinator tracks the lives of the students, he or she may have little idea about how much fruit comes forth from just a single class. I offer up the 1993 Perspectives Nashville class as an illustration.

It was only the second class I coordinated, so I was still getting my feet wet. But my lack of experience did not hinder the Spirit of God in all he was planning. It was the second year in a row for Christ Church to host the class. The 1993 class built upon the momentum generated a year earlier, spurring increased congregational involvement in mission to the recently dissolved former Soviet Union. Through music, Bible distribution, and the sending of missionaries, Christ Church was sowing heavily into Russia and Ukraine. The Perspectives class added the intentionality of adopting an unreached people group, the Kazakhs. Although the venture was short-lived due to pastoral changes, the missionary the church sent (who was in the Perspectives class) was privileged to participate in worship with the first-ever Kazakh believers.

The spark plug for deep change at another Nashville church sat enthusiastically on the front row of that 1993 class. Sam Clarke was so inspired by what he learned in Perspectives that he convinced the entire missions committee and the youth pastor of his church to take Perspectives. His church, St. Bartholomew's (affectionately known as St. B's), was an unusual evangelical, charismatic Episcopal church in an upscale Nashville neighborhood.

After taking Perspectives, the missions committee wrestled for a couple of years to discern God's global assignment for them as a church. Because of the civil war in Sudan, hundreds of refugees were settling in Nashville, many from an Anglican background. A divine connection was made between the Sudanese and St. B's members, resulting in some extraordinary initiatives.

White wealthy, dignified church members welcomed Black African refugee believers into their church, periodically giving over the Sunday service for the Sudanese to lead them in worship with their indigenous instruments, dance, and African rhythms. It wasn't a "show," but genuine, loving communion. St. B's helped two young men receive education for ordination in order to start and pastor a Nashville Sudanese church.

Church members met with African bishops, learning about the horrendous levels of persecution the church in Sudan was experiencing, so far removed from their own comfortable lives. Members of St. B's accompanied refugee representatives to appear before a US Congressional hearing on the plight of Sudan. They visited Sudanese refugee camps in Uganda, identifying projects they could support. The church conducted an international conference for Sudanese leaders, hosted English-language classes, organized writing workshops to help them tell their stories, and enabled the Sudanese to produce their own worship recording. St. B's members built deep friendships with the refugees, advocating for them both locally and abroad. This comfortable, upscale church was irrevocably changed.

Sam Clarke was ordained into the priesthood—a priest carrying God's heart for the nations. John Stayskal, the youth pastor, started Ultimate Goal Ministries to connect American youth with international and refugee youth in soccer games for evangelistic purposes.

Other members of that 1993 Perspectives class went on to have far-reaching global impact. Physician assistant, Lynn Vander Woude, deciding that she did not want to "waste time providing health care to the rich and privileged," joined YWAM to teach in their Primary Health Care School. In just a handful of years, she recorded over twenty-five nations being served by medical professionals she trained before relocating to the island of Tonga.

Bob Schindler and Werner Mischke of Mission ONE[1] were also in the 1993 class. Mischke relates that the Perspectives course impacted him at the deepest level, especially the message of "The Story of His Glory." Mischke became an impassioned proponent of understanding the Scriptures and the mission Christ gave us through the lens of God receiving love and glory from the nations. He crafted a DVD-based resource called *Operation Worldview*, which he and Schindler presented to scores of churches to mobilize for mission.

A deep-level thinker, Mischke studied the Scriptures from the framework of honor and shame, a framework by which much of the

1 www. mission1.org

world operates. His research produced *The Global Gospel: Achieving Missional Impact in Our Multicultural World*,[2] a major book for those working in cross-cultural relationships. He is a key leader in the Honor-Shame Network[3] which helps facilitate a global conversation about honor, shame, and the gospel in missiology and theology.

The 1993 Nashville Perspectives class also sparked vision for a young couple, Jon and Cindy Clendenen. They received training to coordinate Perspectives, extending the Perspectives movement to a city an hour east of Nashville. The class they coordinated in Murfreesboro produced some very significant fruit, the story of which is recorded later in this book under *Divine Connections with Perspectives Instructors*.

The story of the fruit from this one single class can be multiplied many times over through the thousands upon thousands of Perspectives classes that have been held in locations around the world over the past half-century. Only in heaven will the true story be fully known. For the thousands of Perspectives volunteers, it will be a glorious gift we can lay at the feet of Jesus. What a privilege and joy!

---

2 Mischke, *The Global Gospel*.

3 www.honorshame.com.

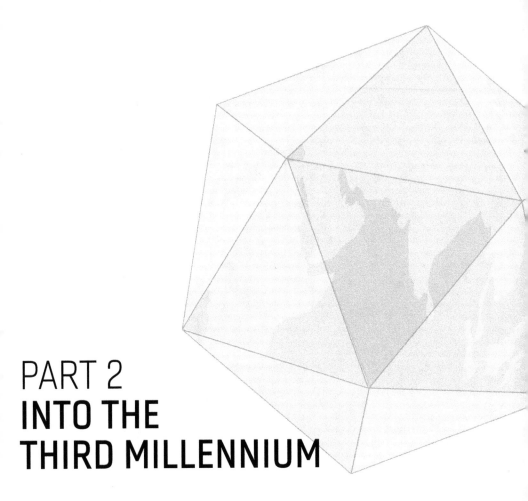

PART 2
INTO THE
THIRD MILLENNIUM

5

Global Events and Cultural Shifts Impacting Mission

Only a few short months into the new millennium the world convulsed as a new global reality exploded onto the scene. September 11, 2001. The fateful day that the World Trade Center towers crumpled to the ground and planes full of passengers became weapons of mass destruction altered the course of history. And with it, the course of mission.

As a result of 9/11, a cascading range of events unfolded during the following decades. Alongside cataclysmic and often horrific global events, massive cultural shifts were also transpiring that would shape the perception and implementation of mission. Underlying it all, technological advances pushed and pulled at the fabric of societies, simultaneously disrupting the status quo and generating new opportunities.

Re-mapping Global Populations

Terror events increased on multiple continents and wars followed terrorism, with Afghanistan, Iraq, Syria, and Yemen suffering the brunt of it. War and terrorism slaughtered tens of thousands and emptied entire regions; over half of the Syrian population was displaced. Ancient Christian communities emigrated from their historic homelands. Wave after wave of refugees flooded nearby nations and washed up onto European shores. Large migrations of other peoples from Africa, Iran, and Myanmar fled political and social repression. And now war has pushed tens of thousands of Ukrainians out of their homeland.

The twenty-first century is experiencing one of the largest refugee crises in history. The population map is being redrawn. Peoples once cut off from gospel witness by governmental and religious structures are now living in accessible lands. The implications for mission are as dramatic now as after the fall of the Iron Curtain in the latter part of the twentieth century.

In the year 2011, another series of unexpected events commenced. Beginning in Tunisia, a wave of pro-democracy uprisings spread across several predominantly Muslim countries. Known as the "Arab Spring," it brought down long-standing autocratic governments in Tunisia, Egypt, and Libya and agitated for political and cultural freedoms in Morocco, Syria, Yemen, Bahrain, and Iran. Huge populations of youth in these Muslim nations remain dissatisfied with stringent Islamic rule and corrupt autocratic control.

The shocking brutality of groups like ISIS and Boko-Haram was unleashed on Christians and Muslims alike. In Muslim hearts and minds, doubts about their own faith began to surface with a yearning for peace and security. A new openness to gospel witness emerged as Christians responded in compassion and love. And then came the great surprise. Muslims began to embrace Jesus as their Savior. Not just a trickle here and there, but in waves of response. New worshipping communities of Jesus followers from a Muslim background formed, for example, in refugee camps, in European cities, and in war-torn Syria.

The challenges of the refugee crisis, war-devasted nations, and ongoing terrorism are immense. But God has been at work in the hearts of those affected in unprecedented ways. More Muslims have come to Christ in the twenty-first century than in all previous centuries combined! Churches in Europe are being revitalized as Muslim refugees are literally knocking on their doors asking to learn about Jesus.

New worshipping communities of believers from Muslim backgrounds are actively evangelizing other Muslims. Iranian believers in Europe are discovering fruitfulness in winning Afghan refugees to the Lord. Unreached people groups, little known and shut off from the gospel, like the Yazidis of Iraq, are suddenly the focus of global newscasts as they suffered under ISIS terror. An outflowing of prayer and compassionate service by Christians led Yazidi's to respond to the gospel, resulting in the first-ever indigenous church among their people.

In Christian congregations across the globe, a new awareness of Islam has fostered increased prayer, missionary sending, and immigrant outreach. God himself is at work in the world of Islam, drawing Muslims to himself in unprecedented numbers; and the church global is joining God in what he is doing to see the harvest increase. We are witnessing a modern illustration of the biblical principle that God can take what Satan means for evil and transform it to bring goodness and salvation to humankind.

Migration, Urbanization, Globalization

Refugees are not the only ones on the move. Peoples all over the world are moving out of their traditional homelands to other nations to escape political, religious, ethnic, or economic repression. Others relocate for educational or employment benefits. According to the UN's Migration Report, the number of international migrants worldwide reached 281 million in 2021, up from 173 million in 2000. That equates to about 3.6 percent of the global population. Global displacement is at a record high, with estimates of 55 million internally displaced and over 26 million refugees.[1] Those estimates were before the flood of refugees out of Ukraine and over the Mexican/US border in 2022!

Urbanization is a twentieth and twenty-first century phenomenon. Throughout human history, rural living has been the norm. The latter half of the twentieth century began to see large population shifts to the city. By the year 2008, the number of global urbanites surpassed that of rural dwellers, with migrations occurring in almost every nation. The UN estimates that by 2050 over two-thirds of the world's population will be living in cities.[2] Christian researcher Patrick Johnstone challenges us,

> The urbanization of the world has important implications for quality of life in every area of human activity: cultural, social, linguistic, and spiritual. … How should this realization influence our strategic planning and our emphases in training and ministry?[3]

As the world's cultures are coming into increasing contact with one another, globalization is happening on a massive scale. The mingling and integrating of diverse cultures are creating a unique global culture that coexists alongside indigenous cultures, especially among the youth of the world. The effect can be a galvanizing of indigenous culture, seeking to resist outside influences, or a casting off of native culture in favor of global cultural traits (primarily Western in origin), or an uneasy mixing of the two. Whatever the effect, for good or for bad, globalization is a societal disruptor.

---

1 UN, "World Migration Report 2022."
2 Ritchie and Roser, "Urbanization."
3 Johnstone, *Future of the Global Church*, 6.

Satellite TV, the internet, mobile phones, and social media have permeated even poor populations in remote areas of the world. The transmission of outside ideas and culture into populations that were isolated only a generation ago cannot help but affect societies. Within urban centers, the impact of technology is even greater. Case in point: the "Twitter Revolution" of Iran in 2009 and beyond.

The rapid advance and distribution of technology in the twenty-first century has created enormous opportunities for mission. Millions of unreached peoples are receiving the gospel for the first time through their cell phones and being discipled or connected to other believers through the internet and social media. Covert Jesus-followers in dangerous conditions can worship with others via services on satellite TV or the internet.

The millennial generation and younger are so exposed to other languages and cultures that they are comfortable in a multicultural, multiethnic, globalized world. For Christian young people, this makes crossing cultures for the sake of the gospel less of a barrier. On the other hand, ubiquitous technology, especially social media, creates a new set of problems.

Technology and globalization have allowed great strides to be made in mission goals, strategies, and partnerships. The cross-pollination of ideas and experiences—especially between Western and non-Western mission strategists, theologians, and practitioners—has enhanced understanding and cooperation in global mission endeavors, as we will see in the following chapter.

Post-Western Christianity and Post-Christian West

Much has been written regarding one of the most momentous global alterations that occurred near the end of the twentieth century—namely, the shift of the Christian church from the Global North to the Global South and East. From a population standpoint, the statistical geographic center of Christianity lies in Timbuktu!

According to the Center for the Study of Global Christianity, in 1910 over 80 percent of the world's Christians lived in the Global North. ["Christians" being those who self-identify as Christian. "Global North" equated to Europe and North America, "Global South" being the rest of the world.] By 1970, the percentage of Northern Christians contracted to 57 percent.[4] By 2018, two-thirds of Christians globally resided in the Global South, with only 34 percent of the world's Christians living in the Global North. And 2018 also marked the first year that more Christians—

---

4   Center for the Study of Global Christianity, *Christianity in Its Global Context.*

numbering 631 million—lived in Africa than in any other continent of the world; Latin America came in second with 601 million.[5] This dramatic shift has happened in a single lifetime!

The geographic shift of Christianity is due to significant population growth in the Global South versus population declines in the North. It is also due to focused mission, over the past two hundred years, to formerly unreached peoples in the Global South. Gospel advance through *indigenous* evangelism proved especially fruitful in the latter half of the past century. The church of the future will look significantly different than it has for the last several hundred years. The forms and expressions of church and worship in the Global South often differ greatly from the Greco-Roman foundations of the Western church. The Bible is interpreted and understood within their context, which can look rather strange to Western eyes.[6]

In contrast, there has been a steep decline in faith in the West. In belief, values, and behavior, nations in Europe and North America are increasingly "post-Christian." An October 2019 Pew Research study revealed a 12 percent drop, in only one decade, in the number of Americans who self-identify as Christians. Concurrently, there was a 9 percent increase in those who said they had no religion, up to 26 percent of the American population.

The generational gap in faith was the most startling. Of those born before 1946, 84 percent identified as Christian, versus 49 percent of the millennial generation (those born between 1981 and 1996).[7] A September 2022 Pew Research report projected that if recent trends in religious switching continue, Christians could make up less than half of the US population within a few decades, and that "nones"—those who identify as atheist, agnostic, or nothing in particular—will approach the majority of the US population by 2070. Most of those who switch out of the Christian faith are between the ages of 15 to 29, when personal identities are being formed. The current rate of those in that age bracket who disaffiliate with Christianity is estimated at 31 percent. Additionally, research has revealed that an increasing percentage of those aged 30-65 are also disaffiliating from Christianity.[8]

The dominance of a secular, postmodern worldview has led not only to a loss of faith but to public antagonism and opposition to Christian values and beliefs. Scandals involving church leaders led many to exit the church. The church's own compromise relative to biblical faith contributed to the

---

5 Johnson and Zurlo, eds., *World Christian Database.*

6 Jenkins, *New Faces of Christianity.*

7 Shimron, "Pew Report."

8 Pew Research Center, "Modeling the Future of Religion in America."

rise of secularism. Of course, all of this has major implications for mission.

Early in the twenty-first century another milestone occurred. The number of non-Western missionaries sent out surpassed the total number of missionaries sent out from the West. The historically conditioned impression of a missionary as a white Westerner is no longer accurate. The day of global partnership is here, yet new roles and attitudes must be learned to achieve genuine cooperation and collaboration.

For the first time in two hundred years, the number of long-term workers sent out by Western churches began to subside. According to researcher David Taylor, one of the reasons for this is the perception (once again!) that the day of the foreign missionary is passing. He asserts, "This trend probably would have happened much sooner had it not been for the unreached peoples movement ... which revitalized missionary sending."[9]

Statistics from 2012 reveal that 63 percent of all cross-cultural missionaries are being sent out from the Majority World (non-West). The former mission-receiving nations are now the mission-sending nations. This is a wonderful thing. Taylor affirms,

> The diversification of the global missions movement is the single most important factor that will lead to the goal of world evangelization. The overall impact of the church in the world will be greater as its witness becomes more authentic through diversification. No longer will Christianity be seen as a Western religion, but as a global faith.[10]

An American colleague once shared this story with me. He was living in a remote area of a majority-Muslim nation serving rural dwellers. As he shared with the inhabitants about Jesus, they were attracted to him. But they told him, "We cannot place our faith in Jesus as our Savior; Christianity is a Western religion, not ours. Besides, you have no idea how much we would suffer if we did."

Then, my friend said, Chinese missionaries arrived. With just their presence, they demonstrated that Jesus is not just for Westerners, and they knew full well what it meant to suffer for their faith.

9 Taylor, "An Enduring Legacy," 127.
10 Taylor, 127.

6

Frontier Mission Developments 2001–2020

The twentieth century ended with a crescendo of focus and activity aimed toward unreached people groups. Among a significant number of mission agencies and leaders, the task of reaching the unreached people groups became a primary strategy and goal. Local churches began to embrace the goal of frontier mission, adopting people groups for prayer and witness.

A reaction against this vigorous frontier mission effort emerged as the new millennium took hold. Some voices from within Southern Christianity and the wider ecumenical world began to criticize the frontier mission movement as a Western construct, claiming it has a simplistic aim of sowing the gospel into every people group without a deeper focus on discipleship and the accompanying works of the kingdom within society. Granted, some zealous mobilization efforts contributed to this mischaracterization of frontier mission, but deeper issues were at the root. At its core, the issue was *"What really is mission?"* This question is still being debated.

What Is Mission?

At the turn of the millennium, the urgency of mission activities to meet human need, such as human trafficking, justice and equality, and care for the poor and the environment rose in predominance, sometimes without any reference to evangelism or church planting. Simultaneously, these global problems captured the attention of the youth in the West, particularly the horrific rise in sex trafficking and human slavery. In some circles, frontier mission came to be seen as "yesterday's trend," no longer valid in today's urbanized, globalized world. The task of world evangelization was at risk of fading out of view, replaced by the urging to "be missional," a catch-all phrase.

I vividly recall the comparison missiologist David Hesselgrave made between current mission drift and similar circumstances when he was a young man in the 1940s. I was teaching a Perspectives class in San Antonio when Dr. and Mrs. Hesselgrave stopped in to say hello. Of course, when one of the leading missiologists of the century attends your class, you yield the floor!

The lesson that evening highlighted the enormous contribution to world evangelization that was made by the Student Volunteer Movement (SVM). Hesselgrave was an SVM recruit. He personally witnessed the rapid decline of the SVM as his generation became aware of all the world's problems. Young people turned from evangelism and church planting to Peace Corp activities. The decline in students giving their lives to the spreading of the gospel message continued until the revival of interest generated during the early 1970s, as recorded in an earlier chapter. Dr. Hesselgrave told his story, then pointedly warned the class, "We are in danger of repeating this same error in this generation."

The fulfillment of the Great Commission turns on the definition of "mission." As Bishop Stephen Neill is famously known for saying, "When everything is mission, nothing is mission." If "mission" is equated with everything the church does to instill kingdom values and labors within society—from serving hot meals to the homeless under a bridge to advocating for socio-political reform to healing disease—then the critical task that Jesus gave us to preach the gospel, baptize, and disciple unto obedience every *ethne* is easily lost.

The former things, often referred to as "kingdom works," *are* urgent and important; they are the works the church must engage in and will be about doing until Jesus returns. They are part of the greater mission of God (*missio Dei*). They are a witness to the kingdom of God, they are an expression of the love of God, and they are most effectively accomplished with and through the church within its own society. Once the church is solidly planted within an ethnolinguistic group, evangelism, discipleship, and all kinds of mercy ministry will be ongoing. Implemented within the same culture, these labors are better described as evangelism and ministry. Within a different culture, this type of work is traditionally labeled "missions."

But what about the people groups who still lack an indigenous church? By nature, that involves those from another culture and language going cross-culturally to bring in the first harvest of believers and work until an indigenous church movement is established within that people. That is not a never-ending, ongoing task, but rather a finish-able task. This is the task of frontier, or pioneer, missions. That is certainly not to imply that frontier mission is an evangelism-only endeavor! In practice, pioneer missionaries are engaged in all kinds of holistic ministries—in conjunction with seeking to establish the indigenous church.

Why is this important? Because Jesus has given us a finish-able task to accomplish. Because we know historically and statistically that over 90 percent of the church's resources (money and people) are devoted to societies where the church already exists, with precious little left over for the remaining one-third of the world's population which lacks a sufficient gospel witness. Because if everything is lumped indistinctively under the umbrella of "missions," finishing the task that Jesus gave us to fulfill to disciple all *ethne* is buried under the heavy weight of global problems and the ongoing needs of the church.

Frontier mission is not urgent because unreached peoples are the *neediest* (although usually they are), but because they are the *remaining* peoples. Establishing a self-replicating indigenous church able to evangelize the rest of their people without requiring outside assistance is only the *beginning* of all that God desires to do within that people. Strong kingdom presence within society (i.e., an indigenous body of believers who have themselves been transformed) leads to an array of kingdom works to bring about societal transformation; in other words, the "blessing" for all nations that God promised to Abraham (Gen 12:1–3).

New Agencies and Networks for a New Millennium

The primary energizing force for frontier mission at the end of the previous century, the AD2000 and Beyond Movement, dissolved at the turn of the millennium; but the seeds it germinated blew around the world, multiplying into hundreds of new national, regional, and global mission agencies and networks, incorporating a robust frontier mission focus. COMIBAM, for instance, sowed the seed for national mission networks within almost every Ibero-American country. Africa serves as another illustration.

The Global Consultation on World Evangelization (GCOWE) 1997 meeting in South Africa, coordinated by AD2000 and Beyond, sparked national evangelization initiatives across the continent. In 2001, MANI (Movement for African National Initiatives) was constituted with the aim of mobilizing "the whole Body of Christ to complete the Great Commission within its borders and to send Africans in mission to the least-evangelized of the world."[1] Their first large continental meeting in 2006 brought together 520 mission leaders from 49 African nations. A second continental association, the Africa Missions Association (AfAM),[2] was founded in 2013 for the purpose of creating national mission associations in every country in Africa and assisting in the development of African sending structures.[3] One of those associations, the Nigeria Evangelical Missions Association (NEMA), can serve as an example of a national network. NEMA has a membership of over 150 Nigerian entities committed to frontier mission, sending out over fifteen thousand missionaries into 197 countries.[4] Similar associations have developed in most African countries.

A glance at another region of the world, Asia, gives a picture of how the non-Western world has energetically embraced the pursuit of completing the Great Commission. Organizations bearing names like Korea Frontier Mission Network, Korean Society for Frontier Missiology, Asia Society for Frontier Mission, Indonesian Peoples Network, and SEALINK (South East Asia Unreached Peoples Network) are a sampling.

The surge of mission-sending from the Global South has spawned most of these new agencies, associations, and networks. They are being undergirded by new non-Western theological and missiological associations. Journals, papers, books, and conferences emanating from these associations inform the growing mission endeavors.

Yet the need was still felt for global cooperation and networking to fill the void left by the dissolution of AD2000 and Beyond. Of course, the two largest evangelical global networks—the Mission Commission of the World Evangelical Alliance (WEA) and the Lausanne Movement—are still very active. The felt need, however, was for a global network that focused specifically on the who, where, and how of *frontier* mission. It didn't take long to fill the void. In 2001 a new global, mostly non-Western movement sprang up: *Ethnê*. Hosting the first of their global triennial gatherings in 2006, *Ethnê* focuses on accelerating movements to Christ among the world's least-evangelized people groups through evangelistic and holistic cooperative mission and prayer initiatives.[5]

---

1 www.MANIafrica.com.
2 www.AMAafrica.org.
3 Taylor, "Ghana 2013 Report."
4 www.NEMAnigeriamissions.org/.
5 https://ethneprayer.org/.

Many other global networks arose after the year 2000 with an unreached people group focus, as can be seen in their name. One of the most prominent, pushing mission agencies and denominations everywhere to embrace the frontier mission concept of closure, is Finishing the Task,[6] founded in 2005. Another large, active network, Call2All, founded in 2007, seeks collaboration of believers to "go where the Church is NOT, rather than where it is" to bring about kingdom transformation in all spheres of society.[7]

There are a number of global networks that focus upon a single people group family, such as FULNET (Fulani Network) or a category of the unreached, such as the Nomadic Peoples Network. As mission activity among the unreached deepened over the decades, new insight and understanding of culture and communication has spawned other international networks, such as the International Orality Network and the Honor-Shame Network. One could go on and on. There are international agencies or networks with a frontier mission vision that focus specifically upon refugees, urban environments, media, the arts, relief and development, business, research, training, students, women, children, prayer, mobilization, church planting, etc.

Among the older Western mission agencies and associations, many changed their name and a few consolidated, rebranding themselves for a new generation. The two largest North American associations of the twentieth century, IFMA and EFMA, joined together in 2012 to become Missio Nexus,[8] proffering a deep well of resources and training for churches and agencies to engage in effective mission. Pertinent to the Perspectives story, after the passing of founders Ralph and Roberta Winter, the U.S. Center for World Mission reorganized and rebranded to become Frontier Ventures[9] in 2015. The name changed, but the passion and commitment to the unreached remain the same.

One Hundred Years of Progress

As one would expect, the proliferation of mission associations and networks generated an escalation of conferences. Often the smallest meetings are the most strategic, but from a global perspective, one particular year should be highlighted. The year 2010 marked the one-hundredth anniversary of the legendary Edinburgh 1910 World Missionary Conference. To commemorate it, several global-level meetings were held.

---

6 www.finishingthetask.com.
7 www.call2all.org.
8 www.missionexus.org.
9 www.frontierventures.org.

Naturally there had to be a conference in Edinburgh, Scotland. Aptly named Edinburgh 2010, it was potentially the most diverse and inclusive mission conference in history. It brought together 250 invited representatives from every major denomination and confession of the global Body of Christ for celebration, study, and reflection on global church and mission issues.

In South Africa, the Lausanne Movement hosted Cape Town 2010: The Third Lausanne Congress on World Evangelization in October of 2010. Drawing together over four thousand evangelical leaders from two hundred countries, the Lausanne Congress encouraged unity and cooperation in mission through evangelism, discipleship, and tackling the world's urgent needs.

The meeting that focused specifically on frontier mission was the Tokyo 2010 Global Mission Consultation held in May of that year. Structured in the vein of the 1910 and 1980 Edinburgh congresses, participants had to be delegates of mission agencies that could actually act on decisions made. Exhibiting progress since 1980, over two-thirds of the delegates were from non-Western mission agencies (in 1980, only one-third were non-Western; and in 1910, less than 1 percent). The consultation was the brainchild of Ralph Winter, although he never saw its realization since he passed away the year before. The purpose was to celebrate progress since 1910, assess what remains to be done in completing the Great Commission, and facilitate plans and cooperation needed to finish the task. Participants were urged to adopt and engage the remaining unengaged, unreached people groups. Recognizing that a focus on evangelism-only misses the mark, the theme was "making disciples of every people in our generation."

In a visual display of the peace and reconciliation the gospel engenders between peoples, the congress was co-organized by former bitter war enemies, the Koreans and the Japanese. Americans and Japanese also took the opportunity to apologize to each other for World War II. Many conferencegoers, however, would have agreed with Allen Yeh, an Asian-American professor of missiology at Biola University:

> But the most moving and memorable moment of the conference was when a Swedish mission leader, Stefan Gustavsson, gave his plenary speech on the state of Christianity in Europe. This was followed by a spontaneous outbreak of prayer, where the non-Western mission leaders cried out for the restoration of the Christian faith to secular Europe. What a reversal of Edinburgh 1910![10]

---

10 Yeh, "Tokyo 2010 and Edinburgh 2010," 120.

Nationally, regionally, and globally, Christians of differing ethnic and ecclesial backgrounds are gathering for the purpose of seeing Jesus lifted up in every place and among every people. The multiplicity of conferences is promoting community, dialogue, and synergistic collaboration that is pushing forward the fulfillment of the Great Commission. Yet now the Global South has a seat at the table; their voices and leadership are reshaping the way mission is understood and practiced. They are from, or near neighbors to, the cultures that are still lacking flourishing kingdom movements. The theological and missiological reflection they provide is enriching the conversation and leading the way forward to fulfill the mission that God entrusted to us.

Changing of the Guard

In 2005, *TIME* magazine named Ralph Winter one of the "25 Most Influential Evangelicals in America." There, among the preachers, theologians, and culture-changers, is a missiologist! Not an expected choice.

The maturation of the discipline of missiology and embrace of mission as a core component of theological education can be witnessed in a comparison between the 1960s and today. In the decade of the sixties, many seminaries were eliminating their mission programs. A turn-around began to happen in the 1970s, as evangelical schools and seminaries established departments of mission. Today we see mission professors ascending to the presidency of three top seminaries: Gordon-Conwell, Asbury, and Denver theological seminaries. This bodes well for establishing a foundation of mission in future ministers and theologians.

If one were to list the individuals most influential in the evangelical mission movement of the latter twentieth century, the list would reveal a collective weight of insight and experience upon which the frontier mission movement rests. They are the professors that college and seminary students studied under, the authors whose books they read, the missionaries whose lives they were inspired by, and the executives whose leadership guided church and mission. Not unexpectedly, the Perspectives text is built upon their scholarship. Quite a number of them also had a direct hand in the development of the Perspectives course.

What is striking is when one considers how many of these mission giants have finished their earthly assignment and are now part of the great cloud of witnesses in heaven. Appendix C lists fifty highly influential mission leaders who are no longer with us, most of whom are mentioned in this recounting of the history of frontier mission and the Perspectives movement.

The mission leaders arising to take their place are now writing and speaking from multiple points on the globe. They are men and women from varied backgrounds and ethnicities. The frontier mission movement will hugely benefit from their contributions, as we stand on the shoulders of the giants who have gone before us.

Therefore Pray to the Lord of the Harvest

Jesus instructs us to look out and see that the harvest is plentiful; but just as in his day, the workers are still far too few. The solution? Prayer. It is the One who is most vested in seeing the harvest reaped who raises up and thrusts out laborers. But he asks us to partner with him by *asking* him to do so. Who can fathom his self-limitation to involve us?

Andrew Murray reminds us in his classic book that the key to the missionary problem is prayer. But it is also the key to opened eyes, softened hearts, and the destruction of the fortresses of Satan that hold entire peoples in bondage. We are seeing a mighty movement of the Holy Spirit in this century in the ingathering of peoples from some of the most restricted environs. This is no doubt a direct result of a surge of focused global prayer movements that began in the latter part of the previous century.

Public worship of Jesus took the stage in the 1980s with citywide "March for Jesus" events. Beginning in the United Kingdom, thousands of Christians took to the streets with banners flying and songs ascending in a public celebration of Jesus as King. A cascading flow of worship swelled during the following years, expanding to thousands of global venues. Each event culminated in corporate prayer for cities and nations.

I have seen up close the galvanizing effect of unified worship and prayer. I participated in the first American March for Jesus, attracting about two thousand participants in Austin, Texas, in 1990. I helped organize the first March for Jesus in St. Petersburg, Russia, in 1994, which involved ten thousand brave believers only three years after the fall of Soviet communism. In 1996 I had the sobering responsibility of leading fifty thousand people in fervent prayer for the nations at the March for Jesus in Nashville, Tennessee. At its height, an estimated ten to twelve million believers from 170 nations lifted their voices to celebrate and pray together. The rapidity with which the annual event spread revealed that God was up to something, stirring his church to worship and prayer.

One of the first global prayer movements focused on the unreached was "Praying Through the Window," a multiyear event beginning in 1993 to focus prayer on the "10/40 Window," where most of the unreached live. It was promoted in thousands of churches and schools, with millions of Christians participating. In the same year, "30 Days of Prayer for the Muslim

World" began, an international prayer event involving millions occurring during the month of Ramadan each year.[11] This prayer movement educates Christians about Muslims, helps break the fear that is often generated through the media, and stirs God's love for Muslims in Christians' hearts as they pray for them. A similar focus of prayer for Hindus and Buddhists was developed, with the hope that they will experience similar engagement.[12]

Emerging from South Africa, a Day of Repentance and Prayer, held on Pentecost Sunday each year, began in 2001. It spread rapidly across the African continent and then the world. By 2005, Christians in 156 countries participated in what became the "Global Day of Prayer." By 2009, each of the 220 countries of the world registered participants, as millions of Christians joined together in unified intercession.[13]

With historic levels of Christian persecution today, the "Day of Prayer for the Persecuted Church"[14] is a critical prayer event that involves millions of believers around the globe annually. Prayer movements are vast and varied: Some have sprung up around specific unreached people groups; others flow out of mission networks in various nations; some focus on women or children; others, like the International House of Prayer (IHOP),[15] establish 24/7 worshipping prayer centers. Widely used publications, such as *Operation World* and the *Global Prayer Digest*, have generated focused prayer for decades. In 2021 the *Global Prayer Digest* merged into the Joshua Project's *Unreached People of the Day*, a digital prayer initiative, and was also incorporated into *Mission Frontiers* magazine.[16] Prayer networks have been established, providing resources and collaboration.[17]

Prayer preceded Pentecost in Acts 1–2. Historic revivals and global awakenings have always been preceded by united, intense prayer. With such global, united, and focused prayer initiatives during the past decades, is it any wonder that we are seeing the greatest turning to Christ among Muslims in history and the steady increase of people movements among other groups long-thought impossible to reach? Or as Steve Hawthorne queries, "Why else would there be a global prayer movement unless God is about to act in a global way?"[18]

---

11 www.pray30days.org.

12 https://pray15days.org/; https://worldprayerguides.org/15-days-of-prayer-for-the-buddhist-pdf/.

13 www.globalvoiceofprayer.com/global-day-of-prayer.

14 www.persecution.com/idop.

15 https://ihopkc.org.

16 https://operationworld.org/; https://joshuaproject.net/pray/guides/gpd; https://joshuaproject.net/pray/unreachedoftheday.

17 Examples are the Global Prayer Resource Network at www.globalprn.com, and Ethnê Prayer at https://ethneprayer.org.

18 Hawthorne, "Rise of Global Prayer Movement," 12–13.

Globalization of Mobilization

Mission mobilization as a profession and a calling was a notion just getting its feet wet in the twentieth century. Today it is a concept fully submerged in an ocean of Christians needing mobilizing. Mission mobilization is a prophetic voice to the existing church on behalf of the yet-to-be church. The prophetic calling of mobilization necessitates grace gifts for fruitfulness. Only through grace, not merely abilities or passion, are mobilizers able to fulfill their calling.

Ralph Winter was known for declaring, "If I had one hundred mission volunteers, I'd encourage them all to stay home and mobilize. The second one hundred I would send as field missionaries." He fully understood the importance and power of mobilization. One dedicated mobilizer can multiply their life into one hundred who go as missionaries. And equally important, mobilizers develop ordinary believers into passionate "World Christians" who support those who go and who pray for the harvest fields. Mission mobilization has always been at the heart of the Perspectives movement.

Since the year 2000, several organizations have sprung up for whom mission mobilization is their sole purpose. Some, like The Traveling Team and Café 10/40,[19] are focused on mobilizing students and young adults into active mission engagement among UPGs. Other organizations, like Global Mission Mobilization Initiative (GMMI, formerly SVM2) and Via (formerly the Center for Mission Mobilization, or CMM),[20] are focused on raising up and equipping not *missionaries*, but *mobilizers*.

As in all other mission output, this impetus to increase the number and quality of mission mobilizers has gone global. As the former mission-receiving lands have become mission-sending lands, there are generally more missionaries ready to go than there are churches informed and impassioned to send them. Thus the need for mobilization.

In the year 2013, the first Global Mobilization Consultation (GMC) was held in Indonesia. The consultation came into being primarily through the impetus of leaders of Perspectives, CMM, Kairos, and Encountering the World of Islam, and it was hosted by the Indonesia Peoples Network and a Chinese megachurch. Global leaders of the programs had been meeting together for some time, but they saw the need for a larger gathering that would encompass all who had a calling to mission mobilization. The consultation was scheduled to precede the separate gatherings of Perspectives Global

19 www.thetravelingteam.org/; www.cafe1040.com/.
20 www.globalmmi.net/; www.vianations.org/.

and Kairos International.[21] The event was a huge success, with 130 attendees from twenty-five nations building friendships and sharing best practices for mobilizing the global church toward Great-Commission participation. A highlight of the consultation was visiting an unreached people group that had hardly been touched with gospel witness. The opportunity for prayer-walking among this people came through prayer-shopping!

The Global Mobilization Consultation generated such enthusiasm that it was repeated two years later in Kenya. Around 250 mobilizers from forty nations participated in the second GMC. At this Kenyan GMC in 2015 a proposal was adopted and a board was formed to establish the Global Mobilization Network.[22] Subsequent GMC meetings have been held every few years, with increasing attendance in rotating global regions, each time hosted by local national mobilizers.

The Harvest Force

So if a primary goal in mission mobilization is an increase in missionaries, what does the harvest force of the twenty-first century look like? Who is being sent, and how are they sent?

We have already indicated that more missionaries today are from the Majority World rather than the traditional mission-sending continents of Europe and North America. In some nations, churches are the primary recruiting and sending structure; in others, it is the mission agency. In places like China or North Africa, it may be a small home fellowship that dedicates one of their own to go out.

Students continue to be a deep well for mission recruits, as their whole lives are ahead of them. Scores of international and national student ministries on every continent provide inspiration and opportunity for students to explore mission careers. The Lausanne Movement recognized the need to incorporate the rising generation and developed an influential Young Leaders Track. The Passion Movement[23] exploded on the scenes in America with its first conference in 1997, blending abandoned worship with a passion for God's fame among the nations. Touching the heartstrings of a new generation, it has impacted millions around the world, stirred intense prayer for the nations, and prompted many to respond to God's call on their lives in mission.

Many megachurches are taking a more direct role in sending out their members, some operating their own in-house mission agency to train, send, and superintend their missionaries. A high-profile example of this

---

21 Renamed *Simply Mobilizing*; https://simplymobilizing.com.

22 www.globalmobilization.org/.

23 https://passionconferences.com/about/.

is Saddleback Church in California. In 2003, Pastor Rick Warren engaged his church in a transformational mission project in partnership with the government and churches of Rwanda, entitled the PEACE Plan. The Plan is focused on community transformation and coming alongside churches that are near-neighbors to least-reached people groups in efforts to reach them. Encouraged by success, the PEACE Plan expanded to multiple nations, multiplying their efforts through training churches worldwide in the model they established. In the process, tens of thousands of Saddleback's own members have engaged in local outreach and short-term mission.[24] This grassroots model was both applauded and criticized, receiving quite a bit of media coverage in both Christian and secular outlets. Saddleback Church is the most visible of numerous other churches that have chosen, at least in part, to bypass the traditional mission agency with direct sending.

As mission mobilization increases in churches and campus ministries, the trend in short-term missions has not abated. Short-term trips help local churches see beyond their own community and engage the world with their prayers, giving, and service. Some discover or confirm their call into career mission because of a short-term experience.

While recognizing the many positive outcomes of short-term mission, a significant downside needs to be addressed. Ralph Winter highlighted the disparities in 2007:

> There are now almost two million short-termers leaving the United States each year compared to 35,000 long-term missionaries. Note that the overall cost of short-termers is at least five times as much as the overall cost of long-term missionaries. This means that instead of doubling or tripling the number of long-term missionaries, we're investing at least five times as much money in short-termers. Short-term trips are a wonderful education, but a very small accomplishment in missions.[25]

The answer is not to abandon short-term missions, but to be cognizant as churches and organizations concerning the balance of investment between short- and long-term field commitments.

A trend that began as a trickle in the 1980s, generally referred to today as Business as Mission (BAM), has also not subsided. Business professionals and entrepreneurs possess knowledge and skill that are both highly esteemed and needed in developing economies. Christian business professionals add value to the environments where they settle, and if that

---

24 www.thepeaceplan.com/history/.
25 Ralph D. Winter, "Learn from Our Mistakes."

is combined with a demonstration of Christ's character and intentionality in witness, they are valuable contributors in mission today. But this is also a challenging goal to pursue.

Over the past decades, numerous books and conferences have addressed this challenge, and all the associated problems of trying to run a for-profit business and pursue mission objectives simultaneously. Early efforts yielded some glaring errors; much has been learned through the years. As is the case with everything else, organizations and networks have been established to educate aspiring BAM practitioners. In 2002, a Lausanne think tank was convened and a business as mission website was launched, out of which flowed resources, training, and conferences. To study and facilitate fruitful practices, the BAM Global Think Tank was established in 2011, heightening international collaboration and learning, coalescing in BAM Global Congresses in 2013 and 2022.[26] The Business as Mission model may prove to be one of the more strategic avenues for early Christian presence among restricted-access groups.

Compared to only fifty years ago, the harvest force for world mission has vastly diversified to include multigenerational, multinational, multi-occupational servants of the Lord being sent from churches and agencies and businesses from everywhere to everywhere. Even more exciting, however, is that new mission-engagement strategies are producing harvesters within the unreached peoples themselves.

The Harvest Field

In the parable of the lost sheep (Luke 15:3–7), Jesus makes clear that even one sheep is so important to him that it is worth leaving the ninety-nine to search for the one lost sheep. How much more valuable, then, is an entire people group? In an effort not to overlook—or worse, to neglect—even one unreached people group, mission researchers and mobilizers have sought to bring greater clarity and definition to the frontier mission task.

During the latter part of the twentieth century, many churches and mission agencies "adopted" an unreached people group for prayer, research, and compassionate ministries with the goal of putting a church planting missionary team in their midst. As a result, many unreached peoples were "engaged" by receiving their first-ever local witnesses to the gospel. But the concern was always, who is being overlooked?

As field research brought greater clarity, early in the twenty-first century new descriptors emerged: "least-reached peoples" and "unengaged

---

26 www.businessasmission.com; www.bamglobal.org.

unreached people groups" (UUPG). The Finishing the Task (FTT) network put out a clarion call for churches, denominations, and mission agencies to select these UUPGs and engage them with missionary teams implementing church planting strategies. Many responded. In December of 2012, Paul Eshleman, the director of FTT, rejoiced that in the previous seven years FTT had tracked more than seven hundred UUPGs that had been engaged by more than seven thousand missionaries. But he also bemoaned that "nearly forty years after Ralph Winter challenged us to prioritize the unreached people groups of the world, there are still three thousand groups unengaged."[27]

Counting unreached people groups, far from being "Western managerial missions" or a numbers game, as some critics have characterized it, has resulted in the gospel being published for the first time among peoples that have been without access to the saving knowledge of Jesus for two thousand years. Compare the 2012 report to the report FTT released in August 2020. Because of collaborative efforts, FTT reports 3,158 least-reached people groups engaged by 42,805 vocational and over 89,000 bi-vocational missionaries since 2005, resulting in almost 3.6 million reported new believers worshipping in over 156,000 new churches.[28] That is worthy of celebration!

Trying to wrap your arms around terms, definitions, and statistics can be like trying to wrangle a greasy pig; just when you think you've grasped it, it twists and turns and eludes you. Questions began to be asked, "What determines if a group is truly engaged?" or "What happens if they become unengaged?" The complexities are similar in trying to define the "reachedness" of a particular group. Yet terms and statistics are important for understanding, collaboration, strategy, and mobilization.

Three predominant entities provide comprehensive people group listings: the World Christian Database; the Southern Baptist International Mission Board (IMB); and the Joshua Project.[29] If you were to visit the different websites, you would find variations in statistics. This is because they utilize different sources and look through different lenses when tallying the number of unreached people groups in the world. Even though there is close collaboration between these three entities, the differing lists can be confusing. The statistics are also continually changing because (1) the world is not static, and (2) on-site presence reveals the actual boundaries between peoples that can hinder a gospel movement, the goal for listing unreached

---

27 Eshleman, "Reaching the Unengaged."

28 Finishing the Task, "2020 Global Update," 19.

29 www.worldchristiandatabase.org/; www.peoplegroups.org/; www.joshuaproject.net.

peoples in the first place. One people group may actually be found to be three or four, or two groups may be discovered to be only one.

If the goal is to see a vibrant, multiplying church planting movement among every people group, allowing every segment of humanity the opportunity to respond to the love of Jesus, then we must continue to seek comprehensive understanding of the world's peoples and be comfortable living with a level of ambiguity. There will never be a precise list of unreached people groups. What we do know is that since Ralph Winter's first stabs at numbering UPGs, substantial progress has been made. Hundreds of them now have energetic people movements to Christ, and thousands more which were previously overlooked are now engaged.

Startling Discovery Unveiling Unfortunate Consequences

In 2016 Rebecca Lewis, one of the daughters of Ralph and Roberta Winter, was examining lists of unreached peoples when she noticed something shocking. The Scottish people, with many believers and historic churches, was listed as the largest "unengaged, unreached people group," whereas many extremely large Hindu and Muslim people groups with zero believers and woefully few missionaries were listed as "engaged" UPGs. As she stared in disbelief, she wondered, "What's gone wrong with the demographics?"[30]

Over time, the definition of the term "unreached people group" had drifted from its original meaning of those "groups without an indigenous church planting movement sufficiently large enough to evangelize the rest of their group," to groups that are "less than 2 percent evangelical," regardless of the amount of access to the gospel or the presence of a culturally appropriate church planting movement. The "less than 2 percent evangelical or 5 percent Christian" were acceptable benchmarks but led to unintended consequences. Furthermore, when "engaged" came to mean even one missionary was working among the people regardless of group size, the result distorted the portrayal of the remaining mission task. Since these lists are used by mission agencies and churches to prioritize deployment of mission workers and funds, and by mobilizers to challenge the church regarding where we fall short of God's global purpose, an inaccurate portrayal could leave millions still sitting in darkness.

Lewis concluded that a new category of unreached peoples was needed. She coined the term "Frontier People Groups" (FPGs) to refer to those groups that do not yet have a self-sustaining indigenous church planting movement—an apt descriptor because they require frontier mission workers

---

30 Lewis, "Losing Sight," 6.

(cross-cultural witnesses from outside the group) and frontier mission strategies. New maps and charts were also needed because

> current maps and charts of unreached peoples do not clearly distinguish between (1) people groups that have not had any movements to Christ (Frontier People Groups); (2) people groups that now have sustainable indigenous movements among them, though small; and (3) people groups with a lot of nonevangelical or even nominal Christians who still need help with renewal and outreach to their own group.[31]

Turns out that Frontier People Groups comprise over half of all UPGs. Working with other demographers, the people group lists were realigned and another startling discovery was revealed. Fewer than one percent of all global missionaries are going to these Frontier People Groups that make up almost one-third of the world's population! Lewis believes the primary reason for this is a lack of clear demographics. She also identifies another reason.

> Since most churches prefer to send people to partner with existing Christians and church movements, the Frontier People Groups are inadvertently eliminated from deployment options. The result is that the areas with the most Christians receive the most missionaries: Oceania receives 300 foreign missionaries per million people, Latin America receives 162, Europe 146, North America 113, and Africa 93. However, all of Asia receives on average only 13 foreign missionaries per million people, with India coming in very low at 7 foreign missionaries per million.[32]

As most of the FPGs are in Asia and India, this is a grave injustice and poor stewardship of the precious gift of the gospel.

Lewis and other demographers set about creating new charts and maps to better reflect the true mission picture, revealing them to the public in late 2018. Of significant interest is a comparison of Ralph Winter's early "pie chart" to a "pie chart" reflecting today's realities, revealing the places the church has made substantial progress and the places still wanting.[33] Joshua Project then created numerous mobilization tools (prayer guides, videos, presentation slides) and made them available for free download.[34] Within the FPG's, thirty-one stand out as significantly large and significantly underserved.

---

31 Lewis, 6.
32 Lewis, 7.
33 Lewis, "Remaining Peoples."
34 www.frontierpeoples.net.

The 31 are those Frontier People Groups with over 10 million in population. They make up almost half the population of all Frontier People Groups. With less than one in a thousand being a Christian of any kind, a person in these groups has virtually no chance of ever hearing about Jesus from someone within their people. All 31 of these Frontier Peoples are either Muslim or Hindu and all but nine of them live in South Asia.[35]

The Joshua Project tools, with their colorful graphics and elucidation, represent a significant step forward in frontier mission. May they generate a giant leap forward in world evangelization.

Exploring New Strategies

The bulk of frontier mission dialogue since 2000 has been about specific strategies to reach the unreached. Ralph Winter expounded in 2005,

> We used to feel like we were pushing a heavy wagon uphill, promoting unreached peoples. But now the hill has been crested and we are running down the other side trying to keep up with the momentum. Unreached peoples is not something we have to promote anymore. … Now we are more than ever focused on revision of mission strategy. Now many more people are getting into missions without knowing what they are doing.[36]

Because the largest blocks of unreached people groups are Hindu, Muslim, or Buddhist, much discussion and innovation is transpiring concerning appropriate and contextualized strategies of evangelism and church planting. It has not been without substantial controversy.

Initially most discussion revolved around how to contextualize the gospel message and the messenger (missionary) so that both can be understood and accepted by the receiving community. It became increasingly clear that the new worshipping community also needed to be contextually formed. As new movements to Jesus began to happen among unreached people groups along a spectrum of contextualized models, heated debates ensued within the global mission community, particularly regarding what was termed "insider movements." How much of the religious practices of the new believing community should be rejected and how much can be retained as they follow Jesus? How much of the recipient's scriptures can be legitimately used in evangelism? When does it become syncretism (the blending of two religions)?

---

35 Wood, "The Path Forward."
36 Winter, interview.

The chief issue at hand concerns issues of identity. We have approached people groups in terms of ethnolinguistic identity. As missionaries intensified efforts to penetrate the global religious blocks, a deeper awareness ripened of the socioreligious identity that the peoples themselves hold.

In the West, with an exalted value of individualism, we freely choose our religious and social identity. That is not true with much of the rest of the world.

> Traditional societies tend to fuse collective identities of religion, ethnicity, and nationality. Therefore, a person who changes one element of these is seen as betraying them all. It means "going over to the other side" or even "going over to the enemy's side."[37]

I visited Bosnia and Croatia ten years after the Yugoslavian war that split up the country. Everywhere I saw the bullet-ridden, bomb-dropping evidence of warfare between groups that identified in both ethnic and socioreligious terms. To be Bosnian is to be Muslim; to be Serbian is to be Orthodox Christian; and to be Croat is to be Catholic.

This fusing of identities that glue peoples together makes it extremely difficult, and often dangerous, for would-be Jesus followers to suddenly identify as a "Christian." The term *Christian*, especially in the Muslim world, is loaded with political, economic, moral (not in a good way), doctrinal, and cultural baggage, much of which Christians themselves would reject. But beyond that, to self-identify as "Christian" within Muslim, Hindu, and Buddhist contexts is often perceived as betraying one's family and community, usually divorcing the new believer from any further relational or evangelistic contact.

The critical questions then become, How can someone within such a context follow Jesus without committing familial, social, and cultural suicide? How can one remain in relationship to foster a church planting movement within his or her people? How can unreached people groups see the beauty and blessing of following Christ by one of their own, up close and personal?

Most of these debates swirled around those working within Muslim contexts. Reams of articles and volumes have been written on the subject. Much of the same deliberations, however, apply in Hindu and Buddhist contexts. Herbert Hoefer wrote a book in 2001 entitled *Churchless Christianity* based on extensive research of believers in Jesus in India who have remained in their Hindu communities, do not take on the "Christian" label, but sincerely follow Christ. Workers in the Buddhist world are

---

37 Green, "Conversion," quoted in L. D. Waterman, "LIFE Scale," 154.

exploring new evangelistic tools and methods that make sense in the Buddhist worldview to bridge the divide to the biblical worldview.

These questions of identity and contextualization are extremely important if we are to see Christ-following movements among most of the remaining unreached people groups. They are also difficult questions for Western Christians to explore. Western civilization was built upon a Greco-Roman foundation. As the Christian faith quickly moved from a Judaic environment into the Greco-Roman world, early Christianity adapted the linguistic, philosophical, and cultural expressions of that world. As a result, Christianity is comprehensible within Western culture.

That is why it is so difficult for Western Christians to fathom how one can follow Christ within a completely foreign socioreligious culture and stay true to God's Word. Just as the early Jewish Christians had difficulty separating their Jewish socioreligious traditions from the essentials of believing faith (only solved by the Jerusalem Council in Acts 15), so Western Christians struggle with what indigenous expressions of biblical faith should look like within other socioreligious contexts. To us, "church" should look like "our churches." Consequently, this remains a much-debated issue.

Fruitful Practices

Through years of discussion and research, innovation and evaluation, consultations and symposiums, argument and collaboration, a consensus of fruitful practices among Muslims began to emerge. One substantial contributing factor was that more and more missionaries were seeing people movements emerge among Muslims, witnessing firsthand what God was blessing.

Some of the fruitful practices have to do with how the gospel message is delivered. Since the remaining unreached people groups are predominantly oral learners, new emphasis was put on learning how to present the gospel and disciple through oral means. Early on, in the 1970s, New Tribes[38] missionaries pioneered chronological Bible storying methods. Training and tools on discipling oral societies began to emerge from field practitioners. Through the leadership of Paul Eshleman of the Jesus Film Project and Avery Willis of the Southern Baptist IMB, the International Orality Network (ION)[39] was established in 2005. The work of ION continues to play a strategic role in the goal of completing the Great Commission. Strategies are now being developed for theological education via orality methods, which will serve the maturing church well.

---

38 New Tribes Mission is now Ethnos360, www.ethnos360.org.

39 www.orality.net.

Other fruitful practices focus on how to evangelize and disciple those of other faiths in such a way as to avoid dislocation of the new believer from their relational networks. Broadly sowing the seed of the gospel until one discovers a "person of peace" (an influential person whose heart God has already prepared to receive the Word of God—see Matthew 10) establishes an entrance for the message and the messenger within the community. Sharing the message with entire families rather than individuals, and then asking them to share what they learned with others, spreads the message widely through natural networks.

Focusing on obeying the words of Jesus rather than mental assent to doctrines results in discipling people into salvation and Christlikeness from day one. Praying for healing or deliverance as Jesus instructed his disciples to do opens the way for Jesus to reveal himself experientially to unbelievers, often resulting in the salvation of all those around. Gathering new believers together immediately in home fellowships led by one of their own (coached by the church planter) keeps the movement indigenous and less exposed to persecution.

Expecting those fellowships to multiply through each new believer widely sowing the gospel message sets the stage for the beginning of a movement. Training movement leaders to disciple and multiply other leaders in simple, reproducible means minimizes foreign influence and money, which have proven to be deadly to church planting movements. When it comes to the contextualization of the worshipping community and how Scripture is best applied within their own socio-religious-cultural context, it has been discovered that those decisions are often best made by insiders as they mature under the guidance of the Holy Spirit, the Word of God, and disciple making coaches.

All of these "best practices" are what Jesus modeled and taught his disciples during his time on earth. It is how the early church grew exponentially at its onset. It has taken us these many centuries to rediscover what has been before us all this time in the Gospels and the book of Acts!

Twenty-First Century Surprise

In 2000, Southern Baptist mission executive David Garrison published a little booklet that immediately got everyone talking. Entitled *Church Planting Movements*, Garrison reported on a few rapidly multiplying church planting movements that were occurring among unreached people groups.[40]

Up until then, most missionaries in the Muslim world would be ecstatic

---

40 Garrison, *Church Planting Movements*, 2000.

to see a handful of converts or a single church established over the course of a lifetime. Suddenly Garrison was begging the question, "Are we expecting too little? Have we been going about this all wrong?" He cast a light on what God was quietly doing.

Garrison's little booklet created so much excitement and curiosity that it was translated into more than twenty languages. Reports began to come in from other areas concerning people-group movements. Are we living in a new season of history? The description of these movements sounded like something out of the book of Acts. God was clearly up to something. Garrison got the ball rolling with his little booklet. He followed up with more extensive research, producing a larger volume, *Church Planting Movements: How God Is Redeeming a Lost World,* in which he described the commonalities of the movements that seemed to encourage their emergence and growth.[41]

Many others joined him in researching and reporting on escalating reports of people group movements to Christ in multiple regions of the world. Some sounded too fantastic to believe. Thousands of new churches in just a few years? Hundreds of thousands of new believers in just one people group? Indigenously led movements with little outside interaction?

Skepticism prompted numerous validation visits, only to discover that these amazing reports revealed what God was doing, most especially in the Muslim world. But the research also confirmed commonalities among these movements, meaning that wise mission catalysts could partner with God by implementing fruitful practices. Many of those commonalities are mentioned in the previous section, "Fruitful Practices" just prior to this section. Research also uncovered factors that slow or stop church planting movements; several of those factors turned out to be traditional church planting models.

It became obvious that if we are going to partner with the Lord of the Harvest in how he is preparing the harvest fields, then we need to evaluate our time-worn methods for sowing and reaping and the role of outside resources. A radical paradigm shift was needed in mission vision and practice, especially in the most resistant regions of the world.

Missionaries who were involved in these various movements began to train others. Several methodologies were used, though they all had similar characteristics. Today we generally refer to these movements and the underlying strategies as church planting movements (CPM) or disciple making movements (DMM).

---

41 Garrison, 2004.

Garrison energized and startled the world again with his follow-up book in 2014, *A Wind in the House of Islam*. In it he documented the greatest turning of Muslims to Christ in history. Up until 1980, Garrison could find only two voluntary movements of Muslims to Christ, numbering at least one thousand baptisms, since the time Mohammed walked on earth. Yet between 1980 and 2000, he documents eleven more such movements. That alone is a dramatic increase over only two decades versus 1,300 years. Yet in only the next twelve years (2000–2012), an additional sixty-nine movements emerged of at least a thousand *baptized* Muslim-background believers or a hundred new worshipping communities. These movements are appearing in all regions of the Muslim world. As Garrison concludes, this unprecedented surge of new followers of Jesus tells us that we are living in historic times.[42] The wind of the Holy Spirit is indeed blowing in the house of Islam!

Collaboration for the Sake of the Name

Understandably, those within Jesus movements in the Muslim world want to keep a low profile. Security issues are a prime concern. Consequently, participants were reluctant to share information and talk openly with others involved in similar movements. But there was much to learn from one another!

The Vision 5:9 Network (its name is taken from John's prophetic vision in Revelation 5:9) took on the challenge. In 2007 they brought together five hundred men and women from seventy-eight organizations and forty-six nationalities who were working among 149 Muslim people groups to collaborate around the question, "What must be done to reach all Muslim peoples?" The data collected from this historic consultation was published in the insightful book, *From Seed to Fruit: Global Trends, Fruitful Practices, and Emerging Issues Among Muslims*.[43] The consultation spurred mutual learning and collaboration and even the engagement of three hundred previously unengaged Muslim UPGs between 2008 and 2017.[44]

A second consultation was held in 2017 with even greater participation. Close to a thousand delegates from four hundred organizations and 103 nationalities participated. Over half were from the Global South and 25 percent were Muslim Background Believers (MBBs). Besides collaboration, the emphasis on abiding in Jesus and just being together was highly encouraging for the many isolated workers. An elderly gray-bearded MBB movingly responded, "For all these years, I thought I was the only hammer chipping away at a giant mountain. Now I know there are a multitude of other hammers helping me."[45]

42 Garrison, *A Wind*, 18.
43 Woodberry, ed., *From Seed to Fruit*.
44 Becker, "What Must Be Done?"
45 Daniels and Becker, "Abide, Bear Fruit," 40.

In his book, *Church Planting Movements: How God Is Redeeming a Lost World*, Garrison insightfully declared that the laborers are in the harvest. New believers within a UPG, effectively discipled to multiply and train others to multiply are the key to church planting movements. Outsiders (missionaries) are still needed to catalyze the movement, but the goal is for the movement to take off without them. Disciples making disciples. Churches planting churches. Movements multiplying movements. The harvest field is simultaneously becoming the harvest force.

CPMs and DMMs are not happening only within Muslim peoples, but also among Hindus, Buddhists, atheists, secularists, and even post-modern Westerners. The methods change per the context, but the same biblical principles are at the core. Many organizations, churches, agencies, and individuals have begun implementing CPM/DMM principles. Experienced indigenous leaders of CPM networks are serving as regional and global trainers to catalyze movements in other peoples. In North America, the Zúme Project put CPM training online, with free access, to train everyday Christians in multiplying disciple making movements.[46]

In 2017 a group of CPM global leaders formed a global movement network they called the 24:14 Coalition,[47] named after Jesus's declaration in Matthew 24:14. The 24:14 Coalition pulls together all those implementing CPM principles, practitioners from both within and outside the unreached people group. The mission of the 24:14 Coalition is to engage every unreached people and place, through an effective kingdom-movement strategy, with sacrificial urgency, by the end of 2025. In prayer, the leaders felt the need for a target date to stir urgency, as statistics reveal that even though the number of UPGs has declined, the population of the remaining UPGs is growing much faster than the rate of evangelization. Only Christ-followers working in partnership with Almighty God to foster rapidly multiplying movements can stem the tide of a burgeoning unevangelized world.

The trust generated through the 24:14 Coalition prompted many movement leaders to open up and share for the first time how God was working in their midst. The work of God is far bigger than anyone dreamed! In April 2017, it was estimated that there were 162 viable church planting movements (CPM) with 20 million new disciples. A CPM is defined as a movement of at least four separate streams, each at least four generations deep (churches planting churches), that multiply rapidly in a short period of time. By the end of 2017, the Coalition could confidently report 650 movements of 50 million new disciples![48] By December 2022, the number

---

46 www.zume.vision.

47 www.2414now.net.

48 Butler, "A Decade's Progress."

of global CPMs had more than doubled to 1966, encompassing around 116 million disciples.[49]

Quite naturally, such explosive growth stimulated suspicion and criticism from some Christian voices, particularly voices from the West. Valid questions were raised about exaggerated numbers, risk of syncretism or heresy, and depth of biblical instruction. Many critics had little to no personal interaction with the movements themselves and based their opposition on a lack of information or understanding of what was actually transpiring within these movements. Others analyzed the movements from a Western construct of church and historical mission models.

A new network, the *Motus Dei* Network arose in 2017 to study and discuss movement issues at a deeper missiological level. "*Motus Dei*" is Latin for "movement of God." According to their website, the *Motus Dei* Network aims to foster quality research, edify and empower frontier workers, constructively critique and mature the evangelical missiological discourse on discipleship movements, investigate how biblical discipleship movements lead to human flourishing and holistic transformation of lives and communities, and to facilitate publishing of training materials and tools for church and mission.[50]

In the height of the COVID pandemic, in the fall of 2020, a substantial Movements Research Symposium was held virtually, initiated by the *Motus Dei* Network. Theologians, missiologists, and field practitioners from both the Global North and the Global South participated. A very helpful book emmanated from this Symposium, *Motus Dei: The Movement of God to Disciple the Nations*.[51] The book explores movement research methodologies and results, theology and dynamics, and addresses theological and missiological objections to church planting movements. Four case studies are presented from diverse religious and geographical regions. The book also helpfully examines today's movements in the light of historical people movements to Christ, including those we find in the scriptures.

Although there have been church planting movements periodically throughout history, what we are seeing today is unprecedented. God is on the move, and he is teaching us how to move with him. "Look among the nations! Observe! Be astonished! Wonder! Because I am doing something in your days—You would not believe if you were told" (Hab 1:5 NASB1995).

---

49 24:14 Multiplying, "Global Dashboard December 2022."

50 www.motusdei.network.

51 Farah, *Motus Dei*.

College Student to Church Planting Movement

"My name is Jay. I'm a student at Union University. I heard about this Perspectives course from a man named Steve Shadrach, and I would like to see if we can have a class in Jackson, Tennessee. I'm working to mobilize college students to pray for unreached people groups."

This phone call enticed me to make the drive from Nashville to visit with Jay. In God's providence, we were launching our first Perspectives class in Memphis, less than an hour's drive from Jackson. Jay enthusiastically enrolled. The year was 1997.

The instructor roster for the Memphis class included Dr. George Patterson, who taught at Western Seminary and was well known for his teaching strategies to enable multiplying movements to Christ.

Jay recalls, "I was in awe as this old guy jumped around the room in the most creative and biblically based presentation of leadership issues I have ever seen. I had never heard someone talk as if the multiplication movement in Acts was actually possible and even expected of the church today!"

What began as email exchanges became a lifelong mentoring relationship between Patterson and Jay. Jay enrolled in Western Seminary to receive direct instruction from Patterson.

"The first day of class in the fall of 1999 my first assignment was to start a temporary underground-training church. This training exercise was the most paradigm-shifting experience of my life, other than my commitment to Christ."

Patterson engaged in obedience-oriented education, rather than typical academic-oriented education. Lessons learned were expected to be applied. God was preparing Jay for the assignment that lay ahead of him.

Jay prayed for God to send him to the hardest least-reached peoples on earth. He landed in "one of the hottest, smelliest, darkest corners of Burma (Myanmar). I had read somewhere that having a faith goal was helpful, so I prayed that God would start seven new churches within the next year."

One day in 2003, Jay heard a knock on his door. Future movement leaders, "The Major" and "The Farmer," as Jay later called them, were standing there. Jay began meeting with them in a temporary training church, encouraging them to worship Jesus in a way that Burmese Buddhists would feel comfortable. Most churches in Buddhist nations do not worship according to the style of the majority-Buddhist peoples. The majority of believers in those nations are drawn from minority tribal groups, not Buddhist peoples. The churches are often Western, the model adopted from early missionaries.

"As I was mentoring these two men behind the scenes and encouraging them to 'just obey Jesus in your own way,' a miracle began to happen. Buddhist friends and family members of these two men started to come to Christ in February 2004. Much to my astonishment, the first seven house churches were started by April."

This was the beginning of what was to become a multiplication movement far beyond anyone's wildest expectations. Jay used Patterson's leadership-training course to train leaders in the movement. He encouraged The Major to develop his own method for sharing Christ with Buddhists. The Major chose to use the laws of Buddhism to help seekers understand their sinfulness. By starting with the Four Noble Truths of Buddhism, he explained that Jesus came down from the "Golden City" to forgive us and grant us release from the cycle of sin and suffering. This method enabled thousands of Buddhists to understand the gospel and thereby turn from serving idols to worshipping the risen Lord.

As the movement grew organically, it spread to other unreached people groups, including a large Hindu group in Burma, and the Muslim Rohingya. Even though their own people were at war with one another, Burmese Buddhist-background believers engaged in compassionate ministry toward their Rohingya Muslim "enemy," sharing the gospel with them. Before long, the gospel movement began to multiply rapidly among Rohingya Muslims, bringing tens of thousands into relationship with Jesus as Lord.

Of course, it hasn't been without opposition, both spiritual and human. Early on, Jay was diagnosed with kidney failure for no apparent reason. This, along with relational storms, almost derailed Jay from the mission. New believers faced their own storms of religious persecution, war, displacement, and devastating cyclones. One particularly aggressive Buddhist monk went from village to village to persecute the new believers, telling them, "Your Jesus is destroying our Buddhism. You must not speak to any more Buddhists about Jesus." Yet the movement continued to grow as God enabled perseverance and turned tragedies into opportunities.

Instead of conceptualizing "church" in the Western sense, new believers were taught through inductive Bible study simply to obey Jesus's commands, share Jesus's stories, and gather in small circles to worship in indigenous ways, all led by locals rather than outsiders. An easily reproducible model. Prayers for the sick, demonic deliverances, compassionate ministries, crisis response, and community-development projects enhanced gospel reception.

The faithfulness of the new believers is exemplary. The story of two believers represents the story of many. A former prostitute chose to follow Jesus in August, and by December had started fourteen house churches three generations deep. And a fire chief, within three months of his baptism, led his entire fire station to Christ and started four new house churches, consisting of sixty-eight former Buddhists.

Adoniram Judson is famous as one of the earliest missionaries sent out from the US, arriving in Burma in 1813. He had great evangelistic success among tribal peoples, but stated, "It is easier to pull a tooth from a tiger than to reach a Burmese Buddhist!"

The tiger of Buddhist resistance to the gospel of Jesus Christ is being rendered toothless in our day! A 2022 evaluation of just this one movement in Burma reveals 26,148 house churches with over 307,000 baptized believers since 2004. This movement has spread into numerous unreached people groups in multiple other nations.

Do you think that young college student sitting in that Perspectives class years ago could have imagined in his wildest dreams that Jesus would invite him into such an amazing movement of God?[52]

---

52 Jay Judson, from personal email correspondence with me and newsletters over many years. Global Catalytic Network (GCN), https://obedience.life/.

7

Catalyzing a Movement

The Perspectives course helps make the local church aware of how a rapidly changing world is impacting the prospect and practice of mission. New missionaries raised up out of the local church, with new vision and understanding gleaned from Perspectives, are better equipped to partner with God in what he is already doing. As are ordinary church members who are mobilized to pray, support, and establish church mission strategies.

Continuing the story of the Perspectives movement, we will see the twenty-first century challenges Perspectives USA encountered in continuing to educate and mobilize the church.

Struggling to Catch Up

As the number of Perspectives courses and students proliferated following the 1999 curriculum revision, the national Perspectives USA office found itself struggling to catch up. Adding to the challenge, the steady leadership of the Perspectives program experienced turnover. At the turn of the millennium, Lee Purgason, after fourteen years directing the national Perspectives Study Program, assumed the role of director of operations for the U.S. Center for World Mission. The directorship of Perspectives was turned over to Steve Halley, who had been working in the Perspectives office under Purgason since 1992. Halley led the Perspectives movement through times of strong growth—a 60-percent increase in the number of annual classes during his watch—but also times of conflict, transition, and frustration.

Steve Halley was mobilized toward mission among the unreached as a college student in the mid eighties. The student mission groups on his campus and his own father, a Nazarene pastor and Perspectives alumnus, introduced Halley to the concept of reaching the remaining unreached people groups. When Halley first took the Perspectives class, it was not so much new information to him as a continuation of his journey. After graduation, Halley and his wife joined the staff of the USCWM and he began to serve in the Perspectives office. Eight years later he was tapped to direct the national Perspectives Study Program.[1]

Steve Halley, Perspectives USA director 2000-2004,
is the tall blonde in the middle, surrounded by colleagues.

Although the numbers of classes and coordinators and students continued to experience robust growth, the size of the staff in the national office serving that growth remained stagnant, handicapping progress and effectual service to the movement. In the void, a new grassroots entity emerged, with the Perspectives office's blessing, to help meet the growing needs of coordinators and to move past maintenance to development. At a meeting of veteran Perspectives coordinators in Washington, DC, in 1998, the idea of an Executive Coordinators Council (ECC) was birthed. The purpose of the ECC was to work alongside the national office, helping to develop and expand Perspectives in the US in ways that the personnel-strapped national office could not.

---

1 Steve Halley, interview by author, February 15, 2008, transcript.

It must be stated, however, that the impetus for the ECC grew out of a season of discontent with the U.S. Center for a lack of leadership and responsiveness to coordinator needs. The ECC set about serving as an advocate for coordinators, providing leadership and accountability, but on the flip side it also magnified disgruntled voices.

Experienced coordinators elected representatives to sit on the ECC for three-year terms. The first ECC meeting was in the summer of 1999, on the heels of the major curriculum revision of the third edition. That only added to the tension and discord. U.S. Center personnel were anxious to recapture a Perspectives movement that had drifted away from the standard Perspectives text into differing curricula.

Questions of ownership began to emerge. The Perspectives course had grown into a movement of awareness, education, and equipping for mission to unreached peoples. Many other Bible studies, curricula, and courses had emerged from the seed of the Perspectives course. The question began to be asked, *What is Perspectives?* Is it a course developed and conducted by the U.S. Center for World Mission? Or is it more? Can the name "Perspectives" be attached to an entire movement representing various organizations, curricula, content, and goals, as long as they relate to frontier mission?

The debate over alternative curricula being used in a Perspectives class continued for many months, with Halley and ECC Chairman Scott White serving as mediators and seeking reconciliation between parties at variance with one another. The final conclusion recognized that even though Perspectives had indeed become a movement expanding in many directions, for the sake of integrity and clarity the name "Perspectives" must refer only to the course developed and owned by the U.S. Center for World Mission. Otherwise, there is not only confusion, but Perspectives could become associated with concepts and outcomes that are not aligned with the core teaching of the course. Other courses and curricula that grew out of the Perspectives seed and carried the same core values and ideas as Perspectives came to be referred to as being in the "Perspectives Family." From 2003 onward, only the standard Perspectives curriculum could be used in an official Perspectives class.

According to White, another point of contention was how much ownership the ECC could have to develop initiatives and direct the Perspectives program. The U.S. Center viewed the ECC as an advisory council, but the ECC saw themselves as an activist board.[2] Halley and the ECC were operating during a vacuum of visionary leadership for Perspectives at the U.S. Center. A maintenance mentality and severe personnel shortage

---

2 Scott White, interview by author, May 8, 2008, email.

limited the intentional growth Halley longed to see. Those were frustrating years for all, Halley recalls, yet several steps forward were taken.[3]

It was painfully clear to all that Perspectives had to catch up with the information age. The Perspectives website was revamped from an information-only page to an interactive site that would provide resources and digitize record-keeping, relieving local coordinators from a mountain of paperwork. Much more needed to be done in this area, but at least they had made a strong start.

Under Halley's direction and the ECC's active leadership, Perspectives coordinator training was completely revised. With the drift away from national leadership, regional networks of coordinators had developed their own coordinator training. Veteran coordinator Sundee Simmons was recruited to garner the best training of each region and create a single training manual and workshop. In the process, Halley worked hard to reestablish and strengthen relationships with regional leaders. Halley also introduced a one-week pastors' and leaders' Perspectives Intensive course for those who could not attend a normal fifteen-week course. The format was successful, becoming part of the permanent schedule.

In July of 2001 a field council of over a hundred coordinators convened in Denver for three days of networking, resourcing, and equipping. Such a large national event had never been held in Perspectives' twenty-seven-year history. The event was planned and executed by the ECC in conjunction with the Perspectives office, and hosted by Caleb Project. It was a tremendous success in bringing unity, consistency, and training to the national network of coordinators.

During its four years of existence, the ECC gave visionary leadership to the Perspectives course and movement, investing much time and energy in strategic planning, program development, and increasing funding. In 2004 the ECC disbanded at its members' own initiative because of disagreement with the USCWM over how much ownership and decision-making ability they were allowed. That same year, Halley resigned from his position as director of the national Perspectives office.[4]

Through the turbulence of those four years, the necessity for major modification of the infrastructure of the national office was made visible. The USCWM renewed its commitment to invest in and nurture the Perspectives movement it had birthed. Unexpectedly, a substantial transition in Perspectives' trajectory was emerging on the horizon.

---

3 Halley, interview.
4 Halley.

A New Start: Fresh Faces in New Places

The year 2004 proved to be a pivotal year for the Perspectives Study Program. It marked thirty years since the inception of the course at Wheaton in 1974. In all those years, the U.S. Perspectives national staff lived and worked within the greater community of the U.S. Center for World Mission in Pasadena, California. For years the U.S. Center had regional staff who oversaw Perspectives classes in their region, but the national headquarters had always been in Pasadena. That was about to change.

In 2004 U.S. Center leadership entered negotiations with veteran mission mobilizer Steve Shadrach to take the helm of the Mobilization Division of the USCWM. Shadrach was interested, especially if it included the Perspectives Study Program. The dilemma? Shadrach was heavily vested in his own student mobilization ministries headquartered out of his home state of Arkansas. Could the U.S. Center possibly consent to move a major division out of the bosom of the Center itself?

As a young man, Steve Shadrach was profoundly influenced by Bob Sjogren, only five years after college-aged Sjogren participated in the remarkable 1980 Penn State Perspectives class. Sjogren brought a team of mission mobilizers to Fayetteville, Arkansas, where Shadrach was serving as a college pastor. When Sjogren's team addressed the college students, the individual most impacted was Shadrach himself. At Sjogren's urging, Steve and Carol Shadrach headed out to Pasadena to take the Perspectives Intensive class in the summer of 1985. Their lives would never be the same. Shadrach recalls,

> I didn't even finish the Perspectives class because I was so anxious to get back to Arkansas to put into practice all the great things I had learned. I was so full, to overflowing; I couldn't sit in class and listen to one more speaker or read one more article. I told the coordinator that I just can't take any more. I have to *do* something with what I have been given over the last month. I had come to Pasadena thinking I knew a lot about missions; I was humbled. I left Pasadena with an expanded vision. Previously I was just trying to reach college students for Christ; now each campus became a launching pad and sending base to raise up laborers to reach the world for Christ.[5]

The following year Shadrach coordinated the first ever Perspectives class in the state of Arkansas.

---

5 Steve Shadrach, interview by author, February 22, 2008, email.

Sixty students packed out a room and hung on every word that every speaker shared each week. There was so much excitement and electricity in that room week by week that we thought the second Pentecost had come! Most all of those initial sixty *are in missions or ministry today.*[6]

Continuing to work with college students, Shadrach subsequently founded three different ministries designed to recruit, train, and connect believers to involvement in the Great Commission: The Traveling Team—bands of college graduates visiting campuses to ignite mission vision; Student Mobilization—an evangelistic and discipleship campus ministry focused on creating lifelong laborers for the kingdom; and The BodyBuilders—a mobilization and equipping vehicle to help Christians fulfill the Great Commission.[7]

Steve Shadrach with Ralph Winter.

In 2003, Shadrach was asked to conduct a seminar on personal support-raising for all U.S. Center staff. As he stood teaching in Pasadena, a flood of memories enveloped him as he remembered how his journey in mission mobilization was ignited at that same spot eighteen years earlier. By early 2004 Shadrach was recruited to direct the Mobilization Division of the Center. His acceptance predicated moving both the Mobilization office and the national Perspectives office to his home and ministry headquarters in Fayetteville, Arkansas.[8] Such a decentralized move was unprecedented in USCWM history, and it was especially amazing that it included Perspectives, a flagship ministry of the Center.

---

6 Shadrach, interview.

7 The BodyBuilders was renamed the Center for Mission Mobilization.

8 Shadrach, interview.

Shadrach asked Dave Flynn to become the director of the national Perspectives office. Dave and Elizabeth Flynn had been a part of the USCWM staff since 1999, having left the corporate world to enter ministry. He was not initially interested in the job and did not want to move his family to Arkansas, but after a season of prayer he felt that maybe a fresh voice would be an asset to the Perspectives Study Program. Flynn brought a valuable mix of business experience in marketing and degrees in missiology and management to the Perspectives directorship.[9]

The move was a huge transition for the national Perspectives office. Only a few of the existing staff elected to move, so not only was there a transition in the leadership of Perspectives, but a turnover of the staff as well. New staff were recruited in Arkansas, enlarging the Perspectives office and filling desperately needed positions. At long last the office was staffing up to meet the increasing demands of the program.

Steve Shadrach and Dave Flynn brought new vision and vitality to the Perspectives program. The move to Northwest Arkansas didn't hurt either. The staff discovered that they were able to accomplish a vast amount more being away from the extra demands and distractions of everyday life at the Center. The downside was missing the live-in community and the regular missiology briefings by Ralph Winter and visiting specialists.

Dave Flynn, Perspectives USA director 2004–2012, with his wife Liz.

Transformation began with an administrative overhaul. The Perspectives staff was divided into two teams. Dave Flynn headed up the more visionary aspect as it relates to strategy, marketing, personnel, and outside development. The weighty responsibility for the more administrative functions—finances, administration, information technology, publications,

---

9 Dave Flynn, interview by author, February 1, 8, and 13, 2008, transcript and email.

and relationship management with instructors, coordinators, alumni, and mission agencies—was handled by a team directed by John Patton and Lisa Freyenberger. The United States was divided into fourteen regions; and a full-time or part-time director was placed over each region, with volunteer coordinators serving under them. This increased structure was designed to result in faster multiplication of classes. To promote greater unity and consistency across the regions and to quell previous discontent, an annual meeting of all Perspectives regional directors was instituted, as well as a yearly visit by Dave Flynn to each region.

Rebuilding Perspectives staff in 2006
soon after relocation to Fayetteville, Arkansas.

The next challenge was overhauling the heavy administrative burden of both local class coordinators and the national office. Flynn conducted a study of coordinator retention and discovered that roughly 70 percent coordinated only one time. Granted, many coordinators went to the mission field themselves or transitioned into other roles, but would more trained coordinators remain if the administrative burden were lessened?

To tackle this challenge the Perspectives office outsourced the design of a website that would automate class functions and allow for personalized tracking and interaction with each student. By 2007, almost all class administrative functions, student coursework, and instructor resources were put on the website. Promotion was centralized, with a customizable website for each individual class, strengthening the branding of the course, while saving time and money. These changes were to allow the coordinating team to pour their time and energy into the lives of their students, rather than the machinery. This step alone was a huge leap forward for the Perspectives program.

Another key challenge that had been weighing on Perspectives personnel for years was tracking and maintaining relationships with former students. There were no systems in place to encourage and guide alumni in processing what they learned and in taking next steps. For the first time, a Perspectives staff person was assigned just to the task of alumni follow-up. New resources were put on the website to enable alumni to learn methods of mobilizing their church, steps to prepare for the mission field, ways to support and serve missionaries, how to pray knowledgeably for the world, opportunities to use their business skills in mission, and tips on ministering to internationals in our midst.

The Perspectives course began on college campuses, but over the decades the class composition changed primarily to lay people in church pews. Yet college students are a prime audience for Perspectives. As Ralph Winter was known for saying so many years ago, "God cannot lead you on the basis of facts you do not know." How important for college students to grasp God's global purpose and make lifelong decisions concerning how they can best contribute to it, rather than discovering God's purpose years down the road and regretting how youthful decisions had handicapped them.

The new national Perspectives staff set about recapturing the university audience. Dave Flynn contacted many campus ministers in cities with ongoing Perspectives classes and discovered that many were not even aware of Perspectives. The national office sought to correct this and, while not in any way neglecting those of other ages, fill Perspectives classes up with college students once again. They recruited campus mobilizers and set goals to begin Perspectives classes near campus communities.[10] The intentional focus worked. Today there are many Perspectives classes on the outskirts of college campuses filled with the younger generation.

New Edition for a New Millennium

By the middle of the first decade of the twenty-first century, plans were already underway for another revision of the Perspectives curriculum. A decision was made not to make a complete overhaul of the text, as was done with the third edition, but to update it substantially to reflect new frontier mission realities.

During 2007, a "Fourth Edition Tour" was set up in nine cities having a long history of hosting Perspectives courses to garner input for the revision. The revision team, consisting of primary editors Ralph Winter and Steve Hawthorne, national director Dave Flynn, and curriculum specialist Bruce

---

10 Flynn, interview.

Koch, traveled to each city to meet with key stakeholders. Over 130 people attended the meetings and provided insightful feedback.[11]

And then the completely unexpected happened. Astoundingly not one, but both primary editors, Winter and Hawthorne, suffered major heart attacks within a few months of each other. God was gracious in not only sparing their lives but bringing them to complete recovery. The revision process, however, was delayed.

A large national conference was planned for the introduction of the fourth edition. It was also billed as a celebration of the thirty-five years since the seed of the Perspectives course was first planted at Urbana '73. All who had ever served as coordinators or instructors through the years were invited to the celebration in Dallas, Texas, in June 2008. Global developers of the Perspectives course were invited to share in the celebration and to give reports on how God was using Perspectives in other parts of the world. Over four hundred attended the conference, at their own expense, with a surprising and encouraging representation of over thirty arriving from other nations. A true national conference of this nature, inviting all those who had made Perspectives a reality in so many places through the years, was a first for the Perspectives movement.

Indeed, there was much to celebrate. Statistics from 2008 reveal that Perspectives had become a flourishing movement. Over six thousand people were enrolling in two hundred US classes per year. Those students were being served by fourteen regional directors, over twelve hundred instructors, twenty-six hundred trained coordinators, thousands of volunteers serving on coordinating teams, and a burgeoning national staff. Perspectives now counted over eighty thousand alumni from North American classes, almost 60 percent of whom had taken the class in the eight years since the turn of the millennium![12] Global growth was beginning to accelerate as well. Statistics tell only part of the story. The real story is the transformed lives, churches, mission organizations, and unreached peoples flowing out from Perspectives students carrying God's heart for all nations.

The fourth edition was finished and released in 2009, ten years after the previous revision. It contained sixty new articles, reflecting new dimensions and new voices in mission. In total, 150 mission scholars and practitioners contributed to the *Reader*, with an increased participation of both international and female authors. It also marked the last Perspectives curriculum upon which Ralph Winter would actively leave his fingerprints.

---

11 Flynn, "Perspectives 4th Edition Tour."
12 Statistics compiled from various published and unpublished sources.

Auxillary Curriculum for Strategic Demographics

Near the end of the previous century, key African American leaders burdened with the mobilization of the substantial African American church came together to form the Cooperative Missions Network of the African Dispersion (COMINAD). The goal was to increase understanding of and partnership in the Great Commission, providing mission resources, strategies, and networking for Christian descendants of Africa. The gloomy statistics presented by Vaughn Walston at the turn of the century revealed that even though African Americans made up 12 percent of the US population, they comprised less than 1 percent of the US international missionary force.[13] While Walston enumerated historical and contemporary reasons for the imbalance, this dismal picture was not always the case. From the earliest days of the American republic, the African American church was committed to cross-cultural missions. In fact, the very first missionary to be sent out from American soil was freed slave George Liele in 1783.

With a desire to uncover and recover their rich heritage in global missions, African American leaders such as Vaughn Walston and COMINAD director Brian Johnson, both partly mobilized by the Perspectives course, and Virgil Amos, founder of Ambassadors Fellowship and a perennial Perspectives instructor, partnered with USCWM regional representative Bob Stevens in 2003 to produce a first-of-its-kind resource for the African American church. Entitled *African-American Experience in World Mission: A Call Beyond Community*,[14] the book tells the stories of African Americans in mission and challenges the church to pick up the baton of mission engagement carried by their forefathers and mothers. Initially envisioned as an ancillary volume to the Perspectives *Reader*, and in a similar format, the compendium became useful both in Perspectives classes and as a stand-alone mobilization tool.

Visionary children's workers wanted to see the teachings of the Perspectives course made accessible to the upcoming generation. Brainstorming for how to make this happen began at the International Children's Expo in 2002. Caleb Project staff shouldered the organizational task[15] and in 2007 published *Outside the Lines: Connecting Kids to God's Global Purpose*.[16] The age-appropriate material was written by volunteers across the country, providing creative activities and multimedia lessons for grades K–8.

---

13 Walston, "Ignite the Passion."
14 Walston and Stevens, *African-American Experience*.
15 Tichy, "Outside the Lines."
16 Now available from Via, https://store.vianations.org/collections/family-mobilization.

Nancy Tichy at the USCWM took an active lead, assisted by a young woman named Carissa Potter. Potter took the vision to produce world Christian resources for families and children to the next level. She started a ministry called Weave,[17] producing an array of resources in multiple languages that help parents disciple their children to understand and participate in God's global mission. One of those resources, *The Journey*,[18] corresponds to the Perspectives lessons. These resources have been a tremendous resource for running a children's course alongside a local Perspectives course, enabling entire families to study the same Perspectives themes together.

Another curriculum and course that evolved in part out of Perspectives is *Encountering the World of Islam* (EWI).[19] In the 1990s, USCWM staff member Keith Swartley began working on a tool to educate Christians about Muslims—their beliefs, practices, historical and contemporary outreach—with an aim to replace caricatures and fear of Muslims with God's love for Muslim peoples. He crafted a course and curriculum along the lines of the Perspectives course.

After the shock of the 9/11 tragedy in 2001, curiosity about Islam in the West skyrocketed, along with a deepening hunger by many Christians to develop an intentional outreach to Muslims. Recognizing that God had prepared them for this season, Keith and Ethel Swartley joined Caleb Project (now part of Pioneers mission agency) in 2002 to make the development and administration of this course their primary ministry. *Encountering the World of Islam* has served as an excellent follow-on course for Perspectives students as they gain a heart for the peoples of the world. The program has grown internationally and been translated into several languages.[20]

Yet another curriculum that emerged directly from the content in the Perspectives course is *Operation Worldview*,[21] created by Werner Mischke. Mischke and Bob Schindler had just relocated their agency, Mission ONE, to my hometown of Nashville when they took Perspectives. The two of them mobilized their pastor to host a Perspectives class at their church a few years later.

The second session of that class still resonates in my memory. Steve Hawthorne was teaching on "The Story of God's Glory." I've heard Hawthorne teach this lesson many times, but this night was unique. The presence of God was pulsating through the message of the lesson. Hawthorne went over time, but no one seemed to care. The pastor, who was leaving early the

---

17 www.weavefamily.org/.

18 For a free download, see www.weavefamily.org/publisher/caleb-resources/.

19 Swartley, *Encountering*.

20 www.encounteringislam.org/.

21 www.mission1.org/books/.

next morning for Russia, stayed another hour to talk with Hawthorne and process the message. But it was Werner Mischke's heart that was penetrated most deeply by the "Story of God's Glory." He was never the same.

As a media professional, Mischke developed an interactive DVD curriculum based upon key lessons from the Perspectives course. Released in 2002, *Operation Worldview* consists of eight one-hour leader-guided sessions designed for small groups.[22] *Operation Worldview* is intended to be an awakening course for churches; it actively promotes the Perspectives course for follow-on engagement. Mischke's desire is that participants come away as he did after taking Perspectives—captured by the Story that is above all stories and desiring to discover one's destiny in God's global love story.

Coordinator Training Reboot

In the Perspectives movement, the key stakeholders are those investing a significant capital of personal time and energy, usually volunteers. Sundee Simmons is one of those stakeholders whose contribution to Perspectives has been lifelong and transformative for the movement. Sundee's story not only traces the development of Perspectives' coordinator training, but is also illustrative of the journey of many Perspectives leaders. Not since the early 1980s, when Jay and Olgy Gary instituted coordinator training, has anyone left such an imprint on the development of this key pillar of Perspectives. Below is Sundee's story, told in her own words.

> I first took Perspectives the fall after I graduated from college in 1990. The deepest impact of the class on me was in how I prayed. My prayer changed from "God, help me with my life," to "God, for your glory, what do you want from me?" When your prayer life changes, everything changes. I saw the Bible differently, the role of the church differently, and my purpose differently.
>
> In 1991 the Perspectives class in my area needed administrative support. I was simultaneously taking the class at the certificate level, as was my future husband. This was when I first started developing administrative processes and creating forms to help me keep track of all the details.
>
> My husband and I originally intended to become cross-cultural missionaries. God, however, redirected our paths to become mission mobilizers. Scott became the mission pastor of a large church in Baltimore, Maryland, and I seized the opportunity to coordinate a Perspectives class for our new church in the fall of 1999. The Washington Baltimore Area Office of the U.S. Center for World Mission asked me to join their staff as the Perspectives Administrator.

---

22 www.mission1.org/four-components-of-operation-worldview.

One of my previous occupations was to write training manuals for a computer training company. When I saw the Perspectives training manual they were using, it broke all the rules I was taught. So the first thing I did was rewrite the manual. The next thing I did was centralize the communication and finances for the region. As the training and administration were professionalized, we saw incredible growth.

I eventually became both the director of the Washington Baltimore Center for World Mission and the Perspectives Regional Director of the Mid-Atlantic region. In 2001, I attended the Perspectives Field Council in Colorado, where I met national Perspectives leadership for the first time. They asked me to take the eight different Perspectives Coordinator Workshop manuals being used in the various regions and create one coordinator training manual to be used nationally.

Over the next few years I worked closely with Perspectives national director Steve Halley to design new policies, infrastructure, tools, and training that volunteers would need to conduct a Perspectives class. Two people had an outsized impact on how our coordinator workshops are conducted today. Arizona Perspectives coordinator Meg Crossman and Missouri coordinator Martha Shirkey, a retired school principal, aided us in team-building and implementing various adult-learning techniques into the workshop.

When the Perspectives staff in Arkansas launched a new website, it required another rewrite of the Perspectives coordinator training manual. In the process we also created a trainer version of the manual to train the Regional Directors to conduct the workshops. From this point forward, all Perspectives coordinator training was nationalized and uniform in content, yet regionalized in delivery.

When my husband and I moved back to Florida in 2010, I decided that instead of serving as a Regional Director for Florida, I wanted to be administrative assistant to two Eastern seaboard regional directors. USA Perspectives director Dave Flynn liked the idea so much that he decided every RD needed an assistant, and thus the role of Regional Administrator was born.

In 2012, I became the national Director of Training. In this capacity I worked with all the other Perspectives departments to update coordinator training regularly, develop webinars, and provide resources. Along with the RDs, we continually learn and evaluate how we can do things better.[23]

---

23 Sundee Simmons, interview with author, February 25, 2019, email.

Sundee Simmons transitioned from Perspectives USA to Perspectives Global in 2020 to serve the growing cadre of international Perspectives developers, coordinators, and instructors. Her journey of thirty years provides invaluable assistance to our global colleagues.

Sundee Simmons overhauled Perspectives
Coordinator training, building a strong foundation
for all future training.

Launching Online

For thirty-six years Perspectives was only offered as a live, in-person class. Oh, a few could take it as independent study, but not many did ... well, Steve Hawthorne did! It took an enterprising, seminary-trained biomedical scientist, originally from Sri Lanka, to initiate and build a modern delivery system for Perspectives.

Richard Gunasekera enrolled in the Perspectives course in 1989, when he was a graduate student at the University of Houston. The impact of the class was so great on him that he designed his graduate project on reaching unreached people groups in Sri Lanka. His project did not stay on paper; he spent the next couple of years in Sri Lanka mobilizing the local church to reach out to the UPGs around them. As part of his strategy, he ran a Perspectives program for English-speaking young people in Colombo.

Upon his return to Houston, Gunasekera served as a volunteer Perspectives coordinator, instructor, and professor of record for credit-level students throughout the decade of the 1990s. At a meeting with Dr. Winter and Perspectives leadership in 2004, Gunasekera proposed creating an online option for homework and exams, in addition to the current paper-based practice. That step eventually led to developing and implementing a full online program in 2010. Gunasekera credits Dave Flynn and Lisa Freyenberger in helping frame the original vision, and

Melissa Barron and John Patton as key developers. Ryan Emis piloted the first international run for the online course, serving as coordinator for a class of Wycliffe Bible translators scattered across the globe.[24]

Richard Gunasekera developed the Perspectives online course offering.

The beauty of the online course is that it allows anyone at any place in the world to take the Perspectives class in English, as long as they have sufficient bandwidth to stream the video instruction. Cohorts are encouraged to participate in discussion groups, which are often enriched through international perspectives. It is a valuable resource for missionaries in the field, indigenous leaders, international students, and those in rural areas who are unlikely to have access to a live class. It has also been welcomed by pastors, leaders, businesswomen and men, and moms whose schedules do not allow them to attend a normal semester-long course. In 2012, a group of healthcare professionals took the class together online.

At the very outset in 2010, 200 students registered for one of the several online course offerings during the year. Registration totals jumped to 750 in 2016, registering around 550 students annually since then. Of course, not everyone who registers completes the course; only those who receive credit or a certificate of completion. By the end of 2022, a cumulative total of 3,267 students had completed the video-driven online Perspectives USA course.

Back to the Mother Ship—Headwinds Ahead

In the rolling hills of Northwest Arkansas, the USCWM Mobilization Division continued rapid recruitment of staff. Campus ministries were ramping up, positioning mission mobilization specialists at strategic colleges and universities, all of whom actively promoted or conducted Perspectives classes. The Perspectives program staff was also expanding, enabling long-

---

24 Richard Gunasekera, interview by author, December 20, 2018, email.

held priorities and aspirations to be realized. With a new website, resources, tools, a renewed focus on students, and the first ever national marketing campaign, Perspectives annual class enrollment approached a record ten thousand in 2011! That same year a record number of alumni trained to become Perspectives coordinators, laying a foundation for future growth.

Meanwhile, the USCWM parent organization was trudging through the difficult transition of the closing of one era and the emergence of a new one with the passing of its founder, Ralph Winter, in 2009. Besides adjusting to a change at the helm, the more pressing issue was gaining clarity on the future mission and vision for the organization in a post-Winter era. The staff wanted to maintain continuity with Ralph and Roberta Winter's legacy, while also recognizing the need to move forward in new ways. They struggled with how best to bring the past into the future. It took several years to figure it all out and put new goals and infrastructure in place.

The juxtaposition of one segment of an organization "on hold," as it thoughtfully and prayerfully considered its future, and the other segment driving a robust vision with rapid recruitment and deployment, was jarring to the organization. Tension and frustration mounted.

The physical separation between California and Arkansas highlighted the deeper separation in corporate culture. When Steve Shadrach assumed the leadership of the Mobilization Division, he already had several active mobilization ministries he was managing and carried a broad vision for the future. The Perspectives office started with a staff of five when they moved to Arkansas in 2005; by 2012 there were over one hundred on the Mobilization staff, many spread across the country at college campuses. Although not all staff were directly serving Perspectives, they promoted and undergirded the Perspectives movement. By contrast, the USCWM parent organization made decisions and recruited staff at a much slower pace and carried different operational values. In essence, the USCWM and its Mobilization Division had become two strong entities with their visions and strategies not aligning.

When the USCWM board of directors and Steve Shadrach could not come to agreement on the direction and operation of the Mobilization Division, they parted ways. The USCWM board decided to move the national Perspectives office back to California in mid 2012. At that point, national Perspectives director Dave Flynn resigned, electing to stay in Arkansas with the mobilization ministries that had been developed there. Shadrach launched the Center for Mission Mobilization (CMM) to continue pursuing their vision and activities. Since all but a handful of Perspectives staff had been recruited in Arkansas, none of the staff wanted to move to California. Like dominos falling, almost all resigned in mass and joined the CMM.

This separation of staff from the USCWM was very painful to all involved. Naturally the Perspectives staff loved Perspectives and had given their lives to it. The CMM sought to practice Hebrews 12:15 and not allow bitterness to take root. They covenanted with one another to not dishonor their former organization. Likewise, USCWM staff told each other, "Love is not an option." Even though they also felt a sense of betrayal, they recognized that they had an opportunity to do something that is rarely done well in the Christian world: to separate with love, honor, and dignity.

The following year was extremely difficult and precarious for the fledgling Perspectives staff. The USCWM undergirded the transition by providing office space and loaning staff to support the Perspectives program. However, all but a couple of staff had never worked for Perspectives, requiring them to learn their jobs from scratch while simultaneously managing a full roster of classes. Bruce Koch was appointed Interim Director, and Sue Patt jumped to his aid as Program Director.

Sue Patt is one of the longest-serving Perspectives veterans. She was in the 1980 Penn State Perspectives class as a college student, participated in the 1980 Edinburgh student conference on frontier missions, then joined the young U.S. Center staff in 1982. Patt testifies that Perspectives changed her career path. She had planned to be a Christian counselor; however, during class "I realized that the world would not miss one more counselor, but if my life could be used to see one UPG reached with the gospel, that would be worth it."[25] As a Regional Director in Pennsylvania with her husband Fran, she had valuable field experience to assist in the transition.

The immediate and urgent need was to recruit staff for the Perspectives office. James Mason was tapped to become the new national director. Mason was a pastor for twelve years before joining the USCWM. A member of his Las Vegas church challenged him to take the Perspectives class. It took a few years of friendship mobilization before he agreed. Mason says that taking Perspectives "was like having a brain transplant." Then as he began to teach the course, it "forced the material into his soul." When his church adopted an unreached people group, Mason became an advocate for Bible translation for their UPG. Intrigued by the concept of mission mobilization, James and his wife Kelly joined U.S. Center staff in 2008. When asked to become Perspectives USA National Director in 2012, the Masons took three weeks to pray about it before agreeing, knowing that he would start with no staff, and it would eliminate their planned sabbatical. They said yes.[26]

---

25 Susan Patt, interview by author, February 8, 2019, transcript.
26 James Mason, interview by author, May 17, 2016, February 14, 2019, and October 21, 2020, transcript.

James Mason, Perspectives USA director
from 2012 to present.

James Mason joined Sue Patt, Bruce Koch, and Karen Prater, temporary Operations Director, in trying to keep the Perspectives program from collapsing under its own weight without trained staff. The Center for Mission Mobilization willingly trained the new Perspectives staff in their roles, even donating administrative staff members for a year to help with the transition.

The timing of the transition back to Pasadena could hardly have been worse. The Perspectives staff in Arkansas were in the middle of the difficult task of centralizing finances. Up until that time, all 250 classes across the country had their own bank accounts and made financial decisions. Such a system exposed great vulnerabilities in legal and tax issues. The new system of centralized finance went into effect July 1, 2012 … just as the move was happening.

When the fall semester began ramping up in August, the team quickly discovered that the new IT system couldn't handle centralized finances along with class registration and administration. At the worst possible time, with class registration, payment, and textbook orders in full swing, the entire IT system collapsed. Students and instructors were vexed, and class coordinators were frantic. Financial transactions were delayed, and some classes didn't receive textbooks until several weeks into the semester. New Financial Director Sue Payne was overwhelmed. "We were in tears every day," recalls James Mason.

Graciously, the previous IT Director, Malachi Wurpts, stayed on during the transition. The situation was so bad that for the first time in Perspectives' history the executive leadership team discussed cancelling the spring semester, which typically has three times the number of classes as fall. With Wurpts' cautious optimism, Mason made the decision that they would move forward in faith. The technology stabilized and the spring semester operated smoothly. The fall of 2013 was rocky once more, before all systems began running as intended.

The move to a centralized finance system was also a difficult transition philosophically. Perspectives grew up as a grassroots movement. Class coordinators served almost as independent contractors, with a wide berth of autonomy. The team in Arkansas began bringing organizational identity to the movement, of which the centralization of finance, promotion, and administration was key. Many entrepreneurial coordinators, accustomed to creating their own unique identity, objected to the new degree of national control. Painfully, a few long-term coordinators quit as a result. But new coordinators relished the centralization because it took a lot of administration off their plate so they could focus on people rather than tasks. By 2014 the annual number of classes and students had picked back up again. Mason acknowledges that they still struggle with the balance of maintaining a collective identity without squelching local creativity and ownership.[27]

The transition of the national US Perspectives office from Arkansas back to California was messy, stressful, and heart-wrenching. Sue Patt remembers a mission-agency representative commenting that they were watching the transition carefully and praying for it. They knew if Perspectives failed, they would fail, because so much of their pipeline of recruits came from Perspectives classes. The key to the ultimate successful transition, Patt affirms, is that everyone was committed to honoring everyone else—to work together and not to badmouth anyone. The staff all made the choice to glorify God actively during the transition.[28]

James Mason concurs.

> I feel very fortunate that our friendship continues with Dave Flynn, with Steve Shadrach, and with the CMM as we partner together for the future of frontier mission mobilization. I sense nothing but comradery. I love what CMM is doing; I'm thoroughly behind them.[29]

In 2013, CMM leaders began to evaluate their own mission. They were mobilizing in the US, but recognized that 80 percent of the church lies outside the US, a sparsely tapped field for mission sending and mobilization. They changed their strategy, and by 2015 almost half of their staff had moved overseas. The Center for Mission Mobilization (recently renamed Via) is mostly focused on global mobilization now, planting staff in strategic centers where the global church is most active and ready to send missionaries. And everywhere they go, CMM staff carry Perspectives with them. They actively partner with Perspectives Global, helping to launch or run Perspectives classes in new languages and lands. Dave Flynn reflects,

27 Mason, interview.
28 Patt, interview.
29 Mason, interview.

"If they had never separated from the U.S. Center, this global mobilization probably never would have happened."[30]

In hindsight, the move of the Perspectives office from Pasadena to Fayetteville, Arkansas, enabled the Perspectives movement to thrive and grow in ways it would not have had it stayed put in California. The move back to Pasadena eight years later enabled the Perspectives movement to gain traction globally in a way that would not have occurred had staff not left the Perspectives organization to form a global mobilization organization. *Difficult?* Yes. *Fruitful?* Yes. To God be the glory for the furtherance of his purposes!

Building for the Future

On the backside of the transition crisis, James Mason tackled his most urgent priority: recruiting staff. Sue Patt continued to serve as Program Director, overseeing all functions related to coordinators, instructors, grading, website function, and communication. The vacant role of Operations Director prompted regular intercession. God began answering that prayer in 2010, three years before the need arose, through a businessman who emphatically told his inquiring wife that he had zero interest in missions.

Mike Bain spent twenty-five years in operations and supply-chain management. His wife Lesley had a desire to go to the mission field, but not Mike! In 2010, their church scheduled a mission trip to Africa to visit friends of theirs. Mike knew they should go, but intuitively knew that if he took this first step, his life would forever change. Sure enough, that was the beginning of their journey.

As they sought God for direction, they came across information on Perspectives and signed up for a class. Halfway through the course, they both felt God was calling them to the mission field. For the next couple of years Mike and Lesley coordinated Perspectives classes in their area. As a process-oriented person, Mike observed lots of glitches and inefficiencies in the new finance system of Perspectives. That entailed many calls to the national Perspectives office, and relationships began to be built.

The Bains evaluated many mission agencies to pursue overseas mission, but could not get a firm direction from God regarding any of them. In the spring of 2013, James Mason posted a job description for an Operations Director. For Mike, it felt like someone was reading his resume. The Bains began raising support, arriving in Pasadena to join staff in the summer of 2014.[31]

---

30 Dave Flynn, interview by author, December 13, 2018, email.

31 Mike Bain, interview by author, January 21, 2019, transcript.

In building for the future, national and regional offices began to onboard new staff. The new staff position of Regional Administrator was added in 2010, freeing the Regional Director to focus on vision and strategy. The volunteer roles of Area Mobilizer and Loop Coordinator were added to help serve the growing movement.

Granting graduate and undergraduate credit for the Perspectives course has been an important value since its college–campus beginnings. Over the decades various institutions have granted credit. Trinity Evangelical Divinity School and its associated undergrad institution, Trinity International University, have been the longest standing partners with Perspectives. Yet from the earliest days, Ralph Winter envisioned credit options from secular universities to make it easier to transfer credits for students attending nonreligious schools. In 2014, a more permanent solution to that aspiration emerged. The Perspectives Study Program was approved by the National College Credit Recommendation Service (NCCRS) to satisfy course requirements in several different fields of study. Three semester hours of graduate and undergraduate credit are issued through Excelsior College, a fully accredited institution. High school students may also access this benefit. Parents are increasingly enrolling their older teenagers to attend class with them, allowing more families to study God's purposes together.

Perspectives leaders thanking Trinity Evangelical Divinity School in 2017 for decades of granting Trinity credit for Perspectives students. L–R: Vicky Warren, Yvonne Huneycutt, Steve Hawthorne, Dr. Wayne Johnson of Trinity, Andrew Herbeck, and Sue Patt.

Establishing and maintaining excellent relationships with mission agencies has also been a long-standing value for the Perspectives office, even when staff shortages have not allowed as much progress as desired. It is well known that Perspectives classes offer up a rich pipeline of missionary recruits. Pioneers mission agency demonstrably affirmed the value they receive when they sponsored one thousand Perspectives scholarships at $100 each one year. Likewise, InterVarsity offered scholarships for the first thousand college students who registered for Perspectives following Urbana 2015. Urbana promoted Perspectives as the follow-on to their famous student mission convention—the very thing Ralph and Roberta Winter wanted them to do in 1973!

Being in a semester-long, in-person class is the best experience, yet it was anticipated that many of those Urbana students scattered across the country would enroll in the online option. With that in mind, the decade-old, outdated video lectures used in the online classes would never do! New videos in a new format utilizing the current fourth edition curriculum had to be made, and they had to be made quickly.

Perspectives Goes to Hollywood

Hollywood movie producer Kurt Tuffendsam's life was dramatically impacted by the Perspectives course. At the insistent urging of his pastor, Tuffendsam took Perspectives in 2009. Completing the course, he wanted to find ways to use his skills to contribute to God's global mission. Within months he launched Mission Rise, an organization that produces movies to mobilize the church to mission engagement. When he heard about Perspectives' need for a new set of videos, he volunteered his personal time and his company's assets to make it happen.

The Perspectives office raised several thousand dollars to produce a high-quality product. National Perspectives USA director James Mason called me in late 2014 to ask if I would take on project management for the remake of the Perspectives videos. At the time I was directing a nonprofit association, while also teaching Perspectives classes nationally and coaching Perspectives instructors internationally. I recognized it as God's assignment for me, but I couldn't start right away. That meant that video preproduction, which included content design and instructor selection and coaching, was squeezed into four short months. We didn't realize how nearly impossible such a timeline would be!

The design for the video shoot was a departure from the standard Perspectives structure of one instructor for each lesson. Instead, the content of each lesson was broken into several short modules, with two instructors selected for most lessons. Faithfulness to the content of the curriculum was our core objective. Even though all our instructors had frequently taught their respective lessons, they had to extensively rework them into strictly timed modules that ensured the core content was communicated. As the enormity of the task in the diminished timeline became evident, the more critical our prayer supporters became to achieve success.

Ready or not, the week of the video shoot arrived in September 2015. Tuffendsam had procured a camera and sound team, four cameras, makeup and hair professionals, film editors, a custom designed backdrop, and the theatre at the famous Grammy Museum in downtown Los Angeles. This production was not your typical low-budget missionary endeavor! The professionals had worked on many Hollywood films; they were also individuals with whom Tuffendsam was actively seeking to share the gospel of Christ.

Video producer Kurt Tuffendsam (2nd from left) with some of the video project team, (L–R) Andrew Herbeck, Yvonne Huneycutt, Kelly Mason, James Mason.

Twenty-three instructors arrived from all over the country, including one from India. Tuffendsam remarked that it was a real learning curve for him to work with missionaries rather than actors! The Perspectives office recruited an audience and numerous volunteers to handle a massive amount of logistics. It was all-hands-on-deck for seven straight days, twelve hours a day.

Not even two days into the video shoot, things began to fall apart. Various technical difficulties plagued the production from day one, delaying the strict production schedule. By day three, the technical issues brought production to a complete halt. Tuffendsam recalls, "Even the techs at the equipment company were baffled by the unusual problems we were experiencing. All productions have technical challenges, but we were encountering some extraordinary ones that seemed to really stump a whole team of professionals."[32]

Recognizing we were facing spiritual warfare, intensified by the nature of the venue in which we were filming, the team sent out urgent appeals for prayer. While the production crew, most of whom were not believers, were in the theater fighting with each other, the Perspectives team went upstairs to the greenroom to take authority in the name of Jesus. Breakthrough came.

---

32 Kurt Tuffendsam, interview by author, May 11, 2020, email.

By day four the spiritual atmosphere was different, everything worked, and the instructors were so on-point that we were able to catch up.

A powerful moment came on day six. Stress was mounting because we were so exhausted, behind schedule, and had only one day left, with no options to extend the shoot. The instructor began telling a very compelling story about a Muslim clan leader in Afghanistan who gave his life to Christ. Suddenly all the equipment started glitching out again. Tuffendsam stopped production. He and the instructor publicly prayed and asked God for help, whereupon the equipment immediately started working. We were able to finish, and God was glorified in the Grammy Museum and among the production crew.

Tuffendsam reflects,

> It's just amazing to me how necessary prayer is in everything we do. Even when you have the most seasoned professionals and all the best equipment, doing God's work always encounters warfare from the enemy. I truly believe God used the Perspectives video production to be a powerful witness to people who typically have very little Christian influence in their lives. Praise God for placing us strategically to be signposts for his kingdom where the church is not yet—even Hollywood![33]

Perspectives team that orchestrated the 2015 video shoot at the Grammy Museum in Hollywood.

33 Tuffendsam, interview.

The deadline for putting the new videos online as Urbana students registered for spring classes was met. As with so many episodes in Perspectives' history—curriculum revisions, leadership changes, financial and personnel shortages—faith, prayer, and God-enabled perseverance carry us forward as we co-labor with him toward the fulfillment of his kingdom purposes.

Defining Identity

During the rebuilding of the Perspectives USA national office, leadership recognized that Perspectives as an organization needed to establish a clear-cut identity and well-stated mission to guide it into the future. Perspectives has always been a grassroots movement, directed and shaped at the local level to contribute to local mobilization efforts. That is a strength of the movement. But it can also become a weakness, spawning a mix of understandings of what Perspectives is and should become. The Perspectives program has confronted this challenge more than once in its history.

The uniqueness of Perspectives is that it is simultaneously a movement, an organization, and a course. Without clear organizational identity defining what Perspectives is and what it is not, the entire purpose of Perspectives in all three aspects of its identity can be diluted or derailed. Many think Perspectives is a training course for missionaries; it is not. Others perceive it as a course just for mission fanatics; it is not. Perspectives exists for the purpose of mobilizing the *entire* body of Christ toward strategic engagement with God in the fulfillment of his global purpose. It is ultimately a discipleship course, which expands into a movement of obedience. The organization must reflect and support the mobilization purpose of the course; the movement, then, will carry along and extend the DNA of both course and organization.

Perspectives had never fashioned its own mission statement. While based in Pasadena, it was part of the greater USCWM vision; while based in Fayetteville, it was part of the larger mobilization vision that defined the CMM. Furthermore, with the expansion of international Perspectives programs, each having its own national identity and leadership, Perspectives USA needed to clarify its singular identity as one of many global programs. Over a two-year period, the Perspectives USA Executive Team crafted the *Mission, Vision,* and *Values* of the organization,[34] soliciting input from key stakeholders and accessing the strategic acumen of Perspectives advocate and businesswoman Vicky Warren.[35]

---

34 www.perspectives.org/who-we-are/.

35 Mason, interview.

The Perspectives USA *Vision*, *Mission*, and *Values* statements were introduced at the second national conference of Perspectives USA, held in Timonium, Maryland in July of 2016. Over three hundred Perspectives staff, instructors, coordinating teams, and mission-agency representatives gathered for three days of inspiration and training. Attendees were encouraged in their unique calling of mobilization; it is a privilege and grace gift from God. With a deeper understanding of the Perspectives movement, they were exhorted to move forward together in unified vision and purpose.

Mike Bain, James Mason, and Sue Patt speaking at 2016
Perspectives USA National Conference.

National statistics presented at the 2016 conference revealed that Perspectives had come a long way in recovering from the 2012 loss of staff and subsequent dip in growth. Perspectives USA staff numbered sixty-two, including volunteer staff, with fourteen Regional Directors and fourteen Regional Administrators. The annual number of classes was back up to 250, enrolling over 8,700 new students, plus many returning alumni. In addition, over 700 students were taking the class online. Serving that growth were around 600 active coordinators and over 2,000 active instructors. The cumulative total of US Perspectives alumni since 1974 approached 150,000 in over 4,200 classes.

Long Overdue: Instructor Development

Perspectives began primarily as a credit-bearing course for university students. The earliest instructors were often professors and the course had academic objectives that must be met. When Perspectives classes moved into churches in the 1980s and began national expansion, the roster of instructors began to change. No longer was Ralph Winter the persuasive influence for acquiring instructors. Increasingly, local coordinators were inviting pastors and popular speakers to teach. Instructors began to be called "speakers," revealing a subtle shift in the local understanding of the nature of the course. Because Perspectives grew up as a grassroots movement, developing structure and curriculum as it matured, there never was a requirement that those who taught in Perspectives must first have taken the course themselves!

Over time this produced a number of problems. Any class coordinator who has been around the block a few times can tell you that a significant percentage of those who teach in Perspectives classes do not adequately teach the lesson. Some hardly teach it at all, and a few teach concepts that are completely contradictory to the core ideas of the course. Even though an instructor is provided the curriculum from which to instruct, if they have never taken the class nor read the entire text, they cannot truly understand the significance to the whole of the concepts they are assigned to teach. Perspectives lessons build on each other and are integrated with all the other lessons. Pastors and speakers are accustomed to preparing sermons and lessons from their personal study and insights; professors are trained to teach a set of integrated ideas pertaining to a syllabus. So it is really no surprise that invited "speakers" in many cases failed to teach the actual Perspectives lesson. The most popular instructors became those who were the most engaging and told the best stories, even if they only lightly touched on the content of the lesson.

The instructors are really not to blame for this. For forty years Perspectives did not invest in training and equipping instructors and never required any kind of certification. Following the release of the fourth edition, Steve Hawthorne set himself to the task of helping instructors learn the curriculum. He had previously identified Sixteen Core Ideas that make Perspectives unique and transformational. The task now was to communicate why those Core Ideas are unique, how some are different from conventional mission ideas, and how they integrate with one another. Hawthorne dug deep once more into the curriculum over many months to craft a set of Instructor Guidelines for each lesson. Released in 2014, the Instructor Guidelines became an invaluable resource and are now considered part of the curriculum. They clarified to an even greater degree what makes Perspectives so transformational.

The problem remained, however, of proactively equipping instructors in the curriculum. The Perspectives office had long desired to have a staff member dedicated to instructor development. Angela Zimmerman answered that call in 2014.

Angela Zimmerman enrolled in a Perspectives class in Kentucky in 2005. She immediately wanted to sell everything and become an overseas missionary. She took the course again the following year, serving on the coordinating team. This time she heard the course material in a deeper way and realized that she didn't need to go overseas to be involved in missions; instead, she could utilize the gifts God had given her at home. The next year the local coordinator left for Africa and invited Zimmerman to lead the class. In 2008, she was invited to be the Regional Director for the Mid-South region. Along the way she discovered that God had given her gifts of mobilization, training, and helping others discover their gifts and destiny.

As a Regional Director, Zimmerman began hearing instructors ask how to prepare a lesson and inquire what Perspectives expected of them. She spoke with James Mason about developing an instructor training and development department. As the old adage goes, when you raise the issue, you are usually the one to solve the problem. In 2014 Zimmerman began to transition from her RD role to Director of Instructor Development.

Angela Zimmerman initiated Perspectives
Instructor Development program.

Instructors have dedicated pages on the Perspectives website that serve as an administrative nexus between the national office, the local class, and the instructor. The Instructor Guidelines and new video modules for each lesson were added to the website to help instructors prepare to teach. Zimmerman worked with Regional Directors to conduct two-day instructor development workshops in each region. The first official training was held in Dallas in 2019. Veteran instructors are highly encouraged to enroll in a Perspectives class if they have never taken the course. All new instructors are required to have taken Perspectives at the certificate level in order to teach. Plans are in place to institute a certification program for Instructors.[36]

---

36 Angela Zimmerman, interview by author, December 26, 2018.

A positive difference has been seen already in Perspectives instruction. Returning to the three-legged stool analogy of coordinator, instructors, and curriculum being the three legs that enable the Perspectives stool to stand, the closer coordinators and instructors are tethered to the curriculum, the stronger the stool will be. The more extensively the Perspectives movement grows, the more imperative the stability of all three legs.

8

Fruitful Frontier—Perspectives Global

The room was filled with pastors and their wives, some pastors of pastors with networks of churches. I was participating in one of the early Nigerian Perspectives Intensive classes. After the first two lessons by Nigerian instructors on God's gracious intention toward all peoples, one pastor stood up and startlingly confessed, "I hear what you are saying, but I can't love Muslims after what they just did to us. We need to round them up, burn down their businesses, homes, and mosques, like they did to us."

Another pastor heartily agreed. A pause of stunned silence.

These two pastors had travelled from north Nigeria, where just the week before Christians and churches had been targets of Islamic terrorism. Their painful reaction was certainly understandable. The class leaders called us to prayer.

On the final day of the course, both pastors stood and humbly repented before their colleagues with changed hearts and minds to love their Muslim enemies as Jesus does and seek to reach them with the gospel. Only the Holy Spirit, through the truth of the Word of God, can bring such dramatic change.

If the nineteenth century was the European century for missionary expansion and the twentieth century was the century of American dominance, the twenty-first century will be defined as robust missionary deployment by the rest of the world. The surge of the global church outside the traditional heartlands of the West is overflowing into a corresponding river of missionaries streaming from Africa, Asia, Latin America, the Pacific, and even the Middle East. In more ways than one, the nations are flooding the nations.

The Perspectives movement has been a rich recipient of this flow, and likewise has been privileged to be a contributor to it. By the year 2018 the annual number of Perspectives students outside the USA exceeded the number of students enrolled in US classes. The fertile contribution students and leaders of other nations are making to Perspectives are ensuring that its best days lie ahead!

So how did Perspectives bear fruit in the nations and the nations bear fruit in Perspectives? The story is disclosed in the stories—many exciting, a few agonizing, with numerous lessons learned along the way.

FirstFruits Internationally

South Pacific

Surprisingly, the first Perspectives course held outside the United States was on the opposite side of the globe. In New Zealand, a local pastor convinced retired businessman Don Cowey to go to Pasadena to be trained to run Perspectives courses. Upon his return Cowey sought to introduce the course to those who had never heard of it. He wrote to thirty church leaders in his city extolling the value of Perspectives. He received back only one reply: "Sounds great, Don, let me know how it goes!"

Undaunted, he pressed on; at least his church was fully backing the course. Yet when it came time to advertise it in the morning service, he was given only two minutes to introduce Perspectives to his congregation. Remarkably fifty showed up for the first class. Cowey relates, "For subsequent courses I needed less than two minutes of advertising. I would merely say, 'Stand up, all those who have done the Perspectives course and had their lives changed.' The looks on their faces said it all, and our classes were easily filled."[1]

The course exploded onto the island church scene, growing from one class of forty-five graduates in 1987 to twenty classes of six hundred students only two years later. A prime catalyst of the growth was a student in that first class, Dr. Bob Hall. Hall was a senior lecturer in sociology at the University of Canterbury in Christchurch. By the second session the Holy Spirit had impacted his mind and heart so deeply, he described it as "being born again again."

---

1 Don Cowey, interview by author, June 24, 2008, email.

Hall became a super-advocate of Perspectives, setting up The Centre for Mission Direction, a mission mobilization organization which would serve New Zealand for years to come. Cowey observes, "When Bob came to take over the course, I saw that I had been but the starter motor for his powerful V8 engine."[2] Through Hall's visionary leadership, Perspectives widely penetrated the island nation.

The Perspectives course in New Zealand has operated in a variety of formats. It is primarily church-based, meeting in small groups. A few Bible colleges adopted the course into their curriculum. A correspondence course was developed for those living in isolated areas, graduating many who became coordinators of classes for their region. In the year 2000, Michael and Freda Simkin took over the national leadership of Perspectives in New Zealand. Of the thousands of Perspectives alumni, many are now serving among unreached people groups or with the numerous refugees living in New Zealand.

The Perspectives curriculum was adapted to the "down under" audience in 1991. The Perspectives *Reader* continued to be used, adapted with local idioms, and a new study guide was created for New Zealand and Australian courses. Lessons on Buddhism and the historical expansion of the gospel into the Pacific Isles were added. A major focus was put on the role of *Welcomer* because of the large percentage of internationals in their midst. Consequently, the course was lengthened from fifteen to twenty-four lessons, but split into two parts, each consisting of twelve weeks. Collectively, the two parts are known as *Perspectives on the World Christian Movement: The South Pacific Version*. It has been used in other Pacific and Southeast Asian countries, such as Papua New Guinea, Fiji, Indonesia, and Malaysia.[3]

Whereas many have attempted to shorten the Perspectives course, the South Pacific program developers took the opposite tack, expanding the course to almost double its original size. National coordinator Michael Simkin expounds,

> We have resisted the temptation to produce a condensed version of Perspectives, believing that the whole purpose of the course is to change the worldview of the students from the "Bless me club" mentality to the one of desiring that God be glorified amongst the nations. Our observation over the years is that radical change of mindset does not happen overnight.[4]

Australia is the other South Pacific nation with a national Perspectives program. Dutchman Peter Ruhlman happened to encounter audio tapes

---

2 Cowey, interview.
3 Simkin, "Perspectives in New Zealand."
4 Simkin.

of Ralph Winter teaching some of the Perspectives material in 1991 and proceeded to initiate the first Australian course. Bob Hall assisted him, sharing the course material developed for New Zealand.

In 1996, a different "Perspectives" program was started in another part of Australia by someone who was unaware of the existing program. For several years there was conflict between the two Australian programs, reflecting conflict that already existed between various mission groups. As the leaders of the two differing programs left to pursue other ventures, new leadership arose that committed to working together. In the year 2005 the two separate programs united, catalyzing a new spirit of unity among Australian mission agencies. Joanne and Ray Green assumed the national leadership of the program until 2007, when they handed it over to Warwick and Jessica Coghlan. Perspectives spread across the continent, with classes and coordinators in every state of Australia.[5]

Perspectives in Australia runs in the same manner as in New Zealand, in small church-based groups led and taught by a team of coordinators. Warwick Coghlan relates the remarkable story of one of their graduates.

> We had an ordinary couple—a schoolteacher and an occupational therapist—go through one of our classes. That same year the schoolteacher took his class to an Asian country for their annual cross-cultural exposure trip. While there, he encountered a woman who had initiated several ministries in-country but was limited in her output because of her need to homeschool her own kids. One of those ministries had a tremendous need for a physical therapist. This schoolteacher returned home, told his wife, and within months they relocated there, fulfilling both needs. Years later the government of this restricted-access country shut down their work, opening its own facility. Through their ministry, the government had caught a vision for helping needy young people that had previously been cast out.
>
> Quite surprisingly, the government asked our Perspectives alumna, the physiotherapist, to stay on as a consultant. The grand opening was attended by high-level government leaders and televised across the country. During the ceremony they asked the physiotherapist to speak and tell why she was serving them in this way. Boldly, in a nationwide broadcast with high government officials standing behind her, she proclaimed Jesus. This couple were average churchgoers, going to work, buying a home, raising kids, then God turned their world upside down.[6]

---

5 Warwick Coghlan, "Perspectives in Australia."

6 Warwick Coghlan, interview by author, December 7, 2019, transcript.

Canada

Perspectives traveled north of the US border early on. Regent College in British Colombia offered a college course using the Perspectives curriculum in the early 1980s, under the auspices of the U.S. Center for World Mission. The first community class was held in 1990. Canadian national director Sharon Walraven was a student in the second class in Canada, a very large class of 250 students. For almost two decades the Canadian programs were part of the North American program, directed from the USCWM. Perspectives Canada did not separate from Perspectives USA and form their own national program until 2008.

Seven of the ten Canadian provinces have held Perspectives classes. Each of the provinces have an autonomous regional team, with a national team overseeing the countrywide development. To reach other large language groups in Canada, classes have been run in Cantonese and Mandarin. Plans are underway for offering classes in the newest Perspectives language version of French, the other official language of Canada.

Canada has a highly diverse, multiethnic population with tremendous potential for reaching unreached people groups. Walraven relates the story of one couple living and ministering among the multicultural, urban poor who had begun to feel they were ministering more out of duty than passion. Encouraged to take Perspectives, they discovered keys for ministry, but more importantly were renewed in their motivation for ministry. "What a blessing," they said, "that we get to be a part of the mission to see God glorified among all ethne, carrying his message of relationship to the nations. Our hope is that because of Perspectives we can be an even greater blessing to our neighbors."[7]

A Root Bearing Offshoots

The history of the Perspectives movement cannot be told without recounting the influence the course has had on books, curriculum, courses, seminars, and even educational degree programs. The influence is so pervasive that the fullness cannot be known. Some college and seminary professors built entire mission majors around Perspectives content. Many churches designed in-house courses utilizing Perspectives material as a foundation. Numerous seminars have bubbled up, inspired by the Perspectives biblical paradigm. The Perspectives office was always receiving reports of someone doing something in some nation along the lines of the Perspectives course. Many called what they were doing "Perspectives."

---

7 Sharon Walraven, interview by author, December 8, 2019, transcript.

In the early days, that didn't seem to be such a problem, until it was discovered how much of a problem it had become. At one point in Australia, three different people were conducting three different courses that they all called "Perspectives"! On the positive side, two courses heavily derived from Perspectives developed their own identity and proceeded to have an outsized influence on nations. One was *Misión Mundial*, which penetrated the Latin American world, as previously described in chapter 4. The other was birthed in the Philippines.

Kairos—*Emerging from the Philippines*

The Philippines have been viewed as a mission field for hundreds of years. This island country is now one of the top mission-sending nations in the world. Helping facilitate this transition, Max Chismon of Living Springs International (LSI), together with his wife and team, produced the *Condensed World Mission Course* in the Philippines in 1994. The course was developed using material from both the *Misión Mundial* (*World Mission*) course that Jonathan Lewis developed for Latin America and the *Perspectives on the World Christian Movement* course. Whereas *World Mission* is a condensed rendering of the Perspectives course, the *Condensed World Mission Course* is even further condensed—hence the name.

The indigenous Asian Center for Missions reported in 1998 that in the four years since their founding, they had mobilized over five hundred Filipino pastors and key leaders using the *Condensed World Mission Course*.[8] By 2008, more than fifteen thousand Filipinos had taken the course, making it a major mobilization tool in the islands. As a result, breakthroughs have resulted in each of the thirteen unreached people groups in the Philippines, almost all Muslim. Now all thirteen groups have churches planted within them.[9]

The structure of the *Condensed World Mission Course* enabled it to spread into other cultures and languages beyond the Philippines. In 2005, a wise decision was made to drop the awkward name and rename the course *Kairos* (a Greek word, meaning a special, opportune season of time). With a nine-lesson format, the *Kairos* course is focused on being accessible to any local church and being easily reproducible. It uses a standard set of DVD teaching materials, translated into the local language, rather than a roster of local teachers.

Graduates of the course can be trained to be facilitators of new courses, with the goal of having one trained facilitator for every six students. The parent organization of the *Kairos* course is Simply Mobilizing. According

---

8 *Mission Frontiers*, "Escalating Filipino Force."
9 Chismon, "Introducing the Condensed Course" updated stats by interview with author, 2008.

to their website, the *Kairos* course is offered in over one hundred countries and has been translated into multiple languages.[10]

The *Kairos* course carries the basic principles and as many of the teachings of Perspectives that can fit into a course carrying less than half the weight. As such, it has been welcomed into the Perspectives family of like-minded

curriculum. Because they carry different distinctives and serve different purposes, both courses have been successfully run in tandem in many countries. The *Kairos* course offers an easily accessible beginning point for mission awareness and mobilization; the Perspectives course adds the depth and breadth of missiological conviction and understanding to sustain and build a sturdy base of strategic mission involvement.

Max Chismon, initiator of the *Kairos* course.

Perspectives and Kairos have always been sister organizations, sharing leadership in many countries. In 2009, a two-week Perspectives Intensive course was held in the Philippines for Kairos international leadership and several Filipino leaders. Chismon wanted his leadership to understand the depth of teaching that underlies the *Kairos* course. Although some efforts have been made, the Philippines is still waiting for its own national Perspectives program.

Bruce Koch playing a popular Perspectives game at Philippines Intensive for Kairos leaders in 2009.

---

10 https://coursemanager.simplymobilizing.com/courses.

The Necessity of Soil Preparation

Not all efforts to develop a national Perspectives program in other lands are successful or sustaining. Difficult labors of love by highly dedicated individuals have at times fallen short of bringing forth a sustainable transformative program. I know this on a personal level; my efforts culminated in a painful failure. Yet, for every misfire, valuable lessons are learned to improve the path going forward. After a multitude of attempts to invent the lightbulb, Thomas Edison famously declared, "I have not failed; I have just found ten thousand ways that won't work."

Russia

I was part of the early missionary wave into Russia after the Soviet Union dissolved in 1991. A chorus began from missionaries scattered throughout the former Soviet Republics for a Russian version of the Perspectives course. As a trained Perspectives coordinator, I was eager to answer that call. Before I arrived, Perspectives alumnus Jim Overton began the work of translating the curriculum into Russian in 1993—thanks to the effective fundraising of USCWM regional director Bob Stevens. His church in North Carolina was especially instrumental, choosing to tithe the proceeds of their capital campaign to the project.

The decision was made to translate Jonathan Lewis's *World Mission* course (being used as a Perspectives text in US classes at the time), as that presented a simpler goal than tackling the heftier Perspectives *Reader* and *Study Guide*. When Overton departed Russia, the unfinished translation was lost. When I arrived in 1994, I searched for the lost translation and finally found it—a three-foot stack of typewritten pages stuffed in a closet at St. Petersburg Christian University! Not only was the translated material unusable because it was not in digital format, but it was also found to be of poor quality.

Even though I had never done anything of this nature before, I took up the challenge of pursuing translation and publication of the curriculum. In addition to my publishing naiveté, spiritual opposition hampered the translation project. My primary translator did a sudden about-face and walked away from his Christian faith two-thirds of the way through. Bob Stevens declared that the *only* way he could get a fax through to Russia was to lay hands on the fax machine and pray during transmission!

When nearing completion of the translation a year later, I delivered it to the most respected Christian publishing organization in Russia. Upon review, they determined that much of the translation needed to be discarded, as it was also of poor quality. They informed me that very few people in Russia at that time had the theological and missiological education necessary to do such a translation.

A few years later, Jim Overton returned to Russia and restarted the project, bringing it to completion with the stateside assistance of Stevens. Finally, in 2001, the Russian translation of *World Mission* rolled off the presses. A Perspectives program was never started in Russia, but *World Mission* became a core mission text in numerous Bible colleges and seminaries. The *Kairos* course also utilized many of the articles for their Russian version. Even though the translation is now outdated, it is still widely circulating in Russian-speaking countries and bearing fruit.

India

Another early attempt to make the Perspectives material available in a major country took place in India. In the spring of 1995, USCWM staff members Ralph and Joanna Budleman relocated to India as mobilizers with a desire to create a South Asian version of the Perspectives course. They chose to use English, widely used in higher education in India. However, their strategy was not simply to reproduce the North American version, but to create a dynamic equivalent course from within the Indian context. They sought to utilize as many South Asian authors as possible, while retaining some articles from the original English version.

Three thousand copies of *Perspectives on World Missions: South Asia Version* were printed and widely used in Bible schools and seminaries. The book was only used as a textbook; a national Perspectives program was not initiated. After the third edition of the *Perspectives on the World Christian Movement* curriculum was published in 1999, indigenous Indian leaders wanted to run Perspectives classes using the new curriculum. To meet their mobilization goals, they decided not to use the South Asian version, as it was better suited to academia. Publication of the South Asian version was eventually discontinued.

Indian national Shibu Mathew picked up the challenge of making the Perspectives course available in India. He was part of a group of alumni who started the Frontier Education Society in 2001 to mobilize believers to evangelize the unreached people groups of India. They chose to target English-speaking pastors and ministry leaders, but also young, upwardly mobile Indians employed in the emerging global-business markets. Beginning in 2002, Mathew ran Perspectives classes in Bangalore and a few other cities. With permission from Perspectives leadership in the U.S., they began to adapt the Perspectives curriculum to an Indian constituency.[11]

---

11 Mathew, "India Preparation Report."

Mathew continued to run classes periodically, but a nationwide Perspectives program never ensued. However, those classes still produced remaining fruit: many alumni began to reach out to UPGs in India; some left valuable IT jobs and went as missionaries; a dozen individuals from one denomination became activists in leading their church to adopt an unreached people group.

A promising restart for Perspectives in India emerged in 2022. Indian leaders from two cities, along with Mathew, conducted two hybrid in-person/virtual classes in two different Indian states. The courses ran as a three-week Intensive, attracting over a hundred students. The process was repeated in 2023, with a third city added virtually. Indian leaders were especially challenged with a new awareness of the unreached peoples in their own backyard.

Other places also experienced promising Perspectives startups, only to fizzle when leadership or conditions on the ground changed. An unexpected example is the United Kingdom.

United Kingdom

One would think that the Perspectives course would easily and early jump "across the pond" to England. In the 1980s and 1990s, the Perspectives *Reader* was used in a few Bible colleges, but only as a text, not producing a course of study. It wasn't until 2001 that the first Perspectives classes were conducted. One class was begun in Liverpool and one in Oxford, by two different groups who were unaware of each other. It wasn't until both groups attended a Global Perspectives consultation in Pasadena in 2003 that the two entities discovered one another! They joined forces to develop a national UK Perspectives program under the leadership of Naomi Gray.

The UK team aimed for qualitative rather than quantitative growth; even so, by 2008 over eight hundred Brits had graduated the program.[12] When Gray left the country to pursue a mission venture, the national program struggled without sufficient leadership. At this writing, the UK program is in suspension, with a hope and prayer for a fresh start.

Even with programs that go into decline due to one factor or another, remaining fruit is produced and multiplied. A couple that met in a UK class is an example. He is British and she is from Singapore. She moved back to her home country with a passion to mobilize the Singaporean church in mission to unreached people groups. He followed her; they were married, trained, and began conducting Perspectives classes in Singapore.

---

12 Gray, "Perspectives in the United Kingdom."

Lessons Learned

The starts and stops, misfires and failures have proffered valuable lessons to future development of Perspectives in other lands. To quote highly successful entrepreneur Bill Gates, "It's fine to celebrate success, but it is more important to heed the lessons of failure."

To be successful and indigenous, the initiative and leadership for launching new Perspectives programs needs to come from national believers, not from outside missionaries. Perspectives must be "owned" by a team, not by an individual, no matter how enterprising a person may be. That team needs to be diverse, representing different denominations, organizations, geographies, and, as much as possible, people of wide influence. A national strategy needs to be formulated from the beginning, with the corresponding aim of mobilizing the leadership to make that happen.

An investment of time is needed to develop a clear identity for Perspectives, rather than letting highly motivated individuals take the course and run with it without collaboration and oversight. Historically, that resulted in many independently created courses that called themselves "a shortened version of Perspectives," but which did not produce the life transformation for which Perspectives is known. Consequently, many were confused by the different "versions" of Perspectives or inoculated against engaging the actual Perspectives course.

The theological and missiological weight of the curriculum requires a team of experienced translators and editors with a sufficient lexicon and conceptual understanding within the target language. It is not sufficient just to produce a textbook; a program of ongoing classes is the objective. If the Perspectives curriculum becomes absorbed by seminaries or Bible schools as a missions textbook, it is difficult to transition to the intended goal of Perspectives: mobilization of the church.

Translating the Perspectives curriculum and introducing it into a new area is always a spiritual venture; Satan will do all he can to oppose local believers from being mobilized to join God in completing the Great Commission. For this reason, a robust prayer strategy is essential.

In all these ways, the soil is prepared for Perspectives to take deep root into a new culture.

Out of all the lessons learned, however, one insight completely changed the way Perspectives is introduced into a new language and nation. But that realization was not apparent until the observation of the following successes.

Fruitful Strategy

Two exemplary Perspectives programs emerged in the early years of the new millennium. One was in Asia and the other was in Africa. They had very different strategies, but did one thing in common. They both insisted on using the North American Perspectives text *as is.* "We will contextualize it later," they said.

Korean Language Version and Korea

South Korean Christians are well known for their passionate mission vision. Seeking to channel this passion into strategic outreach, the Perspectives course was translated into Korean in 1999 by Mission Korea, a mission mobilization organization, under the leadership of Chulho Han. The first Korean class was held in the year 2000 with thirty-five students.

In 2001, Han visited the Perspectives office in Pasadena to learn how to conduct ongoing courses. The U.S. Center for World Mission sent staff member Dave Williams to Korea to assist Han in developing the course. In 2002, Han held an Intensive course for pastors and mission leaders, training them to conduct courses in their cities. That is when the program took off. Two years later over a thousand students were enrolled in Perspectives classes in Korea.

The Koreans chose to make a straight translation of the North American curriculum, then adapt the class experience to its Korean audience. Much emphasis is given to small group integration of the material facilitated by Perspectives alumni. Each small group seeks to interact with

Chulho Han, originator of Perspectives in Korean and Perspectives Asia director.

and learn from a furloughing missionary. To connect the students with their Christian heritage and highlight the cost of penetrating unreached peoples, every class makes an outing to a cemetery to honor the foreign missionaries who died on their soil.

After a decade of running classes, Chulho Han began carefully adapting the curriculum by incorporating some Asian authors. He waited that long so that the authors would have a solid grasp of the material and be able to maintain the Perspectives message.

True to Korean ingenuity, they took the North American program and raised the standard of excellence. Their ancillary materials (guides for students, coordinators, instructors, and classroom activities) have become a model for other global programs. The quality of the classes is kept high by requiring all instructors to study the Perspectives text—being a good speaker is not enough—and requiring a minimum of fifty students to be enrolled.

Initially begun as a follow-up class for university students mobilized by Mission Korea, Perspectives became a premier mission-training course in Korea. Major seminaries have conducted Perspectives classes, and Korean communities in other parts of the world are requesting Perspectives to come to them. Han reports that Perspectives is helping steer the mission trends of the Korean church, providing new insight and helping overcome previous mistakes in mission strategy. The biblical insight alone is transforming the sermons of many church pastors.[13]

In 2010 a new structure, Mission Partners, was spun off from Mission Korea to focus upon mission mobilization by education. Chulho Han resigned from Mission Korea to lead Mission Partners, although the two organizations work closely together. Perspectives enrollment accelerated as a result. Other mission-education programs were developed out of the principles taught in Perspectives to serve the unique situation of the Korean church. In this way, Mission Partners has developed a roadmap for strategic involvement by the Korean church in mission. As a foundational program, Perspectives has played a very significant role in the Korean missionary movement.

As of 2020, the Korean Perspectives program was the third largest Perspectives program in the world, graduating over three thousand students in fifty to sixty classes annually. Since the program's inception, over six hundred classes have been conducted, producing around thirty-five thousand alumni. Around 20 percent of the graduates go on to serve at least one year in cross-cultural ministry.[14]

Su-Min was one of those students. She had served as a missionary in Russia for one year, returning home discouraged. Then she heard about the Perspectives course. She enrolled and was thrilled to discover solutions to many of the struggles she encountered while serving cross-culturally. She was so encouraged, in fact, that she mobilized her family and half of her youth group to take the class. While serving Perspectives for two years as a small group leader, she sensed God calling her back to Russia long-term. She was concerned about her mother, however, as her father had recently passed away. It was her mother who encouraged her to go, as she too had come to understand through Perspectives that our God is a great missionary God.[15]

The goal of the Korean church is to mobilize one hundred thousand young Koreans to active involvement in missions, and out of those to send twenty thousand to the field (sounds like the statistics from the Student

---

13 Han, "Report on Perspectives in Korea," statistical update via email July 7, 2020.

14 Chulho Han, interview by author, email, July 7, 2020; statistics updated June 2023.

15 Perspectives Global Newsletter, September 2013.

Volunteer Movement of last century in which one hundred thousand US students were mobilized to mission engagement from which twenty thousand left home to be overseas missionaries!). The two key mobilization tools in their hands are Mission Korea (a biennial student conference much like Urbana in the United States) and the Perspectives course.

Nigeria

The Nigerian church is strong and has become increasingly missional over the past few decades. In the fall of 2005, at a gathering of over one hundred top Nigerian mission leaders representing eighty agencies, churches, and organizations, the Nigerian church adopted a daring plan to mobilize fifty thousand Nigerians to participate actively in taking the gospel through the nations of North Africa and the Arabian Peninsula in fifteen years. Churches and agencies are actively recruiting, training, and sending Nigerians north.

The Nigeria Evangelical Missions Association (NEMA) is the networking umbrella advocating Vision 5015. Undergirding the vision, NEMA's pioneer Executive Secretary Timothy Olonade put a plan in place to introduce Perspectives to Nigeria in a top-down fashion. Beginning in 2002, NEMA held a series of weeklong Perspectives Intensive classes for top church, mission, and business leaders, so that they could in turn sponsor and facilitate classes in their local regions.

Timothy Olonade, first director of Perspectives Nigeria.

The first class of forty-one leaders crafted a communiqué that they sent out to Christian leaders in the country. (See appendix D.) In it, they acknowledged the benefits of Perspectives, encouraging national promotion and registration. They especially emphasized the potential of Perspectives to bring unity between church and mission in Nigeria. By 2008, over eight hundred Nigerian leaders graduated the course, including an archbishop of the Anglican Church. The archbishop was so impacted by the class that he insisted that all his bishops and priests attend Perspectives over the following three years![16]

The "top-down" strategy employed by Perspectives Nigeria in accordance with their tradition, has proven to be very fruitful. Because so many clergy enroll, classes are held in one-week intensive sessions, two or three lessons per day over six days. Up until 2016, an average of three to four Intensive courses were held per year. The national program then began to proliferate rapidly; now one to two Intensives classes are held per month, spread all over Nigeria.

---

16 Olonade, "Perspectives in Nigeria."

Nigerian Anglican bishops and priests taking a Perspectives Intensive course.

Many Anglican bishops have taken Perspectives, and in turn have required all the priests in their diocese to take the course. Even the most studied among them have been overwhelmed by the content they are absorbing, and it is changing lives. An archbishop of a southern state decided to build a Global Mission Resource Center to train and house furloughing missionaries, provide resources, and host conferences. Professors are encouraging their students to take Perspectives. University students are mobilizing busloads of their fellow students into short-term mission ventures. Churches are adopting unreached people groups and sending missionaries to them. Church planting movements are beginning to happen in Muslim communities in North Africa.

On the other hand, Boko Haram attacks in the north of Nigeria are driving many Muslim Hausa Fulani to immigrate to the South. Yet many churches of the South do not know how to reach out to them because of the great cultural divide; furthermore, they are paralyzed by fear from evangelizing. Perspectives alumni are encouraging the church that this is God's "involuntary come" mechanism[17] of relocating the unreached to gospel-friendly areas. Now many churches are developing effective strategies for reaching their new Muslim neighbors.

National Perspectives director Victor Idakwoji relates a significant breakthrough that occurred in 2012. The leader of a large Nigerian Pentecostal church network was encouraged while in the US to enroll in Perspectives in Nigeria. Upon returning home, he didn't just take the class; he hosted a class for all his top pastors, about forty in total. As the course

---

17 A concept taught in Perspectives of one of the ways the gospel spreads.

concluded, he called them together and deployed around half of them to northern Nigeria to start churches. The church, he said, must send laborers to the unreached fields, not stay in the Christian-saturated areas of the south. He went himself to various Muslim-dominated areas to engage in church planting, and together they are seeing fruit. To sustain the vision, he is requiring that anyone pastoring in his ministry network must go through the Perspectives course.[18]

Between its inception in 2002, through 2021, over twelve thousand Nigerians have graduated from Perspectives. The Nigerian Perspectives leadership train their own instructors and facilitators. They have convened two successful national Perspectives alumni conferences. The Nigerians are now helping Ghanaians initiate a Perspectives program in Ghana.

Nigerian leaders believe that one of the reasons that they have been successful is that they intentionally chose *not* to contextualize the North American Perspectives curriculum, at least not until they felt they were ready to do so. There is a richness in the Perspectives paradigm that they wanted to drink deeply from themselves before they attempted to reproduce it with a localized voice.

The global leadership of Perspectives initially thought that it would be best to contextualize the curriculum as it first entered any new nation, retaining some of the English articles and replacing, adding, or commissioning similar articles from local authors. After all, contextualization is a key value taught in the curriculum itself. The Nigerians and Koreans pushed back on that. After seeing the spectacular success they enjoyed and the failure of contextualizing too early in other lands, the model the Koreans and Nigerians chose was recognized to be the best model. As Perspectives Global director Bruce Koch has often said, "They know how to eat the meat and spit out the bones." It is best to let the Perspectives content deeply penetrate the hearts and minds of indigenous leaders; they can contextualize it through their teaching, and later in the curriculum itself.

Cultivating the Movement

No proactive global leadership was given to the expansion of Perspectives internationally for almost thirty years. Courses popped up in various places as enterprising individuals, impacted by Perspectives, initiated classes on their own. As it was the nature of Ralph Winter and the USCWM to give away whatever is helpful, no real thought was given to a specific Perspectives identity.

---

18 Victor Idakwoji, interview by author, December 8, 2019, transcript.

First Perspectives Global Huddle, Amsterdam 2003.

With the turn of the millennium, global demand for Perspectives increased, yet there was no one to respond to inquiries, much less provide assistance. In 2002, Perspectives veteran coordinator Julie Gamponia did an internship under USCWM staff leader Tim Lewis, in which she researched the spread of Perspectives globally, discovering numerous derivative courses. Lewis, in turn, spoke with Steve Hawthorne, Bruce Koch, and USCWM director Greg Parsons concerning the need to take responsibility for the development of Perspectives internationally. Those four formed an ad-hoc Global Desk in 2002 in an initiative to begin providing leadership. They extended an invitation to leaders of the curricula uncovered by Gamponia's research to gather in Amsterdam in the spring of 2003. This meeting later became known as the first Perspectives Global Huddle.

Initial Perspectives Global Desk: Tim Lewis, Greg Parsons, Steve Hawthorne, Bruce Koch.

The third edition of the Perspectives curriculum had recently been published, with 40 percent change in content, but more importantly, with a new motivation and theological base for mission. Focus was shifted to a theocentric base for mission (an invitation from God to pursue his glory and kingdom purpose among the nations) rather than an anthropocentric base of mission (a response to human need and an obedience-oriented motivation). In the Amsterdam meeting, Steve Hawthorne articulated the 16 Core Ideas underlying the third edition and how a realization gradually dawned upon them that Perspectives is a tightly integrated paradigm with internal cohesion. Bruce Koch recalls Jonathan Lewis, author of *Misión Mundial* (derived from the second edition of Perspectives and from which *Kairos* and other courses stemmed), being quite surprised that the changes in the third edition were of significant substance, not merely cosmetic. This realization made it clear that the derivative courses based off earlier Perspectives editions did not carry all of the same framework and paradigm.[19]

Concern was expressed for the need to establish a clear and consistent identity of the name "Perspectives" so that alternative curricula are not confused with the standard curriculum. Because the attendees were like-minded mission mobilizers, a consensus was quickly reached to honor and protect the identity of Perspectives. Derivative courses were honored for their value and the ways they can be used for different audiences, or as a prequel or sequel to the Perspectives course. In a spirit of collaboration, one attendee suggested it is like having a "Perspectives family of curricula" all sharing the same DNA. The group decided to continue the conversation and expand the reach through convening again in December 2003 at the USCWM in Pasadena.[20]

The Pasadena consultation brought together over fifty people: Perspectives program developers; those seeking to develop national programs; and developers of mission mobilization programs derived from Perspectives. The goal was to build a relational network, clarify and deepen the understanding of the biblical and theological framework of the third edition, and equip Perspectives program developers in the complex task of creating a sustaining national program. At this time, it was still thought advisable to contextualize the curriculum significantly in new lands, adding to the difficulty of the task. Steve Hawthorne crafted a program development manual to guide the work.

It was also announced at this meeting that the Perspectives identity is trademarked and would be protected from this point forward. To both affirm and differentiate specialized courses built upon the Perspectives

---

19 Bruce Koch, interview by author, May 26, 2020, transcript.

20 *Mission Frontiers*, "Mobilizers Meet in Amsterdam."

paradigm, a new designation was introduced. Such courses—be they Bible studies, video courses, shorter adaptations—were invited to join the "Perspectives Family" of mission mobilization resources if they are faithful to the core biblical and missiological DNA of Perspectives. The Global Desk would review and certify the curricula for inclusion. (See appendix E.) The *Kairos* course was the first course to join the Family. A family comradery and spirit of collaboration was established at this meeting that would continue years into the future.[21]

Second Perspectives Global Huddle, High Wycombe, U.K. 2006.

The small Amsterdam 2003 meeting and Pasadena consultation were so encouraging that the Global Desk decided to convene a second Global Huddle outside of London in 2006, again inviting global partners undertaking mission mobilization through education. Twenty-seven participants from twelve countries, eight languages, and seven Perspectives Family curricula attended. The event was graciously hosted by the Perspectives UK program. Deeper partnerships were fomented as the various programs shared reports and prayed together for the global expansion of Perspectives and Perspectives Family curricula. Reports on the initial efforts in translating the Perspectives material into Arabic, Chinese, and Portuguese hinted at a future surge of global programs. Jason Mandryk, editor of *Operation World*, dropped by to encourage the group to stay the course and not let the current pushback against frontier mission derail or deter us in our mission. The designation "Global Huddle" originated at this meeting, with plans initiated to meet every few years in diverse locations.

---

21 *Mission Frontiers*, "Advancing Perspectives Globally."

Praying over a map for God to bless the extension of Perspectives globally
is a regular feature of Perspectives Global Huddles.

The next Perspectives Global Huddle met in Bangalore in 2009, hosted by the Indian Perspectives program. The focus of this Huddle was primarily on the Perspectives curriculum itself, as it followed on the heels of the release of the fourth edition. The Bangalore Huddle provided a significant boost to emerging initiatives in Egypt, Ethiopia, Indonesia, and China. A global Perspectives movement was arising.

Sowing and Reaping in Rocky Soil

The idea of establishing Perspectives programs in the heart of the Muslim world might seem preposterous to some or like faith-filled boldness to others. The soil may be rocky with persecution, but good soil also abounds. National leaders are persevering in faith to cultivate Perspectives programs in the Middle East/North Africa region. The Church of Jesus Christ is growing in these areas, and God does not slight any part of his body from the privilege of active participation in completing the Great Commission. These nations may still be receiving nations, but they are also sending nations.

Arabic Language Version and Egypt

A medical doctor and early missionary sent out by the Egyptian church, Dr. Swailem Sidhom Hennein, first encountered Perspectives in the year 2000 in Chicago. He was given an old edition of the Perspectives Reader.

As he read it, he was amazed at its depth and richness. Later he met Steve Hawthorne, who presented him with a current edition of the Perspectives text. Dr. Swailem, even more impressed, desired to see the curriculum translated into Arabic.

In 2003, Swailem was invited to teach in the largest seminary in the Middle East, the Evangelical Theological Seminary in Cairo. Although he was already in retirement, he returned to his native country to start a missions department at the seminary. Swailem chose to use the Perspectives *Reader* and *Study Guide* for course material. The Presbyterian Frontier Fellowship offered to fund an Arabic translation of the curriculum. Swailem recruited an Arabic translation team while continuing to pour a vision for mission into the hearts of the students and professors.

Dr. Tharwat Wahba, who later ascended to chair of the mission department, and Dr. Sherif Salah, a fellow medical professional invited by Swailem to teach at the seminary, headed up the Perspectives Arabic translation team under Dr. Swailem's oversight. The work was done in stages and took many years, graciously funded by both the Frontier Fellowship and the Outreach Foundation of the Presbyterian Church in the US. A setback came when the fourth edition of the US curriculum was published in 2009. Distressingly, much of the translation work needed to be restarted. To fully grasp the breadth of the course, some translators went to other countries to take Perspectives and one leader was trained in a Coordinator's Workshop in Dubai.

Despite the chaotic "Arab Spring" revolution of 2010, a very successful Perspectives Executive Orientation was held in the spring of 2011 with about thirty church leaders. After receiving an extended overview of the content of the course, these leaders exuberantly began to engage a vision of mobilizing the Egyptian church for mission and laid plans to start an Egyptian Perspectives program. Over the following years a few courses were conducted, utilizing translated materials produced to date. One significant outcome during this time came through a relationship Dr. Salah had with a priest of the Coptic Orthodox Church. Utilizing the Perspectives material, this priest held a class in the Orthodox Cathedral for about two hundred parishioners, exposing them to the richness of the content.[22]

Finally, in March of 2018 the Arabic translation of the Perspectives *Reader* and *Study Guide* was published with a celebratory launch at the seminary. Dr. Swailem, at the age of ninety, was able to see the fruit of his labors before passing away. He left an enduring legacy on the Egyptian church.

---

22 Sherif Salah and Rafik Wagdy, interview by author, December 4, 2019, transcript.

Dr. Swailem and his wife were heroes of the church in Egypt. They had responded to the call to go to a place unlike their native Egypt. Further, they had responded to the call of God again in retirement to help the church in Egypt renew its mission vision. The effect of Dr. Swailem and his key disciples in the seminary is that the whole seminary has developed a missional heart. This vision is articulated from the president on down to the students.[23]

The Perspectives course in the Arabic language may have had a long and slow start, but the strategic significance cannot be overestimated. Arabic is the primary language of twenty-five nations. The average time it takes to learn Arabic is seven years; the average length of stay of mission workers is five years. The discipling of the Arab world will be accomplished by Arabs.

Arabian Peninsula

Many are startled to discover that Perspectives classes are conducted on the Arabian Peninsula. After all, it is the heart of the Muslim world. Most residents are Arab Muslims, right? Actually, no. Over 50 percent of the population of many nations on the Arabian Peninsula is comprised of expatriate workers from all over the world. An estimated 80 percent of the United Arab Emirates (UAE) are nonindigenous. The percentage is even higher in Qatar. These communities of expatriates originate from countries spanning the globe, including large numbers from unreached people groups. If you want to reach the peoples of the world, go to Dubai!

That was the motivation of Matt and Lori Burns when they relocated from Arkansas to the UAE in 2006. They wanted to mobilize the expanding expat community to reach out to the peoples around them. "I didn't know where to start," Matt said, "except to refer back to what mobilized us: the Perspectives course." As trained coordinators, Matt and Lori began to lay the groundwork for a UAE Perspectives program, developing a faithful team and focusing on building relationships. In 2008, they launched Perspectives, sponsored by local churches, in the four major cities of the UAE.

The response was unexpected. During the first two years of the program, they welcomed 360 into the classes. The students were from numerous nationalities and represented diverse segments of society. An average of fifteen to twenty participated in coordinator training after each semester.

One of those who received coordinator training was a South African banker who attended the first ever class in Dubai. He went home after the first night and could not stop talking about what he learned. His wife called

---

23 Ritchie, "Mentors on My Journey."

Matt and asked, "What did you do to my husband? I've never seen him like this before! Is it too late for me and my two sons to register?" That family became the backbone of Perspectives in the UAE for the next several years.[24]

The UAE program has graduated more than one thousand students in over forty classes. They have stimulated a few one-off classes in nearby countries for the Christian expat communities there. Many of those graduates live in-country for a few years on work contracts, returning to their home countries transformed with a vision to partner with God in his kingdom work, wherever he places them.

Although not a standard Perspectives program run by and for indigenous locals, the UAE Perspectives program is highly strategic in awakening Christians of many nationalities to the amazing opportunities God has placed all around them for reaching the unreached. Executives, pilots, doctors, dog-trainers, nannies, engineers, teachers, bankers ... so many say the same thing: "Now I know why I am here. My company sent me here, or I came here to get out of debt, but now I know why *God* sent me here." One retiree stated, "We came here with the oil industry, but when that work was over, we decided to stay. We would rather leave footprints in the sand for the kingdom than return home with a pocket full of money."[25]

Ethiopia

Ethiopia is in the Horn of Africa, considered a bridge to the Middle East. Ethiopians are geographically and culturally close to North African Arabic peoples. Officially a "Christian" nation, Ethiopia has a very large Muslim population and is home to many unreached people groups. These factors strategically position the large Ethiopian Orthodox Church to be gospel harvesters.

In our story about how Perspectives came to Ethiopia, we once again encounter Dave Williams, a true global mobilizer who also helped initiate Perspectives in South Korea. Williams came to Ethiopia as a missionary and began to speak to the leaders of Horn of Africa Evangelical Mission about developing an Ethiopian Perspectives program.

Ethiopian physician, Dr. Markos Zemede, took the Perspectives course in the US in 1999. His life, he says, "was ruined for the ordinary." In 2002, he started the Horn of Africa mission to plant "Christ-centered and culture-affirming churches in the Horn of Africa and beyond."[26] So when Williams approached the ministry's leaders, they were eager to participate.

---

24 Matt Burns, interview by author, July 2, 2020, transcript.

25 From a personal conversation with author.

26 https://hornofafrica.org/dr-markos-zemede. Accessed June 16, 2023.

In April 2009 they worked together to host a two-day "Introducing Perspectives" event, with twenty-two selected leaders. Convicted of the need to mobilize the large Ethiopian Orthodox Church, the second day occasioned serious discussion. How to mobilize millions of Ethiopian evangelicals into mission? Several attendees committed to serve on a Perspectives steering committee, with Tariku Gebre Kersima serving as chairman. Out of this group arose a new mission mobilization ministry, Mission Engagers, which served as the host organization for Perspectives in the country.

The first Perspectives course was run in English as an Intensive course in late 2009 for fifteen prominent church and mission leaders. The first semester-long course was run in 2010 in collaboration with the Evangelical Theological College. Nearly fifty-five students from many schools enrolled in that class, almost all on the credit level. Over the next decade, the team conducted one to two Intensive or semester-long classes per year.

Mission Engagers merged with the Horn of Africa Evangelical Mission and continued to serve Perspectives for several years as a host organization until the time was ripe to create a multiagency network carrying a singular focus of mission mobilization. In 2019, mission directors of major denominations and mission organizations joined together to form the National Mobilization Network (NMN). Along with Perspectives, they have a basket of mobilization tools that they use with churches and university students. Perspectives helped sow a seed of mobilization in Ethiopia. That seed has now sprouted with hundreds of church and campus mobilizers.

From the beginning there was a desire to translate Perspectives into the Ethiopian language of Amharic. English is spoken only at the college level, which limits the spread of the course. The *Kairos* course in Amharic has been broadly used to spread mission awareness. Now mobilization has gone wide, and many are asking to go deep. Leaders are requesting Perspectives in their language, and the timing is ripe. Undergraduate theological education is increasingly being conducted in Amharic.

The challenge is the absence of missiological terminology. For example, Kersima and his team needed to create an Amharic word for "mobilization." They invented a term by combining three words representing three goals they want to accomplish in mission mobilization: to educate; to connect; and to deploy. Despite the linguistic challenges, Ethiopian mission leaders are embracing the translation project in the quest to mobilize the large Ethiopian Orthodox Church.

Kersima sums up the huge opportunity and the bright future:

> Culturally we Ethiopians are very close to the North African and Arab world culture. That calls for a time of obedience

for us. We have been disobedient people. We are the unsent people, with a huge sending potential. Instead, we have always been receiving. Thank God that is now changing. There is an amazing desire, especially among university students, to go to the unreached. They are asking, "Please train us; please send us." Our desire is to mobilize one out of every one hundred and send one out of every one thousand of the twenty million evangelicals in Ethiopia.[27]

Do the math. That is a goal of twenty thousand Ethiopian missionaries sent out from a highly mobilized church!

Establishing the Movement

An ad-hoc team giving the Global Desk their spare time could not service the growing Perspectives movement. In 2007, Bruce Koch was assigned to work with the global movement, but that also happened to be the same time the fourth edition curriculum-revision process was beginning, in which he was heavily invested. With requests pouring in from around the world and programs popping up, the need for dedicated staff was critical.

Matt Burns returned to the US after helping pioneer Perspectives UAE with an interest in launching Perspectives in global gateway cities. He was asked to administer the global extension of Perspectives, with the enthusiastic agreement of Koch. From 2009 to 2014, Burns led the Perspectives Global team.

Matt Burns, director of Perspectives Global, 2009-2014.

Steve Hawthorne and Bruce Koch had experience launching new programs; Burns added administrative and financial-development leadership. They changed the Global Desk name to the Perspectives Global Service Office (PGSO) to reflect the fundamental value of serving national partners. Together they were able to move several key projects forward, including the massive Spanish and Chinese translations. Burns spearheaded development efforts to fund these strategic programs. Administratively, Burns led in launching the first Perspectives Global website and executing two Global Huddles. Under Burns's relatively short leadership term, Perspectives Global gained a steady footing, ready for the massive growth that was to come.

---

27 Tariku Gebre Kersima, interview by author, December 9, 2019, transcript.

After the US Perspectives office moved back to Pasadena and the CMM began a transition to global catalytic mobilization teams, Matt Burns slowly transitioned out of Perspectives to lead a catalytic team in Southeast Asia. At that point, Bruce Koch assumed the full leadership of Perspectives Global.

God had been preparing Bruce Koch his entire life for this leadership role. He entered college to study architecture, a lifelong dream. One day while walking to his dorm room, God clearly spoke to him, "Bruce, I do not want you to be an architect to build buildings; I want you to build my church." After a few days of wrestling with God, Koch switched his major to anthropology in preparation for mission work. Many years later, while speaking at the first Nigerian Perspectives national conference, those words came back to him as he realized, *This is what God meant.*[28]

Bruce Koch, director of Perspectives Global, 2014-present.

While in college, a friend gave Koch a chart that would change the trajectory of the rest of his life. It was Ralph Winter's famous "pie chart," depicting the vast number of unreached people groups. The chart dramatically showed that there were not enough believers in the huge religious block of Muslims to be even represented by a speck of ink on the page. Koch could not escape the stark reality that after two thousand years so little had been done to reach Muslims; he gave his life to change the ink on that chart. He was one of the early signers of the famous Caleb Declaration.

After marrying, he and his new wife intended to pursue church planting in the Muslim world. Family needs created a delay, so they joined the USCWM as a first step. Koch enrolled in a summer Intensive Perspectives course in 1986. He remarks, "Taking Perspectives was like taking a can-opener to my brain; it blew out the dust and cobwebs and let in light."[29] He immediately followed the Intensive class with an early version of coordinator training—a long, five-day workshop. Over the next several years, Koch facilitated Perspectives courses at the U.S. Center, which deeply sowed the content into his soul, preparing him to lead Perspectives Global.

---

28 Koch, interview, 2020.

29 Koch, interview, 2020.

For a few years, the Perspectives Global office would simply run one or two Intensive courses in a country to kick-start a national program. But they began to see some countries struggling for lack of training. Koch extracted portions of the Perspectives USA coordinator training manual to use for the first Perspectives Global-sponsored coordinator training, held in South Africa in 2010. A few years later he recruited Perspectives USA training director Sundee Simmons to rework the American coordinator training manual for global programs.

From 2009, all the funding to help global programs get started during the next decade—over $1 million—came from Perspectives alumni, family foundations, and contributions of the team members themselves. Even after Frontier Ventures (formerly the USCWM) began budgeting for Perspectives Global, almost 95 percent of the budget still came from visionary donors.

The Perspectives Global Service Office team has always been small. The lack of staff actually helped Perspectives Global cultivate beneficial developmental principles; it forced the PGSO to lead through relationships and influence rather than control. Guiding principles and protocols are codified, but nearly all decisions are left to national leaders. The PGSO comes alongside national leaders for initial modeling, training, and guidance; but the national programs assume all leadership, ongoing training, and oversight of finances. The PGSO is not an international controlling office, but an international serving office.

In the same vein, the PGSO does not export Perspectives. There is not an international distribution plan. Because local leaders must own Perspectives themselves for it to be successful, they also must initiate the process of bringing Perspectives to their nation. That initiation is not with the hope that the PGSO will make it happen; instead, they must make the commitment and do the work themselves to make it happen. When the soil in a nation is fertile for mobilization, Perspectives usually follows.

Instead of delivering a cookie-cutter package to be implemented in diverse cultures, Perspectives delivers a program and curriculum to be adapted to individual cultures by indigenous leaders according to the Perspectives ethos and protocols. That adaptation, however, will happen in degrees over time. Perspectives is an integrated, coherent, transformative paradigm; attempts at contextualizing the course with local authors who have not deeply absorbed the content rarely, if ever, produces the same fire within the students for which the course is renowned. As Steve Hawthorne has often said, "If you have not taken the course, you will take it off-course."

Promising Yield

Jesus promised that the good seed sowed on good soil will produce fruit—thirty, sixty, and a hundredfold. Yet that good soil can be in quite diverse environments. We will use two plants as an example. Many people know that Brazil is the world's largest coffee producer, producing one-third of global supply. It is Brazil's largest export, and most Brazilians enjoy a good cup of joe.

On the other hand, few know that China is the world's largest potato producer. Yet the potato is not a food staple for the Chinese; most of the crop is exported or fed to livestock. The coffee crop grows above ground on large plantations. The potato grows underground, usually by rural farmers on small plots of land. The church in these two nations is analogous. In Brazil, most of the population imbibe not only coffee, but also Christianity, where even a president identified as an evangelical Christian. The evangelical church is very visible and growing.

In China, most of the population does not participate in the Christian faith, and the atheistic government opposes the faith. Yet the evangelical church is alive, although mostly "below ground." The church is among the fastest-growing on earth in *both* nations. The good seed in good soil will multiply. These two very opposite environments characterize two of the fastest-growing language programs for Perspectives: Portuguese and Chinese.

Portuguese Language Version and Brazil

Eight years. That is how long it took for the dream of three Brazilian mission mobilizers to become reality. In 2001, Kevin Boot, an American who was born and raised in Brazil, began dreaming about making the Perspectives course available to his countrymen. Boot took Perspectives and coordinated a few classes in the US. Simultaneously, Willem Zuidema, a Dutchman married to a Brazilian, was introduced to Perspectives while serving as chief engineer of an Operation Mobilization ship. He began pursuing his dream of a Portuguese Perspectives program. The third prime mover was Kevin Bradford, an influential and respected seminary professor in Brazil.

The three dreamers came together in 2006 to lay a foundation for the translation and implementation of Perspectives in Brazil. Boot and Bradford attended the Perspectives Global Huddle in the UK in 2006 and returned home to establish a Perspectives national team with six Brazilian leaders. Translation into Portuguese began, and a pilot course was run in 2008 for key leaders, potential instructors, and coordinators. *Perspectivas Brasil* was officially launched at a national congress of Brazilian missions in October 2008. The Portuguese curriculum was released the following year.

It was very important to the founders that Perspectives speak with a Brazilian, rather than a North American, voice. The course was shortened from fifteen to twelve lessons and included thirty articles from Brazilian missiologists and theologians. The indigenous voice aided greatly in the course's national adoption. Today it is a key reference for missiology in Brazil and is used as a textbook in many seminaries. *Perspectivas Brasil* leaders are now exploring how to incorporate all fifteen lessons of Perspectives more fully into the next *Perspectivas* Portuguese version.

For the first few years, leaders were just trying to get courses started in different cities. Most class leadership was haphazard, without a national standard for promotion, training, or implementation. Then, in 2014, God brought Israel Saraiva, a dynamic young mission mobilizer with a burning passion to mobilize his city, on board. Saraiva implemented everything he learned from Kevin Boot, then aimed higher. He recruited a large coordinating team and intentionally focused upon church leadership. The team personally visited with almost three hundred pastors.

The strategy worked. Out of one hundred students in the first Rio de Janeiro class, forty-five were pastors. When those pastors saw firsthand the quality and content of the course, it created a buzz in the city. The following year was maxed out with 120 registered students and a waiting list of thirty. As the team repeated this strategy in each region, standardized the program nationally, and changed their promotion to attract those who were not yet mission mobilized, the reputation of the course soared. The numbers of courses and students multiplied, with pastors averaging around 15 percent of registrants.[30]

Israel Saraiva was appointed national director, leading an executive team comprised of regional coordinators, buttressed by Kevin Boot and an engaged board of directors. The national team poured a lot of energy into developing local and regional leadership. They invested in the spiritual life of their leaders through ongoing discipleship and annual retreats. They developed a coordinator training that focused on training coordinators to first and foremost be mission mobilizers. Instilled within the *Perspectivas* movement is the concept that our God is a mobilizing God; he is not only on mission to reach all peoples, but also to mobilize his people. The objective of the coordinating teams, therefore, is far more than running successful classes; it is to partner with God in mobilizing their churches and cities.[31] These emphases deepened and broadened the movement even more. By 2018, Brazil became the second largest global Perspectives program, trailing

---

30 Kevin Boot, interview by author, December 5, 2019, transcript.
31 Israel Saraiva, Interview by author, March 18, 2019.

only the US. As of the end of 2021, *Perspectivas Brasil* had processed 19,863 students through 484 classes.

Perspectivas Brasil celebrated their tenth anniversary in December 2019 with their first national congress. Geographically, Brazil is almost the size of the continental United States, yet around one thousand people travelled from all over the country to attend the congress. The apex of the gathering was not the plenary talks by Brazilian and international luminaries, but the historic covenant the delegates adopted to become intentional mission mobilizers.

Perspectivas Brasil used their tenth anniversary occasion to host the next Global Mobilization Consultation (GMC) and the seventh Perspectives Global Huddle in São Paulo, Brazil in 2019. Not only did the GMC continue to grow in numbers of global participants, but there were double the number of participants at the Perspectives Global Huddle from the previous Huddle four years earlier in Kenya. The increase in both gatherings reflected the continual increase in mission mobilization worldwide.

Perspectivas Brasil 10th year Anniversary gathering, 2019.

As the fastest growing Perspectives program in the world, *Perspectivas Brasil* is impacting the international mission movement. Between 2017 and 2019 alone, over twelve hundred Brazilian pastors took the *Perspectivas* course, sowing a missional worldview into the huge Brazilian church. One church changed their mission statement from "training leaders to impact our community" to "training workers to impact the nations."[32]

Perspectivas has become a launching pad for many other ministries and has influenced other mission mobilization organizations. With over

---

32 Perspectives Global Newsletter, June 3, 2016.

eight hundred volunteers and an alumni base exceeding twenty thousand, *Perspectivas* is the largest mission mobilization movement in Brazil. Without question, it has contributed to the doubling of Brazilian missionary deployment in the past decade. The latest research by the Association of Brazilian Transcultural Missions (AMTB) discovered that the number of Brazilian cross-cultural missionaries since 2010 increased from 5,500 to over 12,000. Agencies are even asking the leadership of *Perspectivas* to slow down, as they are being inundated with recruits![33]

The leaders of *Perspectivas Brasil* stand in awe of what God has accomplished through this ministry. They don't take credit themselves, but recognize that God himself is mobilizing a powerful South American missionary force to co-labor with him in completing the Great Commission. *Perspectivas Brasil* is riding the winds of the Spirit of God.

Chinese Language Version and China

According to Ethnologue 2019, Mandarin Chinese is the second largest global language, slightly trailing English. China is the second most populous nation on earth, only recently surpassed by India in 2023. The country consists of over 450 ethnolinguistic groups, a large percentage of whom are UPGs. With an estimate of over one hundred million Christians among the Han majority people, China ranks in the top five of nations with the most Christians. When you add in two to three million Christians in the Chinese diaspora, the potential for Chinese mission-sending is colossal.

China has experienced significant changes since the turn of the millennium, which present significant opportunity. The nation's economy grew robustly, elevating millions into the middle class. China has undergone one of the largest migrations in history, as rural dwellers move to the cities. Significantly, the Chinese opened their nation to the outside world. External global gatherings and internal natural disasters have facilitated a greater level of trust and relationship between church leaders. Globalization has dispersed millions of Chinese across the globe.

Numerous attempts have been made, as early as the 1980s, to translate all or parts of the Perspectives curriculum into Chinese. However, they never produced a course of study, only books of various lengths and composition. The books were useful; and even though some were called "Perspectives" at the time, they were, in fact, derivatives. No one ever created a true Perspectives curriculum.

In late 2009, new momentum arose to translate the Perspectives curriculum for the purpose of a program of study. The catalyst was the Urbana student gathering. The Chinese delegation to Urbana knew about

---

33 Boot, "Perspectives in Brazil."

Perspectives and arranged a visit to the USCWM while in the States. During their visit, they persuaded the Perspectives Global office to pursue translation. That led to two attempts with groups in Hong Kong that had been offering English Perspectives classes; but, due to lack of resources, nothing came of them. At this point God brought just the right champion to the table to see the project through.

Dr. Kam Idur had been mobilizing the Chinese world for decades, spending time in both the East and the West. He, also, had been waiting for years for Perspectives in Chinese. As he was very connected with Chinese Christian leadership in many nations, Dr. Kam was able to assemble a translation team while the Perspectives Global office raised funds for the project. The Chinese version became the first Perspectives Global managed and sponsored translation project. Perspectives alumni in the US were excited to give to this strategic venture, as were key family foundations. A $100,000 matching grant was met in only twenty-eight days.

The translation process, however, was not that swift and easy. Not surprisingly, many of the translators encountered serious illnesses, family issues, unusual workload spikes in their day jobs, and depression. Spiritual warfare often accompanies the introduction of Perspectives into new areas. In early 2013 the new translation was beta-tested with Chinese Perspectives classes in Toronto, Seattle, and a class in Asia. Noting deficiencies, the team recalled the translation and put it through a rewrite. The Korean Perspectives program offered their abundant classroom resources to be adapted for Chinese students. All in all, the entire process took five years.

A field test of the completed curriculum was conducted with one hundred top Chinese leaders in November 2013. The relaunched course was well received. Chinese leaders have tremendous interest in mission and realized Perspectives would supply them with valuable mission education and cross-cultural awareness. They commented that this course of study would supply the depth needed to build a mission movement. Over thirty of those leaders were trained as coordinators and instructors. Two key leaders from Taiwan volunteered their time to polish and publish the material in simplified characters and aid in getting it produced into complex (traditional) characters.

Project leader, Dr. Kam, explained their program development strategy:

> We translated the entire US Perspectives curriculum; we did not leave anything out, even if it was irrelevant or very American. We wanted the Chinese church to have the same depth of teaching and paradigm shift for which Perspectives is globally renowned. What we indigenized were the teaching, trainings, and resources. We look to incorporate Chinese-oriented

material in a later revision. The Asian publisher reports that the first printing was sold out within two to three years.[34]

The growth of the Perspectives program in Chinese has been phenomenal. Students are highly motivated and have some of the highest course completion rates in the world, even though most study at the credit level. Programs are indigenously led, self-sustaining, and expanding to many Chinese-speaking communities around the world. Currently, if all the Chinese courses were in one country, it would be the fourth largest program in the Perspectives Global Network, only surpassed by the USA, Brazil, and Korea.

The Chinese church is reporting that they are gaining a global vision, numerous missionaries and mission mobilizers are being raised up, and new sending structures are being established. The time is ripe. Perspectives is a tool God is using at this critical juncture in history to equip the global Chinese church to take their place in the global mission of God.

Fourth Perspectives Global Huddle, Seoul, South Korea, 2011.

Seeding into Other Asian Nations

Perspectives program expansion proliferates additional program expansion. Word gets around and more Christians clamor to see Perspectives developed in their own language and country. A seedbed for that growth was the fourth Perspectives Global Huddle, held in Seoul, South Korea, in 2011. The Korean Perspectives program hosted the gathering, which brought together fifty-six participants from twenty-three nations and four Perspectives Family

---

34 Kam Idur, interview by author, July 15, 2020, transcript.

organizations. The focus of the Huddle was on sharing insights and resources on running a successful Perspectives program and how to integrate various mobilization tools. Attendees represented a continuum along the program development process. The continuum was given definition, used to this day: "Interested Countries," "Emerging Programs," and "Established Programs."

The most profound takeaway from the Seoul Huddle was not programmatic, but a devotional message by Max Chismon, founder of the *Kairos* program. Expounding on Ephesians 4, Chismon encouraged participants that God has lavished grace gifts on his people for the building of his church. Mission mobilization serves in the prophetic role to exhort the church to fulfill the purpose of God. Mobilizers are to take courage; God has generously gifted them to fulfill the prophetic role to which they are called.

The enlarged participation in the Huddle made it apparent to the PGSO that leadership and equipping needed to be regionalized to keep pace with demand. A strategy of addition—adding one country at a time at a pace limited by the capacity to send teams from the US—needed to shift to a strategy of multiplication. The leadership of established global programs needed to be empowered to serve startup programs within their region. Facilitating multiplication also required creating clear guidelines and standardizing resources and training to be adaptable and transferable. A high value of the PGSO is that Perspectives Global be a peer-to-peer network in which global programs can learn from each other.

In Asia, Africa, and Latin America appeals for Perspectives were accelerating. In the two-year period of 2013–14, nine new national programs emerged. The PGSO could not possibly serve this growing movement alone, nor did they want to. The first regional director to be appointed was Chulho Han, director of the flourishing Korean Perspectives program. Julie Gamponia, working in Thailand, joined Han as assistant Asian director. Together they were given responsibility for serving, guiding, and overseeing development of all Asian programs.

Two significant initiatives emerged from Asian regionalization. The first Perspectives Asia Regional Huddle was held in 2017, gathering twenty-two attendees from eight nations. Dr. Todd Johnson, director of the Center of Global Christianity at Gordon-Conwell Theological Seminary, addressed the group. He affirmed the direction in which the Perspectives Global ministry is heading as a peer-to-peer network. The degree to which the PGSO has entrusted global partners with program formation is highly unusual, he said—something he would like to see more Western agencies practice. The synergy created at Perspectives Asia Huddles has quickened development of additional Asian programs.

The second initiative in 2017 was a consultation on how to adapt the historical section of the Perspectives curriculum into Asian contexts. A small group of leaders convened, with the invaluable contribution of Asian history specialist, Dr. Scott Sunquist, formerly dean of the School of Intercultural Studies at Fuller Seminary and now president of Gordon-Conwell Theological Seminary. Out of all the sections of the Perspectives curriculum, the historical section is the portion that most needs adapting into national and regional contexts. This consultation was the first step in what will be a similar process in many regions for years to come.

Indonesian Language Version and Indonesia

Indonesia is the fourth most populous country on earth and the largest Muslim nation. Yet over 10 percent of the population are Christian, making it a nation with one of the largest Christian populations in Asia. In previous decades there have been some significant people movements to Christ, including among the substantial Chinese diaspora. Indonesian Christians have embraced mission to unreached peoples over the past forty years, researching the numerous UPGs in their own country and deploying missionaries nationally and abroad. A strong indigenous prayer movement supports the work. The Indonesian church is a rising mission force, with enormous potential ahead. Just the type of soil that is ripe for Perspectives.

In 2006, an Indonesian youth-mission mobilizer, whom we will call AJ, took Perspectives in the US and was trained as a coordinator. He dreamed of bringing the course to his homeland. Other mission mobilization courses, such as *Kairos*, were already running effectively in the islands of Indonesia, but AJ wanted to also bring the depth and breadth of Perspectives. He organized a course in 2007 utilizing the English Perspectives curriculum for forty hand-selected students. Those students were spurred to begin *Kairos* courses on their university campuses. With limited resources, AJ produced a rough translation of Perspectives into Bahasa Indonesia, the national language. In 2010, key church and mission leaders gathered for an Introducing Perspectives event with PGSO leadership. A program leadership team was established, but the launch of a truly Indonesian course was delayed by the recognition that the translation needed further refinement.

The international leadership of the Perspectives and *Kairos* programs, which had been meeting together at biannual Global Huddles, decided to hold the 2013 Huddle in Indonesia. They extended, for the first time, a broad invitation to all mobilization ministries to a three-day Global Mobilization Consultation (GMC), followed by a three-day Perspectives Global Huddle.

Fifth Perspectives Global Huddle in 2013 in Surabaya, Indonesia
compared to first Global Huddle in 2003 in Amsterdam.

The 2013 Perspectives Global Huddle that followed on the heels of the GMC spurred a burst of energy and momentum among the increasing number of global programs represented. The Huddle provided an opportunity for reflection and discussion of lessons learned over the years concerning program development and adaptation of curriculum, and a deeper understanding of the uniqueness of the Perspectives paradigm.

The PGSO and the Indonesian leadership team took advantage of the presence of global Perspectives trainers in Indonesia to hold an Intensive Perspectives class in English for thirty strategic leaders who could serve as future instructors and coordinators. The Intensive course was conducted in two weeklong sessions, one immediately following the Huddle and another six months later. Meantime, the translation work continued. Two years later a similar split-Intensive was conducted with about one hundred students using a beta-version of the Bahasa Indonesia translation. The translation is now complete, and plans are underway for a relaunch of a full Perspectives program in the Bahasa Indonesian language.

Singapore

Seeds have the potential to travel great distances on the wings of the wind to repopulate. One Perspectives seed travelled almost 11,000 km from the northern to the southern hemisphere on the opposite side of the world, took root, and bore fruit. This is the unexpected love story of how God used a Singaporean attorney and a British climate scientist to bear kingdom fruit far from the original source.

Ailene left her homeland of Singapore to study in the United Kingdom. While pursuing her degree, she enrolled in a Perspectives class. Inspired, she dreamed of seeding the course into her homeland. She briefly returned home in 2010, just as Steve Hawthorne and Bruce Koch were passing through Singapore on a short layover. Ailene arranged a meeting, in which they agreed that she would bring together a few key mission leaders to meet with Hawthorne on his return trip. Despite the interest generated from that meeting, no one arose as a torchbearer to make the course a reality.

There was some familiarity with Perspectives in Singapore from the late 1980s. Michael Jaffarian, a lecturer at Singapore Bible College, conducted a modular three-year missions course, open to lay people, leaning heavily on the Perspectives curriculum. The mission pastors of two churches that hosted Perspectives twenty-five years later had originally been impacted by Jaffarian's course.

Ailene did not feel that she could initiate a project as big as Perspectives herself ... that is, not unless she married Benjamin. Benjamin was a Perspectives coordinator she met in England; however, far from being engaged, they were not even dating. But God has ways of accomplishing his purposes. Benjamin moved to Singapore, and they married in 2013. Shortly after marrying, God again prompted them to initiate a Perspectives program. PGSO helped them orchestrate a "Taste of Perspectives" for potential partners, resulting in several organizations getting behind them. In 2014, they legally incorporated Perspectives and attended coordinator training in Hong Kong. That fall they held their first two semester-long course with fifty-three students.

In the first seven years of running Perspectives classes in Singapore, Ailene, Benjamin, and their team have been instrumental in sowing mission vision into the lives of 314 students and their churches. God orchestrated a love story between two professionals from two distant parts of the world in order that his eternal love story might be told to the peoples who have yet to hear of his love for them.[35]

---

35 Ailene G., interview with author, email, July 27, 2020.

Taiwan

The expansion of Perspectives into Taiwan is a case study in the advantages of regional networking and leadership. A Taiwanese pastor and his wife with decades of experience in Christian publishing attended the large Perspectives class in Hong Kong in 2014, in which the newly revised Chinese Perspectives curriculum was being field-tested. They volunteered to polish the text in simplified Chinese characters and then to convert it into traditional characters for other Chinese speakers, including Taiwanese.

This couple's son, Ray Peng, was the executive director of United Mission of Taiwan (UMOT). Peng took a Korean pastor with him to Korea to help him learn about the Korean Perspectives program. The Taiwanese were so eager to hold a Perspectives class that they didn't even wait for the published Chinese curriculum, but initiated their first class in 2014. The Korean program shared all their ancillary resources with Taiwan, making it feel quite Korean; the instructors, however, were all Chinese. When mission agency leaders discovered that Perspectives was being conducted in Chinese, excitement grew.

The staff of UMOT took responsibility for organizing and coordinating classes, seeing Perspectives as a flagship vision course to mobilize the nation's churches. When UMOT conducted a survey in 2017 of all the churches and mission organizations on the island, they discovered that less than 10 percent of all Taiwanese churches participate in missions. Only six hundred missionaries had been sent from the four thousand churches on the island, and only a handful of those missionaries were working among the least-reached.[36]

In 2015 UMOT staff accessed Perspectives coordinator and instructor training in Thailand, enabling them to conduct trainings in their country. The Chinese Perspectives *Reader* was published in Taiwan at the end of the year, and the Korean ancillary materials were revised to fit their culture. From 2016 onwards the Taiwanese Perspectives program has run fall and spring semester courses, averaging five classes per semester.

Mobilizing churches is a priority for Perspectives Taiwan. To date, over forty churches have hosted a class. One such church was on the verge of closing their missions department. One of their own missionaries persuaded them to host a Perspectives class, and 107 students filled the room. The church's mission vision was reignited; they are now rebuilding what they were about to shutter.

---

36 Ray Peng, "Transforming the Church to be Missional," www.lausanne.org/content/lga/2018-11/transforming-the-church-to-be-missional.

In eight short years, 2014–21, Perspectives Taiwan held sixty-five classes with more than twenty-five hundred students from four to five hundred different churches. About 20 percent of the participants have been pastors and ministers. Even though the course is only offered at the more demanding credit level (equivalent to American college level), an astonishing 60 percent completed all the requirements for credit. A highly dedicated thirteen-year-old boy went further than that. Attending the class with his mom, he not only finished all the credit requirements but also read through the entire Perspectives *Reader*! He knows he is young and cannot do much yet, but he has committed to praying for the nations.

How has Perspectives Taiwan borne so much fruit? Most of the people on the coordinating teams are single women in their twenties and thirties who have no traditional cross-cultural experience. Not the type of individuals you would expect to mobilize pastors and churches! The answer these young people give: "We know that we are not the most qualified people, so we know that this is definitely God's work."[37]

Thai Language Version and Thailand

The Chinese language program was directly instrumental in seeding Perspectives into the Thai language and culture. In 2011, the translators of the Chinese curriculum went to Chiang Mai, Thailand, to take the course in English. Thai pastors were invited to join this Intensive class. One of those Thai leaders, Chumseang Reongjareonsuk, was the founding director of Wycliffe Bible Translators in Thailand. He had previously translated the *Kairos* course into the Thai language, enabling its countrywide spread as a foundational mobilization tool. Deeply impacted by the Perspectives course and its potential for transformational discipleship and mission sending, he declared, "This is what God wants me to do; he wants me to translate this course and bring it to the Thai church."

Filipino-American Perspectives veteran Julie Gamponia, employed as a teacher in Thailand, had been praying toward this day for many years. Assembling a group of pastors, they began to discuss how to make Perspectives a reality in Thailand. Reongjareonsuk began the long translation process with the help of Phanu Dopphoopha and a team of editors. Kam Idur, facilitator of the Chinese program, met regularly with them to coach and encourage. Jonas Kang, a Korean missionary in Bangkok, initiated conversations with denominational leaders in Bangkok, and along with Reongjareonsuk introduced the Thai curriculum to the

---

37 Cheng-Yen Yan and Cynthia Wu, interview with author, December 9, 2019.

Protestant Committee of Thailand, a board overseeing the major Protestant denominations in the country. The committee enthusiastically endorsed it as a primary educational tool for the Thai church.

A Perspectives working committee was formed, and in 2016 a half-day "Taste of Perspectives" was held for forty key Thai leaders. The Thai language curriculum was completed and published the same year. The ground was prepared for the first Thai Perspectives course to be held in 2017. Following the Indonesian Perspectives model, the course was divided into two weeklong Intensives, separated by several months in which the students would complete their coursework. Almost all the initial instructors were Thai-speakers, whether indigenous or long-term missionaries who had taken Perspectives in the US.

One of the firstfruits of the first Thai class is Bangkok Perspectives coordinator, Linee Jutrakul, a highly experienced educator. She testifies,

> I believed God was calling me to do something, but I did not know what. I resigned from my job and enrolled in the Perspectives class. Afterward I knew for sure that this is what God wanted me to do—to mobilize the Thai church by volunteering to coordinate and expand Perspectives classes in our country. I am so happy.[38]

During the first three years of the national program, nine classes were conducted in three large cities in Thailand, enrolling around two hundred students. Four major seminaries grant credit for Perspectives, appreciating the enhancement the high-quality curriculum adds to their programs. Each year the coordinating teams strive to contextualize the course and instruction deeper into the Thai culture. The Thai Perspectives program is bearing good fruit in prayer meetings, short-term mission involvement, engagement with diaspora populations, and the sending of at least five alumni to the mission field.[39]

Malaysia

The newest Perspectives Global program in Asia launched in 2019 in Malaysia. This peninsular nation in Southeast Asia is an ethnically and religiously diverse nation, with significant minority populations of Chinese and Indians, the predominant populace of the church. Large numbers of UPGs live in the nation and surrounding countries, including the dominant Muslim Malay people group.

---

38 Linee Jutrakul, interview by author, December 9, 2019, transcript.
39 Julie Gamponia, interview by author, December 9, 2019, transcript.

Perspectives course content was sowed into Malaysia over three decades. In the 1990s, the IMB conducted classes for their missionaries in the region, opening enrollment to locals. Perspectives course director Peter Shankar Nambiar took the course at that time. In the early 2000s the *Kairos* course entered Malaysia; its widespread use is an entry point to mobilizing God's people into God's purpose. The CMM relocated several of its staff to the country around 2014. As Perspectives is a key tool in their tool belt, they set about creating an appetite for the course. They organized a "Taste of Perspectives," in which close to ninety local leaders were introduced to the course.

Peter Shankar Nambiar, Secretary-General of the Malaysia Center for Global Missions, worked closely with the CMM staff over the succeeding years to launch the first official Perspectives course in 2019. The class was indigenous from the first, led by national Malaysians. It was conducted in English, on a weekly basis, attended by mission and church leadership. Because of the language diversity in the Malaysian church, the following year presented two course offerings, one in English and one in Chinese.

In 2020, Perspectives Malaysia launched its first ever online program in both English and Chinese. The online format garnered students from the US, Philippines, Indonesia, Kenya, Uganda, Hong Kong, India, and a few other students from restricted-access nations. The virtual program was designed using the Discovery Bible Study approach for weekly two-hour small-group discussions. To date, Perspectives Malaysia has over one hundred graduates. Expectations are high for the contribution the Perspectives course will render for mission mobilization of the church in this strategic nation.[40]

Propagating into Other African Nations

The potential for mission-sending by the African church over the next three decades is astounding. By 2050 the continent of Africa is projected to have more Christians than all of North America, Europe (including Russia), and Asia—*combined*![41] Currently 44 percent of all Protestants are African, with an estimated 55 percent by 2050.[42] Imagine if just a fraction of those African Christians could be mobilized to envision an evangelized world and actively embrace God's purpose for them in achieving that outcome. That is the passion of African Christians seeking to use the Perspectives course to light a mobilization fire. Beginning with Nigeria in the west and Ethiopia in the east, the Perspectives program slowly began propagating across the continent.

---

40 Peter Shankar, interview by author, July 11, 2020, email.

41 Zurlo, Johnson, and Crossing, "World Christianity and Mission 2020."

42 The Center for the Study of Global Christianity, *The Inquiry*.

South Africa

Very early in the frontier mission movement, Perspectives course content contributed to the rising South African mission movement. Pastor Richard Verreynne visited the U.S. Center for World Mission in 1982, met Dr. Ralph Winter, who gave him the Perspectives *Reader* and *Study Guide*. Returning home, he used the Perspectives curriculum to develop a four-semester missiology course in the newly established School of World Mission at the Christian Reformed Theological Seminary. The mission education flowing out of this seminary resulted in many local churches acquiring a mission vision and sending out hundreds of missionaries in the 1990s. Several local-church Perspectives classes were organized, and even though the content made an impact, a sustaining national program was not established.

When the fourth edition of the curriculum was published, Steve Hawthorne and Bruce Koch approached Richard Verreynne about formally establishing a Perspectives Study Program. They conducted a Perspectives Executive Orientation in 2009 with a dozen key mission and church leaders. It was followed by a Program Development and Coordinators Workshop in 2010. Verreynne stepped down from national leadership in 2017, handing the baton over to Suzy Abrahams. Abrahams is a full-time pastor, and thus serves Perspectives in a volunteer capacity.

Since 2010 an all-volunteer leadership team has conducted twenty-five classes and ten coordinator trainings, printed their own textbooks, and established national and regional leadership teams. A particular challenge for Perspectives in South Africa is that the nation is linguistically quite diverse, with eleven official languages. Perspectives is offered in English, a governmental and business language, but not in the most widely spoken language. Nevertheless, the program is spreading from Cape Town into other regions of the country, and even into neighboring nations. South African national leadership introduced Perspectives to Angolans and assisted Malawi in running their first class in 2020.[43]

Kenya

The Perspectives course and the *Kairos* course work hand-in-hand in many nations, one course influencing the development or spread of the other. In Kenya's case, they shared the *Kairos* course with Ethiopia, and in turn received the Perspectives course from Ethiopia. Kenyan national director, Sam Ngugi, relates the story.

> In 2006 I enrolled in the *Kairos* course, and the world of global missions was opened up to me. That same year I became

---

43 Suzy Abrahams, interview by author, August 3, 2020, email.

acquainted with the Perspectives course through the *Mission Frontiers* magazine. The organization I worked for subscribed to this journal, where I saw an advertisement for Perspectives. I really wanted to take this course, but the closest place it was being offered was Nigeria.

Six years later I was contacted by Tariku Gebre to help him start *Kairos* courses in Ethiopia. To my great joy I discovered that Ethiopia had the Perspectives course! I told Tariku, "We have been waiting for Perspectives in Kenya for many years and had no idea it was being offered in a nation next door!"

Tariku helped us to initiate the Perspectives Study Program in Kenya in April 2013. Many mission leaders in Kenya had heard about Perspectives, so when we announced that we were going to run a class, there was great excitement. We held our first Intensive course in Nairobi, with numerous mission leaders, missionaries, and Christian workers in attendance. Subsequently, we formed a national coordination team and trained instructors. The Perspectives Global Service Office helped us print two thousand textbooks in Nairobi for the East Africa region. They also introduced us to Jeff Lewis, who journeyed with us and was of great help and encouragement in the initial years of the development of the program.[44]

The Kenyan Perspectives National Coordinating Team continues to run classes in Nairobi every year, graduating over three hundred since 2013. Ngugi's mission organization, Mission Campaign Network (MCN) serves as the structural host of the national Perspectives program.

In 2016 the leadership decided to give greater focus on Christian professionals who were being overlooked in mission mobilization. The strategic impact of Christian professionals is seen in the following story. The head teacher at a school in the slums of Nairobi enrolled in the Perspectives course. Because her understanding of God's mission changed, she began to reach out to the Muslim girls in her school for the first time. As she befriended them, they began to open their hearts to her, giving her an opportunity to share the gospel. To her delight, several decided to become followers of Jesus, and she was able to disciple them. This educator is now walking in the newfound joy of knowing how God can use her for his purpose through her career.[45]

MCN continues to offer both *Kairos* and Perspectives courses, working in synergy to mobilize different constituents at different levels.

---

44 Sam Ngugi, interview by author, December 8, 2019, transcript.
45 Ngugi, interview.

As the *Kairos* course has spread out from Kenya to East and Central Africa, it is creating a hunger for the Perspectives course to add the depth and breadth to mission understanding and engagement. Kenyan Perspectives leadership is ready to respond.

Rwanda

An American medical doctor, Marc Simpao, enrolled in a Perspectives class in Austin, Texas, in 2012. Shortly thereafter, he and his family landed in Kigali, Rwanda. He intentionally pursued an international position where he could combine his skill with his passion to extend God's kingdom. Simpao was eager to help Rwandans establish an indigenous Perspectives program. He worked with the Perspectives Global Service Office to conduct an inaugural Perspectives course taught by international instructors.

Kenyan Perspectives leadership came alongside to help. In May of 2015, thirty-two church and mission leaders gathered for the inaugural one-week Intensive course, which was well received. A follow-up team was quickly formed, and they set about planning for the next class. Pastor Rukundo Rogers was trained as lead coordinator.

Training local instructors is key to indigenizing the course. The Rwandan team took advantage of the presence of Jeff Lewis and myself, who were in Kenya at the 2015 Perspectives Global Huddle, to conduct instructor training in Kigali, Rwanda the following week. A dozen potential instructors, including two from Kenya, participated in the training. A second Intensive course was held the following year, this time for student leaders. The course was completely orchestrated by Rwandan leadership, and five of the newly trained instructors stretched their wings to teach one-third of the course. The thirty-one student leaders in attendance disciple university students through their ministries. They discovered that sowing God's heart for world evangelization into the hearts of those they lead *is* discipleship.

Perspectives has often inspired initiatives that bear fruit for generations to come. Such could potentially be the case in Rwanda. A young Rwandan couple leading a university ministry was discipled into mission through the *Kairos* course and Perspectives, becoming facilitators and instructors of each course. Through their engagement with students, they saw the need for a Rwandan mission agency to send out Rwandan missionaries, with a focus upon the unreached. This young couple took a huge leap of faith to start the first *indigenous* mission-sending agency in Rwanda. This new agency and their missionaries are almost completely supported by the Rwandan church.

Uganda

The catalyst for sparking the Perspectives program in Uganda began at the Global Mobilization Consultation in Kenya in December 2015. Pastors Julius Twongyeirwe and Dennis Kilama from Uganda were attending the GMC and heard reports from Korea and Nigeria about how the Perspectives course was igniting a missionary-sending movement. They realized that this was a program they needed to awaken the Ugandan church.

Pastor Twongyeirwe contacted the Perspectives Global Office but received no response. He contacted the Kenyan program team and received a delayed response. He waited for a year, and finally decided to take the risk upon himself to run a class on his own. He surmised, "I'm going to start this class because we need it so much; if we get into trouble because of copyright issues, then they will come to us, but we will have made a start."[46]

In June of 2017, he gathered a group of fifty students in his home, where he conducted the class over the next fifteen weeks. They only had a copy of the third edition of the text, so they photocopied the lesson for the students week by week. The students were mostly young churchgoers that Twongyeirwe knew from other mobilization and outreach endeavors he had organized. Pastors Twongyeirwe and Kilama taught the class, with Twongyeirwe creating and grading his own reviews. He reported in regularly to the Global Office so that there would be transparency in everything he did. Finally, the Global Office responded, and arranged for the Kenyan program to send texts for future classes. Half of that original class completed the course; out of that group, PGSO staff and Kenyan director Sam Ngugi were able to come and train future coordinators and instructors.

A second fifteen-week class was held the following year, once again in Pastor and Mrs. Twongyeirwe's home. The young students and the pastors who were in these initial courses began to promote Perspectives among their peers and churches, enabling the course to multiply. Pastors began hosting Perspectives in their churches, strategically positioned throughout the large city of Kampala in multiple denominations. Another class was conducted in the western region of Uganda, laying a strategic foundation for the future. In the first three years of Perspectives in Uganda, 230 students graduated from ten courses.

Perspectives leader Sharon Nafuna relates the surprising result that Perspectives is having on the younger generation:

> Eighty percent of Ugandans claim to be Christian, yet many do not really understand their faith. I, myself, was one of them. After the first few lessons of Perspectives, many young people

---

46 Sharon Nafuna, interview by author, December 8, 2019, transcript.

begin to ask themselves, "Am I really a Christian?" They are seeing in the Scriptures for the first time what it means to be a Christian. They are going to their churches and influencing their churches to go back to the basics of the gospel. We are seeing their values and priorities changed through their social media posts. These are young professionals, just starting their families. This is promising for the next generation.[47]

Extending the Movement

The second biannual Global Mobilization Consultation (GMC), followed by the sixth Perspectives Global Huddle, was graciously hosted, near Nairobi, by the Kenyan Perspectives leadership in December 2015. Over the span of seven days, three hundred mission mobilizers from around the world met together to worship, pray, collaborate, and strategize how to best facilitate a mission movement within their nations on behalf of the unreached.

Global Mobilization Consultation 2015, Nairobi, Kenya.

The Perspectives Global Huddle met after the GMC, gathering seventy-two participants from twenty-three countries, a significant increase from two years earlier, reflecting rapid growth and burgeoning interest. Two substantial milestones were reached by this Huddle. PGSO director Bruce Koch explains it best in his own words.

> This particular Huddle marked a significant shift in strategy for the Perspectives Global leadership team. With Perspectives in five languages now, with four more in the process of translation, the demand for Perspectives is exploding. The Perspectives Global Service Office can no longer hope to provide direct support for every new national program. There are far too many countries asking for permission and assistance. The reservoir of experience and wisdom

---

47 Nafuna, interview.

Sixth Perspectives Global Huddle 2015, Nairobi, Kenya.

in our movement has been growing for more than a decade. Now is the time to build on that strength. The theme of the 2015 Global Huddle was Extending the Movement. An invitation was extended to our partner programs to join us in the ongoing missiological inquiry that is needed for ongoing global curriculum development and regional adaptions. That raises some new challenges, but also opens the door to even greater impact.

Ten of the countries that meet our criteria for "established" programs were asked to give presentations that highlighted their strengths and lessons learned in developing their programs. No program has ever had the fast start that China has had with twelve course offerings in their first eighteen months. Brazil is faced with the challenge of maintaining quality while experiencing explosive growth over the last three years. Korea sets the global standard for comprehensive curriculum resource development and training. The Nigerian program has arguably had the greatest national impact of any of our programs. The veteran programs held workshops in which the "emerging" programs could ask and receive inspiration and guidance.

We also articulated for the first time, in clear and concise fashion, our purpose, core principles, protocols, phases of development, and shared practices. We managed to summarize fifteen years of experience into a page and a half. In the long run, that may have been the most significant outcome, because it provides clear rails for the network to run on. Perspectives is in twenty-three countries today. Starting new national programs is often a difficult and slow process. But by extending the movement through multiplication rather than addition, we can anticipate that number growing to as many as fifty to sixty in the next decade. Once again, we left our Huddle greatly encouraged, strengthened by one another's faith and commitment to mobilizing God's people toward world evangelization and transformational development.

Our movement is remarkable is so many ways, but the most important observation is that there is no explanation for what Perspectives Global is accomplishing with so few resources other than Jesus Himself working through us all as weak vessels. Who would want it any other way?[48]

Latin America: Ripe for Mobilization

Only slightly behind Africa, Latin America contains the second largest body of affiliated Christians of any global region. The evangelical church has grown at an astounding rate over the past century. Accompanying such growth has been a vast increase in mission-sending. Since the decade of the 1980s, God has used the international network COMIBAM, the Perspectives derivative *Misión Mundial*, and influential national leaders to sow a frontier mission vision into Spanish-speaking countries. Numerous indigenous mission agencies, networks, and publications arose. Mission departments were established in seminaries and Bible colleges.

All this activity created a pent-up demand for the Perspectives course in Spanish. For many years, *Misión Mundial* was promoted as the Perspectives course. Latin American mission leaders became familiar with the "mother course" Perspectives through their education or international contacts. The Perspectives Global Service Office (PGSO) was increasingly receiving requests from numerous countries for the standard Perspectives course to be translated and made available in their nation. The fact that there are twenty-two Spanish-speaking nations forced a change in PGSO strategy from addition to multiplication. It became obvious that a necessary, and indeed better, strategy was to establish strong regional anchor programs which could multiply themselves into near-neighbor nations, rather than responding from a single global headquarters. The shared language and cultural similarities of the Latin American world provided an excellent opportunity to initiate such a strategy.

A Spanish Translation for Ibero-America

The story of making the Perspectives course available to the Spanish-speaking world begins in 2011 through two separate events: one involving a Latino in Central America; the other with former missionaries to Central America living in Texas. We will begin with the story of the missionaries, Ken and Glynis Kintsel.

The Kintsels first took the Perspectives class in 2003 in Oklahoma, having returned to the States after serving in Ecuador. Glynis recalls,

---

48 Bruce Koch, Internal report on Perspectives Global Huddle, December 2015.

I was almost mad at God! Why would he lead us to take this amazing class when we seemingly couldn't do anything about it? It was like pouring gasoline on the fire within us to serve Latinos, yet there were very few Latinos living in our city. We wanted to do whatever we could to share Perspectives with the Spanish-speaking world. To our shock, we were told that the course did not exist yet in Spanish! "Just pray," we were told, and pray we did … for eight long years![49]

The Kintsels moved to the Texas-Mexico border to teach Spanish to prospective missionaries. When Ken assumed the directorship of the school, they initiated the Perspectives course in English for their trainees and for locals in the Rio Grande Valley. For six years they coordinated Perspectives classes, but as drug-related violence escalated near the border, the school's pool of applicants dried up. The future looked uncertain.

Kenneth and Glynis Kintsel, initiators of Perspectives in Spanish.

Then, in 2011, Ken and Glynis Kintsel visited their daughter in college in Fayetteville, Arkansas. While there, they dropped by the national US Perspectives office and encountered the ministry of Perspectives Global. Glynis continues their story,

I began to get really excited. At last! This must be the answer to our prayers! I loved the large map on the wall with pins in it showing where Perspectives was being offered.

But wait! I suddenly realized there were no little flags in *any* Spanish-speaking country. My long bottled-up emotions exploded. Do these people not understand the critical time the Latino church was in? Do they not know that this is a *kairos* time for the Spanish-speaking world?

I went off for a few minutes as I tried to contain myself. The man standing there, Matt Burns, stared at us with wide eyes. "Can you stay and talk?" he queried.[50]

One week later, Matt Burns received a surprise call from Graceway Church in Kansas City offering to donate $64,000 to translate the Perspectives course into Spanish. Burns knew exactly whom God had

---

49 Ken and Glynis Kintsel, interview with author, April 17, 2019, and October 16, 2020.
50 Kintsel, interview.

prepared to oversee the translation project. The Kintsels approached their ministry's board, by now all Perspectives alumni, about pivoting their ministry from teaching Spanish to English-speaking missionaries to mobilizing Latin Americans for mission through the translation of Perspectives into Spanish. The board concurred; consequently, the name of the ministry changed to the King's Way Center for World Mission. Staff member Carl Johnson administered

Carl Johnson,
Spanish translation project director.

the huge and complicated translation project, overseeing a multinational team of native speakers. Having translators from several nations was an effort to keep the end product from exhibiting the colloquial uniqueness of any one country.

Meanwhile, in Costa Rica, a single young woman named Montserrat Antillon took the Perspectives course while visiting in the US. Deeply impacted by the course, she planned and worked for months, with the support of US Regional Director Stan Freyenberger, to enable the course to be offered in her city of San Jose, Costa Rica. In the spring of 2011, Antillon and the strong coordinating team she recruited kicked off the first official Perspectives course in Latin America. Forty-five mostly bi-lingual students enrolled in the English course, including numerous pastors and leaders. The enthusiastic

Montserrat Antillon,
an initiator of Perspectives in Spanish.

response generated a coordinating team for a class in the fall of the same year, enrolling almost seventy.

Montserrat Antillon carried a passion to spread Perspectives throughout all of Latin America, her energy working like a spark plug to ignite a similar longing in others. In 2013, a coordinating team she trained was able to serve the first ever South American Perspectives course, a two-week Intensive in Lima, Peru, conducted in Spanish!

The Spanish translation of the Perspectives *Reader* and *Study Guide* was completed in 2013, carrying the Spanish name *Perspectivas*. In addition to the class in Peru, there were also two Spanish Intensives held in the US. The participants in those three classes represented sixteen of the twenty-two Spanish-speaking countries, and virtually all of them started asking for help to launch *Perspectivas* in their countries. Bruce Koch, now the director of the PGSO, quickly realized they were creating a demand they could not meet.

The Kintsels transitioned to managing a *Perspectivas* Global *Español* Service Office (PGE) to aid in the development of the course as it spread southward. A second PGE Service Office was opened in Lima, Peru, led by former Perspectives US national director Dave Flynn and his Peruvian wife Elizabeth. The PGE planned and coordinated all of the program start-up events on behalf of the PGSO. They also oversaw the printing of books and the translation of ancillary materials, making *Perspectivas* the first curriculum translation to start out of the gate with a complete set of resources.

Perspectivas Programs in the US, Costa Rica, Mexico, and Cuba

United States

One of the beta classes for the Spanish-language version was held in 2013 at the Rio Grande Bible Institute, a seminary for Latino pastors. The academic dean of the school came to the Kintsels in tears after taking the English class, imploring them to offer the class for their pastors to promote a full-fledged mission vision in their students.

One of the students in that first *Perspectivas* class was Marco Murillo, whose ministry vision was transformed into planting churches with a mission DNA. Murillo heeded the call to initiate a Spanish program in the US to enable the enormous Hispanic population to study Perspectives in their mother tongue. He launched courses in six states and Puerto Rico before settling into his goal of church planting.[51] The US Spanish-language program now operates under the regional leadership of Perspectives USA.

Costa Rica

Following the initial Perspectives courses in English in Costa Rica in 2011–12, a strong leadership team was in place to switch to the Spanish-language program. Classes expanded outside of the capital, with four classes conducted in 2013, this time all in Spanish. The Costa Rican program matured over the years, becoming a catalyst in the mission mobilization of the Costa

---

51 Kintsel, interview.

Rican church. Current director Lucía Brenes reports that Perspectives is fostering unity between denominations, mission agencies, and parachurch organizations.[52] Now this established program is building the movement in Central America by helping other countries launch new programs.

The significance of the availability of Perspectives in Spanish is viewed through the personal reflection of this Costa Rican pastor after only the first lesson.

> I have been a pastor for thirteen years and run a Bible institute, and it has been a very long time since I have felt so moved. It is so rich; I just can't pass quickly over so much revelation. Even with a master's degree in theology, I had not taken in the marvelous inheritance that I have received through faith in Christ. For all these years I have rejoiced in being part of the church, but I had not really perceived that this was only part of the inheritance I am going to receive. I am absolutely beyond words to express my gratitude to all of you for making this course available.[53]

Mexico

The editor of the Spanish-translation project, Eugenio Torres, put together a leadership team to launch *Perspectivas* in Mexico. Editing the text sowed a passion deep into his soul. He confessed to the Kintsels that as he edited, he would just stop and weep. He later discovered that his wife was also reading and weeping.

They were able to hold their inaugural Intensive class in 2013, with thirty-nine key leaders and pastors. Following the course, the students created the very first *Perspectivas* alumni group to continue fellowshipping with one another, a feature that was duplicated in future classes. In the successive years, Intensive classes have been conducted in some large cities, while other cities began to hold regular fifteen-week classes.[54]

Cuba

The fourth Latin American country to hold a *Perspectivas* class was Cuba. Cuba, of all places, might seem an unlikely location for an early *Perspectivas* course, but God had gone before, arranging circumstances years earlier. The director of a leadership ministry, Kathleen Peterson, was visiting the director of a seminary in Cuba when she noticed the English Perspectives

---

52 Personal email received from Lucía Brenes, November 17, 2021.
53 Quote from a personal email received from Montserrat Antillon, April 8, 2012.
54 Kintsel, interview.

Reader on his bookshelf. Peterson, who grew up in Panama, the daughter and granddaughter of missionaries to Panama and Cuba, is also a Perspectives alumna. The Cuban educator inquired if she knew anything about Perspectives. To her affirmative answer, he declared, "I know it is God's will for Perspectives to come to Cuba." It was through the invitation of that seminary that the PGE was able to send a team to conduct and model an Intensive course in Cuba in 2014.

Despite a shortage of texts and intermittent electricity problems, the course registered 108 students! A visitor to the island nation reported that everywhere he went they were talking about *Perspectivas* in the churches. One Cuban declared, "Now I understand why God is having our government bring all these students here to study. The nations are coming to us so we can reach them!"[55]

The Cuban *Perspectivas* program today is strong and continuing to grow. Following the initial class and coordinator training, between 2017 and 2021 ten courses have graduated 520. Additionally, forty-one coordinators and twenty-three instructors have been trained. This island nation is off to a great start.

Rapid Multiplication Into Bolivia, Colombia, and Argentina

Communication flows swiftly through networks of relationships in the Latin American world. With the inauguration of *Perspectivas* in Costa Rica, Mexico, and Cuba, the PGSO received a tsunami of interest from other Latin American countries. The PGE and the PGSO worked together to plan and cosponsor the launch of *Perspectivas* in three more nations in 2016: Bolivia, Colombia, and Argentina.

Bolivia

A Facebook post alerted Bolivian Osvaldo Rosales and his wife that Perspectives had been translated into Spanish. They contacted the Flynns in neighboring Peru to ask how to access the course. After a year of planning and prayer, a *Perspectivas* ten-day Intensive class was held in April 2016 for key leaders. Four months later PGE leadership returned to train coordinators and instructors to establish a foundation for a national program. The following year the Bolivians launched their first fifteen-week course; actually, they initiated three courses in three cities. Each year thereafter they conducted simultaneous classes in a circuit of four cities, followed by coordinator and instructor training. There are only nine main cities in Bolivia, and *Perspectivas* is now in five of them.

---

55 Kintsel, interview.

The Bolivian leadership recognized early on the need to establish more than a study program in Bolivia. Students were opening up in class and sharing their hearts. Class leaders responded by developing a mentorship program to invest in the students' lives, aiming for deep-level transformation. Weekly mentorship sessions also dramatically increased student completion rates. The mentorship program became part of the DNA of the Bolivian program, operating at the national, regional, and local levels. Predictably it has generated a larger volunteer base for expansion, which only bodes well for the future of *Perspectivas* in Bolivia.[56]

According to Rosales, in just a few short years *Perspectivas* has been instrumental in launching Bolivians into mission in places like Turkey, Nepal, France, and Ethiopia, as well as to the least-reached ethnic groups within Bolivia's borders.[57]

Colombia

The formation of *Perspectivas* Colombia began with one of the most networked mission leaders on the continent. Victor Ibagón served many years on the board of COMIBAM, including an interval as president. He was introduced to the Perspectives course in 1997 while visiting the U.S. Center for World Mission in Pasadena. While there, he and his wife Yolanda took the course in English. According to Ibagón, everything changed, not only in his thinking, but also in his theology and missiology.

> Perspectives changed all the paradigms I learned in Latin America about missions. My dream was to be a pastor of a megachurch in Colombia, but when I saw the kingdom of God and the commitment by God to bless the nations, the focus of my life and ministry radically changed. My wife had been praying for Muslims. I asked her, "Why are you praying for Muslims when we have a lot of people in our country that need to hear the gospel?" After Perspectives I understood.
>
> When we returned to Latin America from Pasadena, I went to my friends in COMIBAM and told them that we need to use this material. They replied, "The Perspectives course is already available here in Spanish; it is called *Misión Mundial*." "No, it is different," I insisted.
>
> We waited seventeen more years to see Perspectives in Spanish.[58]

---

56 Rosales, "Perspectives in Boliva."

57 Osvaldo Arancibia Rosales, email to author, November 1, 2021.

58 Victor Ibagón, interview with author, December 5, 2019, transcript.

In 2013, Victor and Yolanda finally saw their long-awaited hope: the Perspectives text in Spanish. They took the course again, this time in their mother tongue. Intent on making the course available to their countrymen, they contacted the Global Service Office, resulting in the first *Perspectivas* course in Colombia in 2016. Ibagón recruited forty-five candidates for the Intensive class. A naysayer came along afterwards, persuading half of the candidates not to take the course because it is

Victor Ibagón, director of the Perspectivas Consejo and Perspectivas Colombia before passing away in 2021.

from the US and it is too expensive. However, those who completed the course expressed, "Victor, Colombia needs this course."

As a result, many more pastors attended the course the following year. Other courses in other cities followed in succeeding years. *Perspectivas* Colombia is now emerging as one of the strongest programs in the region. They took the lead in IT development for the entire Spanish program, working with other national programs in the creation and administration of the *Perspectivas* Global *Español* website and a shared online classroom platform.

Ibagón witnessed that *Perspectivas* is really exciting the younger generation. Pastors of megachurches are starting to take notice. One such pastor recently testified, "We have numbers, miracles, signs and wonders; but we forget one thing: our people need to understand the purpose of their lives."[59]

Victor Ibagón used his influence to multiply *Perspectivas* classes throughout Ibero-America. His personal testimony of transformation added weight to the content he taught, especially with other pastors.

> I was teaching the biblical section of the course in the Southern Cone of South America. As I was teaching on the kingdom and glory of God, one pastor in the middle of the room pounded his fist on the table and ran out of class. Everyone was staring at him. He was really angry.
>
> When he came back in, he said, "Victor, I don't have anything against you. But when I understand the global purpose of God and the glory and kingdom of God, I also understand that I lost twenty-five years of my ministry. My paradigm concerning ministry has changed and I must start again."

---

59 Ibagón, interview.

This guy is one of the most influential pastors in that country.[60]

In October 2021, Victor Ibagón received his "Well done, good and faithful servant" from Jesus as he left this earthly life. Ibagón was in Spain helping launch the Spanish national *Perspectivas* program when he had a fatal heart attack. His wife Yolanda faithfully continues on with their life's work.

Argentina

How much determination does it take to get Perspectives started in another country? In the case of Argentina, the startup team of seven travelled to multiple nations at their own expense—paying for airfare, visas, and hotels—just to be able to take Perspectives so they could bring it back to their country. National director Claudia Bustamante had been praying to have the Perspectives course in Spanish since she first encountered the English text on a visit to the USCWM in Pasadena in 2006.

In 2013, Bustamante was invited to attend the inaugural *Perspectivas* Intensive course in Lima, Peru. What transpired next, I'll let her share in her own words.

> Those ten days in Lima were extraordinary for me. I saw God bringing us deep new waters of renewal. While listening to the instruction, I was also listening to the Lord. I wrote down in my notebook the names of 350 pastors in Argentina I needed to tell about this. When I returned home to Buenos Aires, I gathered a group of leaders. Only sixty pastors could attend. I had invited pastor Jeff Adams of Graceway Church in Kansas City to share with the group about Perspectives via Skype. Something unexplainable happened. All the power in the building went out. The only thing that was working was the projector, the laptop, and the Skype connection. I explained to the pastors how this course was for me a theological, biblical, and missional revival in my own heart.
>
> One pastor asked, "What do you want us to do?" "Go to another country where they are doing *Perspectivas*," I replied, "so that we can form a team and bring it here."[61]

Perspectivas in Argentina began in October 2016 with a ten-day Intensive class of pastors and leaders from various regions of the country. The facilitation and instruction in the Intensive class served as a model and on-the-job training for future courses. Coordinator and instructor

---

60 Ibagón, interview.
61 Bustamante, "Perspectives in Argentina."

trainings were held in April 2017, followed the next day by an Introduction to *Perspectivas* event for the city. Six days later classes began simultaneously in three cities. Argentina runs classes in modular fashion, one Saturday a month with two or three lessons per month. The desire to attend was so great that many drove several hours, some even travelling fourteen hours by bus, only to return that night and preach in their churches the following morning![62]

The Argentine *Perspectivas* classes were self-led and self-supporting almost from the beginning. The first generation of modular classes had over 200 students. The following year the course expanded to six cities, with another roster of 180 students. *Perspectivas* Argentina now runs all their own trainings. They have an executive team of ten, about thirty trained instructors, and a volunteer team of ninety nationwide.[63] Even though the leaders and volunteers come from differing church backgrounds, they have a deep level of honor, respect, and friendship with each other. This family connection is of utmost importance to the team; they have contextualized the program into their relational culture.

Only three years into running their own program, *Perspectivas* Argentina began helping other countries get started. They helped facilitate the first Intensive class in Chile and took up an offering to pay for textbooks for forty-four pastors to take the course in Cuba. They are assisting Paraguay in the startup phase, and Uruguay is on their radar.

Bustamante recognizes that God paved the way for the fast growth of *Perspectivas* in Argentina.

> Our field of Argentina was ripe for Perspectives. The mission movement in Argentina has been around for thirty-seven years. *Misión Mundial* has been all over our country. But in the last eight years the missions movement came to a plateau. We had always pushed missions based on the need of the peoples. Perspectives brought a new breath of the Spirit and a new focus, not just to the missions movement, but to the church in our country. It brought a deepening of the theological understanding. *Perspectivas* is now a driving force that is renewing not just all the mission agencies in Argentina, but the whole church.[64]

---

62 Bustamante.

63 Kintsel, interview.

64 Bustamante, "Perspectives in Argentina."

Transition to Full Latino Ownership

A core value for all Perspectives Global programs worldwide is national ownership—directed, led, and funded via local resources. It usually takes years for a national program to realize that goal. In the interim, there is shared ownership between the local program and the Perspectives Global Service Office (PGSO) as they partner together to host startup events needed to launch a program. Those events usually include Introducing Perspectives events, Intensive classes, and trainings for coordinators and instructors.

When the Spanish translation opened up possibilities in twenty-two countries simultaneously, it became obvious that a regional strategy was needed. In 2015 the PGSO invited the PGE team and leaders from seven countries to the first *Perspectivas Consulta* (consultation) in San Jose, Costa Rica. The representatives were from the countries that were deemed most likely to become "anchor countries" for program development in their part of the Latin American world: Mexico, Costa Rica, Colombia, Argentina, and the US. Cuba was also included because it had a strong start, even though it could not serve as an anchor country for the Caribbean. The idea was to focus on establishing solid programs in a few countries and allow them to support the development of *Perspectivas* in nearby countries.

The result of this first *Consulta* was the formation of the Spanish *Consejo* (council) to guide program development throughout the Hispanic world, with the support of the PGE team. The *Consejo* has a representative from each of the six regions of the Hispanic world, meeting virtually every month. It just so happened that *Perspectivas* began with one program within each of the six regions—not something that was intentionally planned. The purpose of the *Consejo* is to give direction, leadership, and stability to all Spanish-language programs, while upholding standards to maintain the identity and quality of the movement. National programs are free to experiment and structure the program as best fits their context, as long as common standards are maintained.

Consulta (later renamed *Encuentro*) gatherings for all established and emerging programs are held annually for the purpose of building relationships, casting vision, problem solving, collaboration, and prayer. At the third *Consulta* meeting in Bogotá, Colombia, in 2017, the *Consejo* assumed full responsibility for all Spanish-language program development. The PGE took a back seat, continuing to serve at the direction of the Latino-led *Consejo*. The *Consejo* select their own leadership, propose and manage the program-development budget, and determine how and where to start new programs.

At the May 2018 *Consulta*, the Bolivian Perspectives program became the first national program in the world to sign a formal agreement with the PGSO. This agreement establishes certain standards and protocols in publishing and program development to ensure continuity across the Perspectives Global Network. This program agreement has become standard protocol for all other national programs.

Spreading North, South, and Across the Ocean

Never in Perspectives' history have programs in a specific language multiplied and spread more rapidly as they have in Spanish. Once the foundation was solidly laid and Latinos assumed full leadership, *Perspectivas* began to propagate into other Spanish-speaking nations with increasing rapidity.

Spain

Naturally the existence of a Spanish translation generated interest from the homeland of the language: Spain. PGE staff Ken and Glynis Kintsel traveled to Spain in 2017 and 2018, meeting with leaders in a few cities to assess interest in initiating a *Perspectivas* program in Spain. The trips were not without incident. Their 2018 trip landed Glynis in the emergency room with a life-threatening condition. Ninety-five days later, after weeks of hospitalization, Glynis was strong enough to return home. If the medical emergency was intended by Satan to halt mobilization of Spanish Christians, it backfired. Global prayer ensued for Glynis, and along with it, for the Spanish program, fostering higher anticipation of what God might have in store.

Startup teams were formed in Barcelona and Málaga to host Introduction to *Perspectivas* events in April 2019, attracting a total of eighty attendees, a mixture of Spaniards and Latinos who emigrated to Spain. A maiden model Intensive course was held in November 2019 in Málaga. The course was truly an international event. The twenty-six enrollees came from several cities of Spain, other European countries, and one from Africa. PGE and *Consejo* leaders travelled from eight countries in the Americas to coordinate, teach, and mentor future Spaniard leadership.

Reports came in of an incredible amount of joy and unity in the Holy Spirit in the daily sessions. As is now standard practice, coordinator and instructor training workshops were planned as follow-up in early 2020; they were, however, cancelled due to the global COVID-19 pandemic. The virus did not forestall all efforts to build a foundation for *Perspectivas* in Spain. Close to thirty from strategic cities enrolled in the 2020 Spanish virtual course. It is anticipated that many of them will form startup teams to initiate a study program in their location.

Spain has the potential to be an early fruit-bearer on the European continent. A Spanish pastor hosting Victor Ibagón in his home during the model Intensive class, told him, "Victor, if I don't like this course, I will leave." But he stayed. At the conclusion of the course he stated,

> This is from the Holy Spirit. I thank the Lord, for now I understand why here in Spain our churches do not produce fruit; it is because our gospel is not contextualized. This is a new beginning for me.[65]

Peru

After the initial Intensive course in Lima, Peru, in 2013, it took a few more years to build a national strategy and team. One lesson learned from the initial class is the importance of planning for a movement rather than simply conducting a class. The 2013 class had forty-four students, but many didn't finish the class, and follow-up was lacking. Yet it was not without impact. One pastor went home to introduce a missional focus in his church and now has missionary candidates headed to the Muslim world. Another student became a spark plug to relaunch *Perspectivas* in 2016 in the south of Peru. That Intensive class of thirty-six students included several Bolivians, who returned home to help launch the program in their country. That class also included a youth pastor from Lima—Yussei Pacheco.

Yussei Pacheco went to Argentina to acquire coordinator training so she could hold a class in Lima. PGE staff Dave and Liz Flynn mentored Pacheco and her team to relaunch *Perspectivas* for the third time in 2019. They followed the Argentine model, holding class one weekend per month for five months. In an effort to bridge the denominational gap, five churches representing five denominations hosted the course. When they held communion on the final night, a pastor commented that it was the first time he had ever served communion to someone outside his denomination. The students from the various churches continued in relationship and prayer together after the course was over. A hallmark of Perspectives worldwide is that it helps break down ecclesiastical barriers.

With a strategy in place to create a national movement, a Coordinators Training was held shortly after the 2019 course. The twenty-one Peruvians in the training selected Yussei Pacheco to be their national coordinator. The Flynns stepped down from active leadership, serving in an advisory capacity only. The Peruvian team planned for two classes in 2020, but after the Coronavirus global pandemic, they created their own virtual format,

---

65 Ibagón, interview.

registering fifty-seven in combined classes. Such resilience at an early stage bodes well for the future of *Perspectivas* Peru.[66]

Chile, Panama, Guatemala, and Puerto Rico

Strong *Perspectivas* programs take responsibility to help nearby countries initiate and launch new programs. Sometimes it takes a few years after an Introduction to *Perspectivas* (IP) event for startup teams to be identified and established before the first model Intensive course is conducted.

The *Perspectivas* program in Chile stands out as the first national program to be launched without teaching and training teams being coordinated by the *Perspectivas* Global *Español* (PGE) team. Rather, the Argentine *Perspectivas* program, only three years old itself, assisted Chileans in launching a national program.

Two young Chilean men attended the first *Perspectivas* Intensive course in Peru in 2013, returning home eager to see the course offered in their country. It took a few years for their dream to become reality. In 2017, an IP event was conducted in Santiago to stir up interest. Mission leaders in Argentina came alongside these two young men to introduce them to mission leaders in Chile. In July 2019, a group of Chileans travelled to Argentina to take the Intensive course being held on board the Operation Mobilization ship *Logos Hope*, harbored in Buenos Aires. Argentine *Perspectivas* leadership then helped Chile run their first Intensive course in late 2019. Despite social upheaval in the city, thirty-four students attended the class. More Chileans enrolled in the 2020 Spanish virtual class, laying a foundation for a national launch in early 2021. Even though the 2021 launch had to be conducted virtually, over fifty new students enrolled, with around twenty volunteers trained for leadership.

Meanwhile, in Central America the Costa Rican *Perspectivas* program leadership assisted Panama and Guatemala initiate programs. An IP event was conducted in 2018 in Panama, followed by coordinator training. Due to COVID-19, the maiden Panamanian class of forty-nine students was incorporated into the 2020 Spanish virtual class. Although Panama has only been able to run virtual classes, one local church is already talking about two eras in their church history: before *Perspectivas* and after *Perspectivas*.

In Guatemala, an Introduction to *Perspectivas* was conducted in October 2019, cosponsored by the PGE and a Guatemalan startup team led by David Puerto. They managed to hold a large Intensive class in January 2020, just before the Coronavirus pandemic broke out. As Spanish-language programs

---

66 Dave Flynn, interview by author, October 9, 2020, transcript.

moved to a virtual format, additional Guatemalan students participated in the 2020 online course, building a foundation for a national program.

The US Spanish program helped Puerto Rico get rolling, holding a couple of Intensive classes before the pandemic quarantined the populace. As with the other young programs, Puerto Rico enrolled numerous students in the 2020 Spanish virtual course.

Dominican Republic

The first *Perspectivas* class to be held in the Dominican Republic happened through a miracle of God. This story is so good that I want you to read it for yourselves, as told by the man God used to initiate the process. Jose Martinez is a Dominican living in the state of Kentucky in the US but ministering in the Dominican Republic.

> My wife and I had wanted to launch Perspectives in the Dominican Republic (DR) for many years, but logistics prevented. When we heard that the Spanish-language program was being offered virtually due to COVID-19, we thought this could be an answer to our prayer. I contacted Victor Ibagón, director of the *Perspectivas Consejo*. He told me the global leadership was meeting the very next day to determine how to work in DR. I replied that I was willing to lead an effort to have the believers in DR take the class virtually, and then hold coordinator and instructor trainings after the pandemic was over.
>
> The next day Victor called me to tell me that the leadership decided to have Costa Rica be the mentoring country for DR and to work directly with Ana Laura Meneses, the *Perspectivas* Costa Rica director. I immediately called Ana Laura. She suggested that those in DR could join their virtual class starting August 9, 2020. But there was the problem of how we would get the books to them. I told Ana Laura, "God will take care of this."
>
> I approached the community pastors we work with in DR and asked how many would be willing to commit the next fifteen weeks to take this course. They said they had the time but not the money, as many were unemployed due to the virus. Our ministry decided to underwrite the cost and asked them to pay what they could. We thought maybe ten or fifteen would sign up. Within one week, forty registered!
>
> The next concern was getting forty texts quickly to the Dominican Republic. We had to have a special printing done, but the publisher said it was too expensive to send them. I told them to ship them to me in Kentucky and God would help me find a way. I contacted international shippers, but they quoted

$6,000 to $12,000 to ship—way too expensive. People in many countries began to pray.

While praying, my wife asked me, "You have a friend, Matt, who has a plane. Why not ask him?"

I had met Matt when I was teaching the Perspectives class that he coordinated the previous year. I was hesitant to make such a request, especially with the Coronavirus. My wife was persistent. "What do you have to lose? He could say no, but if God wants to use him to glorify himself, you will find out."

I called Matt, and to our shock he said yes—with two conditions. First, he wanted me to accompany him, a difficult decision as I was still recovering from COVID. Second, I needed to get authorization for him to land his plane in DR and clear customs. I truly had no idea how I was going to do that, but I said, "Lord, I will trust you," and I agreed to do these two things.

I called my sister in DR and asked her if she could connect me with someone in an airport who could give us authorization. Amazingly, she has a cousin who is the director of aviation for the entire country. She called him, and one of his staff gave her the name of an official at an airport. I called right away and asked him to help me get authorization to land a private plane carrying Christian books for a class and customs clearance. I was delighted how fast he agreed. Within only a few days he was able to obtain clearance.

Matt and I flew his one-engine plane to DR the next week. When we landed, we were warmly welcomed and not charged anything to land our plane, nor for customs. Typically, there is a substantial charge to land a private plane.

Later we met with the individual assisting us. He inquired, "Who did you contact in DR so that I could help you? There is something strange about this operation. I feel like God is involved in it."

"What do you mean?" I asked. He explained that when I called him to request authorization, *a voice in his heart* spoke to him and told him that he needed to help us bring these books to the country.

He continued, "I am not a Christian, nor a deeply religious man, but I think God was speaking to me about this operation to oversee it myself rather than delegate it to my staff."

He then asked me to look at his computer monitor. He showed me the email exchange between himself and customs. Upon asking for authorization to clear a cargo of Christian books as a donation to a local church, the customs official responded, "Do you know these people?"

Our new acquaintance looked at me and said, "I sat on this chair for five minutes thinking how to answer this question. I thought to myself, 'I do not know these people.' I had a dilemma." Drug trafficking is a big problem with small planes. If it were not books, but drugs or weapons on our plane, and he put his name on the operation, his career would be over.

He continued, "Jose, as I sat here on this chair thinking how to respond, the same voice spoke to me again and told me, 'You need to approve this operation. This is my operation and you need to oversee it personally.'"

Turning to me with a puzzled look, he asked, "So who are you and your people that God is speaking directly to my heart to help you? Please tell me."

Matt and I were in awe. I explained that I follow Jesus Christ, the God who created the heavens and earth, sovereign over all things, as he was experiencing. I explained that many people were praying for this operation all over the world and that God has moved to ensure that his mission of making Jesus known moves forward. I added that if God is talking to him like this, God wants him to be part of his kingdom operation by committing to follow Jesus. I then explained the gospel to him. He responded that he was glad that he obeyed God's voice and would like to be a part of our work in DR.

Right after this Matt and I met with the local pastors to distribute the books. When I told them the story, they erupted in worship to God. They said that they felt God's love for them. They said that God's action has inspired them to step out in faith to make disciples in their churches and communities, and that they will go to the ends of the earth to bring the gospel to the unreached.

As I was worshipping with them, God spoke to my heart. "Can you trust me now? Can you place all your faith on me that I will finish my mission? If you step out in faith to reach the unreached and make disciples, I will show up—because this is my mission, not yours."[67]

The participants of this virtual class will be spark plugs to ignite interest in a future *Perspectivas* program. Plans are underway to lay a foundation for the launch of a national program.

As programs spread from nation to nation, those from other countries are ignited with a vision for the benefit of Perspectives for their people. Even though there is not yet a program in his nation, the director of the

---

67 Jose Martinez, from email dated August 16, 2020.

Evangelical Mission Association of Nicaragua, Alfredo Martínez, expressed, "I encourage the brothers and sisters of Perspectives to keep moving forward because it is making an impact on our countries here in Latin America, and it is producing something that is transforming our world."[68]

Expecting A Harvest: French-Language Version

The top five global languages are Mandarin Chinese, English, Spanish, Arabic, and French. The Perspectives course is now in all these languages, welcoming French as the newest offering.

French speakers are present on every continent, but most numerous in France, Canada, and Africa. In Africa, French is an official language in twenty-one countries and a spoken language in many more. Francophone Africa is ripe for mission mobilization. About 90 percent of French-speaking evangelicals live in Africa. The church is growing faster in Africa than anywhere else on the planet. The Francophone church in Africa is in immediate proximity to a multitude of unreached people groups; half of Africa's nearly one-thousand least-reached peoples live in Francophone countries.

Rory Clark, originator of Perspectives in French, with Ralph Winter.

The person responsible for initiating and guiding the process of translating the Perspectives course into French had been dreaming of a French course ever since he first took Perspectives in St. Louis, Missouri, in the early 2000s. Although not French himself, Rory Clark had worked in the French-speaking world, teaching at the university level. Challenged by the lack of gospel access among the unreached, he joined Frontier Ventures, serving as an assistant to Ralph Winter for nine years. In 2011, Clark began meeting with African leaders to assess local interest in Perspectives. In 2014, through several divinely orchestrated encounters,

---

68 Testimony in a video created by *Perspectivas* Guatemala, translated from Spanish, received by author November 12, 2021.

Clark was introduced to Frédéric Mondin, a French translator working for a publishing house.

In God's perfect timing, Mondin and his Bolivian wife were residing in Bolivia at the exact time as the launch of the Bolivian Perspectives program. They joined the first Bolivian class, which propelled them back to France to mobilize for the unreached while also working on the French translation of the Perspectives curriculum. Mondin led an international translation team from three continents and four countries.

This is the amazing nature of the Perspectives Global network: a Frenchman takes Perspectives in Spanish in South America and moves back to Europe to translate Perspectives into French to be premiered in Africa!

The initial launch of Perspectives in the French language was planned for Cameroon and Côte d'Ivoire in Africa. Suddenly the global coronavirus pandemic shut everything down. Plans shifted to developing a virtual class for mission leaders in French-speaking European nations. Then, unexpectedly, a tragedy occurred.

Deep into planning for the French launch, Rory Clark was diagnosed with stage 4 cancer. Fervent prayer went up all over the globe that Clark would live to see the realization of his dream and the fruit of his labor. Yet, a little over a year later, in 2023, God took Rory Clark home. In faith we believe that Rory will one day meet tribesmen from unreached people groups in West Africa who are living eternally in heaven because someone took Perspectives in the French language.

Two of the men on the French leadership team are Fulani tribesmen. The Fulani are traditionally nomadic herdsmen; their cattle is their gold. One of them, Younoussa Djao, has been waiting for a French Perspectives course since 1998. Djao is so excited to finally have the Perspectives course in his language that he declared, "On the day that the first Perspectives class is held in Francophone Africa, I will kill one of my cows and hold a feast!"[69]

69 Rory Clark, interview with author, December 1, 2020.

Divine Connections with Perspectives Instructors

Often one of the most significant things God does in a Perspectives class is spark a meaningful connection between an instructor and a student. An introductory conversation can result in far-reaching impact. Such was the case in a 2001 Perspectives class in Murfreesboro, Tennessee.

Jerry Trousdale was a former missionary in West Africa, then a publishing house executive with Thomas Nelson, and then pastor of a church in Murfreesboro. He worked with freshly trained coordinators Jon and Cindy Clendenen to host the first Perspectives course in his city. In God's amazing providence, Trousdale was also hosting a pastor friend from West Africa in his home, who was seeking medical help for his young son. Since they would be in the States for a while, Trousdale enrolled his friend, Shodankeh Johnson, in the class. Also in God's amazing providence, one of the Perspectives instructors that year was David Watson. Watson was seeing amazing progress with a new methodology in church planting, what is known today as a Disciple Making Movement (DMM).

Shodankeh Johnson had been faithfully pastoring in Africa, but running up against barriers in reaching areas where Christianity was not welcome. As David Watson shared DMM principles, describing how extensive people movements to Christ were happening among those of other religious backgrounds, Johnson and Trousdale hungered to know more. A mentoring relationship was forged with David Watson. When Johnson returned home, he began implementing the principles he learned. God worked in thrilling, unimaginable ways. Through intensive prayer, compassionate ministries, and DMM strategies, previously closed communities began to respond to the gospel.

Johnson elaborates, "Compassion for people is an essential kingdom value found in the DNA of every Disciple Making Movement. We have dozens of different types of access ministries and each one plays its unique role in helping us advance the kingdom of God in Africa." When a felt need is identified within a community, disciple-makers create relationships of trust, work with the community to meet the need, and begin Bible-storying in the process. These access ministries, whether it be education, agricultural projects, business development, or medical and hygiene ministries, result in transformational blessing for the community. About 90 percent of these engagements lead to a church, often several churches within the community.

Johnson emphasizes, "Prayer is the most powerful and effective access ministry and has caused a cascading effect throughout the movement. ... Through persistent prayer we have seen very hostile communities opened, unlikely Persons of Peace identified, and whole families saved. All the glory goes to the Father who hears and answers prayers. Intercession is the undercurrent that supports all we do."

This disciple making movement has resulted in churches planted in every city and every chiefdom in the country, with many religious leaders even embracing Christ. The sustaining motivation for Johnson and his team is to make Jesus famous. "We do whatever it takes to get the gospel to the people, so Christ is glorified. Our work is never about us. It is about him. We are making him known with a strategic focus on unreached people groups."

As the movement spread, within fifteen years churches were planted in thousands of communities in twelve nations. Shodankeh Johnson is now a catalyst trainer for prayer and disciple making movements all over the world.[70]

Jerry Trousdale likewise began training others in DMM principles, multiplying the number of multiplying movements among dozens of unreached people groups. The organization through which he ministers recorded an average of twenty-eight new church plants *per day* in 2021 through the DMM strategy. They have teams of indigenous leaders catalyzing movements in fifty-nine nations, with multitudes of new believers from various religious backgrounds.

Trousdale utilized his publishing expertise to research and record the amazing ways God is at work today. The titles of his books say it all: *Miraculous Movements: How Hundreds of Thousands of Muslims are Falling in Love with Jesus* and *The Kingdom Unleashed: How Jesus' 1st Century Kingdom Values Are Transforming Thousands of Cultures and Awakening His Church*. God is using these books and the teaching of Trousdale and Johnson and Watson to inspire many more to seek God for similar movements.

A small Perspectives class in a college town run by newly trained coordinators. Who would have imagined in such a setting that a connection

---

70 Johnson, "Passion for God."

would be made and a spark would ignite, leading to an extraordinary harvest among some of the hardest to reach? God did. Just as Jesus took the simple offering of a small boy to feed five thousand, we never know what God has planned for the smallest labor of love we do for his name. Take heart, Perspectives coordinating teams!

9

Moving With God into the Next Half-Century

As of this writing, Perspectives is in its forty-ninth year as a course, an organization, and now a global movement. Fifty years is a long time for anything to last. According to recent research, 30 percent of nonprofits do not see their tenth anniversary, and over half of all nonprofits are destined to fail or stall within a few years.[1] Social movements come and go with the times. And yet Perspectives is embarking upon its next half-century. Such longevity and global reach were not envisioned at that inaugural class in 1974.

Naturally, all organizations must innovate with the times to continue to exist, otherwise they become irrelevant. But just as important—or more so— is staying true to the core mission and purpose of the entity or movement. Mission drift is a prime reason for the demise of any organization. The purpose of Perspectives is anchored in the historic, eternal, global purpose of God—an unchanging mission. Looking to the future, Perspectives leadership entered a season of prayerful deliberation about how to move with God in mobilizing the next generation for his mission. And so did Perspectives' parent organization, the U.S. Center for World Mission.

---

1 Ebarb, "Nonprofits Fail."

USCWM Becomes Frontier Ventures

When Ralph and Roberta Winter founded the U.S. Center for World Mission in 1976, they envisioned a center for collaboration, research, strategy, mobilization, and training toward the goal of breakthroughs of the kingdom of God within every people group. A large campus was purchased, anticipating dozens of like-minded organizations to office and partner together. Many did come, and many new organizations were birthed at the USCWM, including the notable mission agency Frontiers. In large part, the original impulses of the USCWM were successful, most especially the embrace of unreached people groups by churches and mission societies. Scores of new mission agencies and networks arose around the world to facilitate mission to the unreached. The Perspectives course became a flagship mobilization tool for the church. The publications flowing out of the USCWM mobilized prayer and furthered conversation regarding strategy and applied research. Ralph Winter and the USCWM were a major force in global collaboration. Most significantly, hundreds of formerly unreached people groups have been reached.

After the passing of Roberta (2001) and Ralph Winter (2009), USCWM staff embarked upon a long season of soul-searching regarding the future vision, mission, and structure of the organization. As Ralph Winter was such a prolific innovator with a toe in many streams, how were the staff going to craft a new way forward that is manageable and maintains continuity with the past, while also reshaping the vision for the future?

It took three people to fill the "Office of General Director" that Ralph Winter once held. One of those individuals, Bruce Graham, who had served with Dr. Winter from the beginning, summarized it this way,

> The last generation of effort has launched all kinds of people to the uttermost and in many cases they have bumped up against walls in making the gospel known. It's time for a new generation to rise up and take their place in God's purpose for the unreached, to build on the work of the previous generation and to carry it further.[2]

Chong Kim and Dave Datema filled the other leadership roles in the Office of the General Director. Datema affirmed,

> We remain focused on catalyzing breakthroughs among the unreached peoples. We remain focused on collaboration that accelerates breakthroughs. And we remain focused on identifying

---

2 Lambert, "Catalyzing Kingdom Breakthrough."

barriers to those breakthroughs and helping find solutions with others. Those remain constant for us, even as we seek new ways to do them.[3]

Like so many other mission organizations in the twenty-first century, the U.S. Center for World Mission rebranded for a new generation and a new start. In 2014, the USCWM became Frontier Ventures, and the campus was renamed Venture Center. A major milestone was celebrated in 2016: forty years of ministry of the USCWM / Frontier Ventures. Cascades of praise ascended to God for his goodness in the amazing ways he has used this ministry.

Difficult days, however, were still ahead in forging a way to the future. Due to the Center's success in mobilizing toward the frontiers, and dramatic global changes in previous decades, the staff of Frontier Ventures felt that the more urgent task today is not mobilizing more missionaries to the unreached but helping them be more effective once they got there. And where is the best place to learn effective strategy? From those working among the unreached. From a strategic point of view, it made more sense for Frontier Ventures to become a multi-site organization, with hubs located close to where God is raising up new mission movements among the unreached.

Due to technological advances, geographic proximity is no longer necessary for ministry collaboration. Over the years, the Venture Center campus had ceased to be a *physical* center of collaboration of like-minded organizations. Maintaining the property had become a greater hindrance to fulfillment of the vision, especially with long-delayed and expensive maintenance projects. From a financial point of view, it made more sense to free up property resources for actual ministry.

The very difficult decision was made to offer up the campus for sale. God brought a new leader on board to shepherd the organization through this controversial and nostalgically painful process. In 2017, Kevin Higgins was appointed President of William Carey International University (WCIU), which Winter founded and which also shared the Frontier Ventures campus. Higgins had a long history of connection to WCIU and the USCWM. He had led other organizations in the past and had the privilege of serving in the midst of a great people movement to Jesus in South Asia. In 2019, Kevin Higgins was appointed as General Director of Frontier Ventures, bringing fresh insight and experience to the organization. He led the staff through a multiyear transition in defining a new organizational vision, a new structure to support the vision, and the difficult sale of the Pasadena campus.

---

3 Lambert.

The campus sale was especially distressing for some; a few of the staff had been in residence there since the founding of the USCWM in 1976.

Frontier Ventures staff are progressing forward with new energy, vision, and strategy. The core of the original USCWM vision is still in place, yet now with a greater emphasis on missiological inquiry and collaboration. Replacing a single centralized location, global hubs are being established to be both learner and accelerator in the ways God is moving among the unreached. Through fostering communities of spiritual formation and training, through collaboration and innovation, through publishing to expand missiological insight, Frontier Ventures seeks to catalyze kingdom breakthroughs at the frontiers of God's global mission.

Perspectives USA Reorganizes for the Future

The U.S. Perspectives Study Program experienced a surge of growth after recovering from the transition back to Pasadena from Fayetteville, Arkansas. Staff were recruited, initiatives were begun, but the national office still struggled to keep up with the growth. As Frontier Ventures was making changes to prepare for the future, Perspectives leadership likewise took time to identify barriers and solutions to foster and service future growth adequately, while positioning themselves for a new generation.

A pressing need was to rapidly recruit personnel. Perspectives has always been a part of the larger Frontier Ventures mission order. The process of joining and serving through a mission order unfolds differently than recruiting for and serving a more task-oriented organization. While Frontier Ventures partners with others to see breakthroughs in mission via missiology, spiritual formation, innovation, and training, Perspectives has a very specific focus on mobilization through education, with a high demand for immediate administrative support.

It became clear to Perspectives leadership that a new and separate structure was needed to position Perspectives USA for a successful long-term future. A decision was made with the Frontier Ventures board to pursue Perspectives USA becoming its own legal entity. Both organizations firmly express that this is an organizational, not relational, decision. The two entities continue to work in close cooperation.

The discussions of legal separation continue at the time of printing of this book. The intellectual property of the Perspectives curriculum remains with Frontier Ventures, who is responsible to national programs for revisions, publication, and distribution. William Carey Publishing (formerly William Carey Library), the official publisher of the curriculum, is a division of Frontier Ventures.

With this in view, the organization that was previously referred to as simply "Perspectives" has officially become "Perspectives USA." Perspectives Global remains under the Frontier Ventures umbrella. Perspectives USA is a colleague program in a global network of national programs serviced by Perspectives Global. Each program is committed to one another and to the global Perspectives movement.

Perspectives USA leadership began strategizing and implementing structural changes to enable future stability and growth. Multiplying national leadership was a top priority. Increasing the number of national regions decreased the geographic footprint for each regional director, allowing for deeper commitment to the staff and volunteers under their leadership. But that also meant enlarging the Executive Leadership Team and adding departmental staff in human resources, staff development, communications, and other functions.

Growth in staff, volunteers, classes, and students required an improved technology platform to support it. An entirely new technology platform and website was designed, improving class and communication functions, but also adding new features, such as instructor certification, data analysis, customer-relationship management, a learning-management system, financial management, video sharing, and multilingual capabilities. A new reality that is still being worked out is managing multi-language classes, with increasing numbers of Spanish and Chinese language classes. The IT project was huge, requiring extensive resources. To meet this challenge, Perspectives USA instituted its first development department to raise funding.

Perspectives USA staff in 2022.

The long-held vision of developing and supporting an extensive alumni network began to take shape. A Next Steps Network was fashioned, enlisting church and mission-agency personnel to mentor graduating Perspectives students. Over forty mission agencies committed to work together to coach alumni. Funds were raised to develop a web platform for networking and showcasing opportunities. In the process, Perspectives was able to broaden and strengthen relationships with churches and mission agencies, who are crucial partners in propelling the movement forward.

Staff, volunteer, and instructor development is another high priority for Perspectives USA. Desiring to move beyond the hard-skills training needed to administer classes, the Perspectives office began adding soft-skills training, such as team building, leadership, communication, and reaching a new generation. This entailed redesigning Perspectives coordinator training and implementing instructor training and certification. The multiplication aim is to build leaders who recruit, guide, and build other leaders. These improvements positioned Perspectives USA to move confidently toward an expansive future.

Perspectives Global Matures

The rapid growth of Perspectives internationally pushed the Perspectives Global Service Office to expand its capacity and output, while simultaneously leveraging the resources of its global partners. From an ad-hoc Global Desk responding to inquiries in 2002, the Perspectives Global Service Office (PGSO) matured into an operational executive staff of four, along with another seven consultants meeting together regularly. A larger global-leadership team of seasoned national program leaders meets quarterly to guide the Perspectives Global Network.

These leadership gatherings solidified the core principles, protocols, and shared values of the Network. The phases of development of a national program were delineated. A new website[4] was launched in 2022 to showcase growth and communicate the distinctives of Perspectives Global.

Operational leadership of the Perspectives Global Network is distributed by region or language. The Spanish, Portuguese, and Chinese language programs each have their own leadership guiding the global expansion of programs in those languages. An Asia Regional Director oversees all programs in the Asian region. English-language programs in Africa are coming together to establish their own leadership structure. Other languages or regions that are not as developed fall under the oversight of the PGSO.

Perspectives Global Service Office in 2022.

---

4 www.perspectivesglobal.org.

Distributed international, intercultural, multilingual leadership is both an enormous blessing and a huge challenge. The Perspectives Global Network, however, is willing to meet these challenges for the benefits it provides. We are stronger and more effective together.

Perspectives curriculum in multiple languages.

Perspectives Curriculum Fifth Edition

With every edition of the Perspectives curriculum, the life-shaping paradigm for which Perspectives is renowned becomes clearer. Steve Hawthorne has often articulated,

> We have been carrying this remarkable gift from God that is deeply transforming lives and producing strategic mobilization output across cultures. Yet we have been unsure of exactly what it is we are carrying. What is it that makes Perspectives so transformational? Through the years we have come to understand that it is a cohesive, integrated whole. It is not just teachings, or the latest mission trend. It is a distinctive paradigm for understanding God and his mission that is often dissimilar to conventional mission approaches.[5]

So often people ask, why don't you shorten the course down to thirteen weeks, or even better, nine weeks, to make it more accessible? Yet it has been discovered that such attempts rob the depth of the transformation that Perspectives achieves. Each of the fifteen lessons contributes in an invaluable way to the overarching whole.

Others suggest jettisoning core ideas for concepts more relevant to today's ever-changing world. To which Hawthorne replies and Perspectives stakeholders agree, "Just because the world has changed, does not mean our

---

5 Not an actual quote, but the essence of what this author has heard Hawthorne elucidate numerous times.

mission has changed. That would be true if our mission is a response to needs. But our mission is ancient, given by God. We are not doing something urgent; we are doing something ancient."[6]

A significant need is for the Perspectives curriculum to incorporate global voices who are singing the same song. At the Perspectives Global Huddle in Saõ Paulo, Brazil, in December 2019, a half-day was reserved for international program directors to give input into the next edition of the curriculum. With a passion for and commitment to Perspectives, Steve Hawthorne once again set aside other ministry commitments to work on the fifth edition of the curriculum. Linguist and field practitioner Pam Arlund joined Hawthorne as co-editor, adding a wealth of cultural intelligence to the team. The curriculum revision team is seeking to enrich the curriculum with more input from international partners. God has raised up leaders from the nations who

Pam Arlund, co-editor of the 5th edition of the Perspectives curriculum.

are equally passionate about ensuring that the distinctive Perspectives paradigm is not diluted or misdirected in the next edition. Together they are aiming at producing a more globalized edition of Perspectives to serve a surging movement of mission mobilization in all nations.

Seventh Perspectives Global Huddle 2019, Saõ Paulo, Brazil.

2020: Unexpected, Uncertain, Chaotic, and Fruitful

Who could have predicted the massive worldwide upheaval that the year 2020 delivered? Day-to-day life was proceeding as normal, when suddenly the whole world shuts down due to the raging COVID-19 coronavirus. The various programs of the Perspectives movement faced the same questions

---

6 Hawthorne, "Working Together."

businesses and organizations everywhere pondered: How do we proceed, or do we shut down also? Nation to nation, even community to community, had varying levels of infection and restrictions on activity. For conducting a national program, the complications were colossal. The uncertainty surrounding even near-term planning was even more debilitating.

Virtual Necessity

The spring semester began as normal for classes in the US. But by mid-March the nation was entering an extensive lockdown. Schools closed, businesses shuttered, and all public gatherings were prohibited. City streets were eerily quiet. When it became obvious that the lockdown was not going to end soon, public interaction moved to "Zoom." Employees worked from home, school instruction went online, and as many churches and organizations as were able shifted to online services and gatherings. With only a few weeks left in the semester, the US Perspectives program was able to effectively shift every single class to a virtual learning environment. All classes finished successfully, a tribute to the perseverance and flexibility of staff and volunteers.

A few areas in the US were able to resume in-person classes in the fall of 2020, but most students continued online. To maintain learning objectives, a large national coordinating team served the virtual class, nurturing discipleship through small groups in online break-out rooms. The COVID challenge persisted into 2021, hindering a full resumption of live classes. As a result, the number of classes and students in the US was reduced by half.

On the positive side, the online classes extended the geographic reach of the course into rural areas and even overseas. One exciting example was an online class held in Seattle, in the far-northwest of the United States. Some of the Seattle Perspectives leadership were friends with a ministry leader in India. They invited him to take the class from India virtually. He did, inviting some Indian friends to join him. After experiencing Perspectives, these Indian believers determined to do whatever it took to develop a Perspectives program in India. With the assistance of the Seattle Perspectives team, two in-person classes were run in India in 2022. A re-launch of Perspectives in India is underway!

Instant Innovation

The rapidity with which other national Perspectives programs pivoted to an online format was astounding. In 2019, before the global epidemic, only three Perspectives programs had online offerings. By 2021, twenty-six had developed virtual offerings. The innovation, creativity, and arduous work involved revealed the high level of commitment by program leadership and volunteers. Rather than regressing during the global pandemic, several programs surged forward in greater breadth and unity of spirit.

With *Perspectivas* Argentina taking the lead, the *Consejo* organized a team from eight countries to develop an online platform that could serve all the Spanish-language programs. Their innovation established a way for each national program to register, receive funds, and mentor students from their own country, while sharing a common platform and instruction by the most experienced instructors. In total, 844 students registered for the 2020 online course, coming from eighteen of the twenty-two Spanish-speaking countries, including the US. A second virtual course was conducted for Central American countries, registering ninety-six. Reports surfaced of entire families engaging as instruction streamed into private homes, of new nations and previously inaccessible rural areas gaining access, and even of field missionaries from Turkey and Japan participating.

Spanish language virtual class of 844 students in 2020.

The role of William Carey Publishing was critical in enabling the Spanish online course to occur. At the height of COVID-19, the textbooks were stuck at the printer and could not be shipped. The staff at William Carey Publishing dropped everything and created an electronic version of the Spanish-language Perspectives text. William Carey Publishing has been hugely instrumental in supporting language translations and in developing printing and distribution channels around the world.

Brazil was only able to run four of sixty-four planned classes before the spread of COVID-19 shut them down. They immediately began planning for a national online program. They chose to prerecord their instructors to simplify logistics, enabling students to learn from some of the best instructors in the country. Before the launch of the online class, national leadership ran a six-week online discipleship training for seven hundred volunteers, led by class coordinators. These volunteers were trained to reproduce this training in small groups as an integral part of the online class experience.

This first-ever Portuguese online program registered 2,300 students! The class registrants were divided into large regional groups to engage the material and pray for the nations in interactive Zoom meetings held every two weeks. Those regional groups were further divided into small groups to process through the discipleship training. The Brazilian program has become a model to other national programs in personalized student mentorship.

Innovation in Angola for connecting to a virtual class.

Through the personal recruitment of a Brazilian pastor, forty pastors and leaders from the African nation of Angola joined the class. On the opening night of the online course, *Perspectivas* volunteers gave a freewill offering to provide scholarships for the Angolan pastors and for indigenous tribal leaders in the Amazon. Besides reaching into new areas of Brazil, this one South American virtual class is kick-starting Portuguese Perspectives programs in Africa and Portugal.

Despite challenging bandwidth capabilities, several African countries pushed forward with online programs and coordinator trainings. The first ever Malawian Perspectives class was conducted online, with assistance from South African program leadership. Reuben Kachala had been dreaming for years of having Perspectives in his country. Carrying a passion to turn Malawi from a mission field into a mission force, in 2015 he founded Frontier Mission International, an indigenous mobilization and sending agency. Perspectives is one tool in his tool belt to undergird the vision of Malawian-led mission sending. As one of his students commented, "Perspectives is the grandmother of all mission mobilization tools."[7]

Perspectives programs in other languages and countries also took the deep dive to go virtual. Malaysia had a particularly challenging scenario. They had planned, for the first time, to run simultaneous English and Chinese language courses. When the pandemic shut the country down, on short notice they quickly arranged for all their instructors in each language to video their instruction. That's thirty videos! They were able to pull it off and successfully advance their program.

Program leaders report advantages and disadvantages with virtual classes. Certainly, an online program offers wider accessibility. It is a more flexible and less expensive option for students. Rwanda, for instance, was able to double their capacity by offering courses every semester for the first time. As we have seen, it can also jumpstart new programs in new areas. But for many parts of the world, internet reliability is a severe handicap, limiting student interaction with instructors and coordinators, and contributing to absenteeism. The depth of student learning and transformation is impacted as a result.

Since an online class cannot model in-person, interactive learning methods which have proven so strategic for multiplication, the potential exists for movement momentum to be stalled. The sense of community acceptance and relational unity across barriers is greatly diminished without in-person gatherings. All these factors are necessary for strong growing programs. Having been developed, online offerings will most likely continue to be one option for many global Perspectives programs. This requisite experience, however, has demonstrated that in-person learning is more productive.

Challenging Recovery

During 2022 the world began slowly opening up to normal activity. By then "Zoom fatigue" had settled in across businesses and organizations. National Perspectives programs were not immune. Enrollments were plummeting. People were not desirous of sitting in an online class in the evening after being on Zoom or another online platform all day at work. The struggle to maintain connectivity and mentor students virtually was also wearing on the thousands of volunteers that make Perspectives courses possible.

---

7 Reuben Kachala, personal interview with author, email, June 10, 2021.

Course offerings were reduced. Class size diminished. Of the thirty-eight nations with Perspectives programs, twelve did not run any classes at all during the pandemic. Restarting after a long pause will take significant effort. By the end of 2021, the annual number of students taking Perspectives globally had dropped 45 percent from pre-pandemic levels. Many programs used the lull in expanding growth to strengthen their bench in leadership. Emphasis shifted to building infrastructure, developing new coordinators and instructors, and mentoring volunteer teams.

Not all global programs stalled, however. One of the largest national programs, Perspectives Taiwan, grew 10 percent from 2019 to 2022. The programs in Malaysia and Colombia experienced a percentage increase in triple digits! The Spanish-language portion of the USA program had more students in 2021 than they had in 2019.

Perspectives is a movement that builds on the excitement and momentum of fresh graduates of previous years. It may take a while to fully rebuild the momentum from the two years of enforced restrictions. God's calling to his church to finish the Great Commission has not abated, however. Perspectives leaders are anticipating in faith that as God has worked to overcome challenges in the past decades of the movement, so he will do so today.

Looking back on 2020–21, Christians around the world testify that beyond the horrific pandemic and what Satan meant for evil, God brought forth good, shining through his people and working with them to further his kingdom on earth. Looking through the Perspectives lens only, the necessity to pivot to online options scattered the seeds of the course further in two years than any time in the previous forty-eight years. The potential for those seeds to take root and grow into Perspectives programs in new places will spur the mobilization of God's people for world evangelization for years to come.

Celebrating the Past, Looking to the Future

Perspectives is on the cusp of its fiftieth anniversary. Planning is underway for a global celebration at Moody Bible Institute in Chicago in the summer of 2024. The expectation is for a couple of thousand attendees for the three-day event, with participants from every Perspectives program worldwide. Besides offering specific training opportunities, anticipated outcomes include a beneficial cross-pollination of ideas, inspiration toward the future, and the furtherance of the bonds of a true Perspectives global family. And, of course, a party! After all, there will be significant African and Latino presence!

There is much to celebrate what God has done through this movement over the past five decades. A statistical look only reveals a portion of the total picture, but it does indicate the breadth of expansion.

In 2019 before the pandemic interruption, Perspectives USA reported an annual enrollment of around 7,400 students in 225 classes. Post-pandemic, Perspectives USA had about a 75 percent rebound in 2022. Around 1,000 coordinators, together with 1,500 volunteers serve those students each year. A roster of 1,000 active instructors bring a variety of perspectives from diverse ministries, schools, church traditions, and life experiences. All this is undergirded by a national staff of 125, with more in the pipeline.

Record keeping was not always consistent in the early years of Perspectives. Best estimates approximate the total number of Perspectives USA alumni in 2023 at 200,000, and the total number of US classes above 5,300. Dozens of mission agencies recognize Perspectives as a major pipeline of high caliber missionary recruits. It is estimated that approximately half of the 40,000 evangelical missionaries from the USA that currently serve overseas are Perspectives alumni.

Outside of the US, Perspectives programs continued to multiply into new nations, especially in the Spanish and Portuguese language networks. The tenth anniversary of the translation of Perspectives into Spanish was celebrated by program leaders in Panama in 2023. Now over half of the twenty-two Spanish-speaking countries have Perspectives programs. The investment that the strong Brazilian program has made in Angola, Africa is bearing much fruit. Dozens of Angolan pastors were mobilized and now they are spreading the course across their nation.

Tenth Anniversary celebration of Perspectives in Spanish.

Chinese language programs were growing significantly through 2019. Strict COVID lockdowns and restricted information flow in Asia has since retarded and obscured program development. A national program restart in India in 2022 was received with great enthusiasm, spreading to three cities in 2023. English language programs in Africa are steadily building, with the first Africa Regional Huddle held in Ethiopia in 2023. The first French-language Perspectives course was conducted online in Europe in 2023, enrolling mission leaders and professors from three nations.

Not surprisingly, as the global church continues missionary expansion, the growth trajectory of Perspectives outside of the US now exceeds that of Perspectives USA, with an estimated one hundred thousand non-US alumni.

Since 1974 when the first Perspectives class was held at Wheaton College in Illinois, over 7,700 classes have been conducted worldwide, in at least forty-five nations, with over three hundred thousand alumni. At least half a million copies of the Perspectives *Reader* have been sold, sowing Perspectives content beyond the Perspectives program.

The astonishing impact Perspectives has had, both directly and indirectly, is indisputable. Ideas flowing from course content have percolated through many cultures, schools, churches, and organizations, shaping new entities and outcomes. More significantly, many unreached people groups receive sustained informed prayer, outreach, and even the beginnings of a disciple making movement due to a spark first ignited in a Perspectives class. Without a doubt, many people groups that formerly sat in darkness, now shine with the light of the gospel of Christ because of the prayers and obedience of Perspectives students.

What is it about the Perspectives course that makes it so life-changing? What is the unique contribution of this course?

David Bryant suggests that it is the course's Christology, woven explicitly or implicitly throughout.

> Perspectives explores how everything—and all peoples—will be summed up, one way or another, under Christ as Lord. Ultimately, that vision is the single greatest blessing we take from Perspectives. In other words, the course unleashes for students an abounding hope focused on the supremacy of God's Son. Biblical hope is not about some wistfully wished-for outcome. Rather it is about a firm and secure confidence that God's promised plan for the nations in Christ will surely be fulfilled. Furthermore, the Father loves each of us so fully in the Lord Jesus that he has ordained a very special place in that plan for each. In the end, Perspectives takes students captive to a marvelous sense of personal destiny grounded in this glorious hope from which they will never get free![8]

Arthur Glasser, the founding father of the biblical section of Perspectives stated, "The inductive method of Bible study informs Perspectives. It drives

---

8 David Bryant, from an email reflection sent at the author's request, September 4, 2008.

you back to Scripture. It is one of the most valuable contributions of the Perspectives program."[9] Indeed seeing Scripture and history afresh through the eyes of God's purposes being fulfilled is what student after student comments upon as being so revolutionary.

Ralph Winter captures the multidimensional aspects of the course in his answer.

> What is it about the course that changes people's lives? Not any one thing. It is the Holy Spirit working through the people that run the course and speak in the course and write the course that changes people's lives. The very idea that God is still around and at work creates a sense of awe in the average student. They may believe in God, but they've grown accustomed to the idea of God and have no more awe of God. The Perspectives course is not what we are really promoting. We are promoting the awe of God. The course is an earthen vessel in which something very much more important is being carried.[10]

Indeed, that is what the Perspectives course gave me and so many of the students that I have encountered. An awe of God, a sure hope in his purposes being fulfilled, a joy that he calls us into strategic and significant partnership with his grand and glorious work … these are life-changing perspectives.

The transformational paradigm interwoven within the course content is a grace gift from God. It is a precious stewardship for which stakeholders within the movement do not take credit but feel a grave responsibility to carry. It is revealed for this time in history, as we draw ever closer to the consummation of his purpose.

Over the past half-century God has favored Perspectives beyond anyone's imagination. Still, the best days are ahead. Considering how God has used this course in North America over the past fifty years, what can be envisioned for its future among Asians, Africans, Latinos, Arabs, Europeans, and others?

What a prophetic word indeed Arthur Glasser spoke from Zechariah at that first class in 1974, "Do not despise the day of small beginnings."

Our response can only be, "Now all glory to God, who is able, through his mighty power at work within us, to accomplish infinitely more than we might ask or think. Glory to him in the church and in Christ Jesus through all generations forever and ever! Amen" (Eph 3:20–21, NLT).

---

9 Glasser, "Personal Recollections."
10 Ralph D. Winter, "Personal Recollections."

CONCLUSION

We've come to the end of our story recounting the history of the Perspectives movement and the larger frontier mission movement. We've told stories within the story and seen how our story is part of The Story above all stories, the Story of God's glory. Just as God's Story is not yet finished, the participants in the Perspectives movement are anticipating many more wonderful stories ahead as they partner with God in the completion of his Story.

Yet, oddly enough, it seems we are almost back where we started fifty years ago as we contemplate today's societal, political, and religious landscape, most especially in the West. The parallels to the 1960s are startling. Racial tension, political divisiveness, riots, looted and burning cities, an escalating crime wave, mounting drug overdoses, unpopular wars, a new rise of Marxism, and a sexual revolution, this time unimaginably extreme. In the 1960s the world experienced massive geopolitical change from colonialism to independent nations. Another massive geopolitical change is underway today with mass migrations shifting historic demographics, and all the cultural upheavals that entails. In the 1960s the church was in despair that it was losing ground. Today, it is clear that we live in a post-Christian and anti-Christian culture in the West. Relativism of truth has been replaced with an abandonment of truth altogether. Religious and democratic freedoms once taken for granted are eroding. The ground has shifted so rapidly under the feet of the church that anger, confusion, and despair seek to replace faith, hope, and love.

Here is where we do well to do as the Psalms tell us: remember and recall the works of the Lord. In the 1960s the Holy Spirit moved upon a lost generation much like ours today, unexpectedly turning stoned rebellious youth into transformed joyful witnesses to the power and love of Jesus. Just five short years after the 1966 cover of *TIME* magazine speculated "Is God Dead?," another *TIME* magazine cover headlined "The Jesus Revolution." The Jesus Movement, on full display at EXPLO '72, cascaded into a new wave of students volunteering for mission.

In expectation of another Jesus Movement, the fiftieth anniversary of EXPLO '72 was held in 2022 organized by millennial evangelist Nick Hall. Hall is known for attracting the next generation to large evangelistic events. He believes Gen Z is ripe for a new move of God. In an interview he states, "I've never seen people more open and more hungry to the Gospel, never seen young people more willing and excited to live this out and share it...

They want to be a part of something bigger than themselves. They want to be a part of a cause; they don't want another event or concert, *they want a movement* (italics mine)."[1]

Hall represents one of millions beseeching God for a widespread, global revival. Darkness and despair are fertile ground for a fresh work of God and prayer ushers it in.

On the other hand, in marvelous ways we are *not* back where we were fifty years ago. The new vitality exhibited in the southward shift of the global church adds thousands of new harvesters to the global mission of God who are in closer cultural proximity to the remaining unreached people groups. Mass migrations are bringing the unreached into closer geographic proximity to the church. Access to the Scripture and the message of the gospel in every language has significantly increased in the last fifty years. The size of the remaining task of planting the church within every people has diminished since 1974, even as we soberly recognize that the absolute number of unbelievers within those groups continues to rise.

The past five decades have given us greater clarity on the scope of the remaining task and best practices in mission strategy. Before 1960, a colonial approach, exhibited most clearly in mission stations and Western-dominated leadership, prevailed in strategy, leading to the call "missionary go home!" With McGavran and Winter paving the way, mission strategy shifted in the 1980s to identifying and resourcing ethnolinguistic people groups where the gospel had yet to take root and flourish.

Frontier mission focus amplified discussions on contextualization and overcoming barriers to the gospel message and messenger. Now mission strategy aims beyond individual conversions only or single church plants to disciple making movements, and even a movement of movements. The pace of gospel advance has accelerated within UPGs where a movement strategy is implemented. God is helping his global church understand how to finish the task he has given us.

The most astounding advance in the past fifty years is the way Jesus himself is drawing peoples to himself in supernatural ways resembling the Book of Acts. In the mid-twentieth century, a missionary would be thrilled to win a handful of Muslim converts or establish a single church of Muslim background believers. Only fifty years later we behold movements of millions of Muslims worshipping Jesus. God is working in history to break religious barriers holding peoples captive, creating hunger in the hearts of those once thought resistant. Could we be approaching the end of the age

---

1   Nick Hall, quoted by Mark A. Kellner in "U.S. Evangelist."

where a new book of Acts of the Holy Spirit is being written to bring in the fullness of God's family through Jesus Christ?

As nations hit walls of destruction and despair, could another Jesus Movement be in the making? Could another Student Volunteer Movement for missions be in the offing?

God is stirring a new generation, a global generation uniquely fitted for cross-cultural relationships in a *kairos* season of global opportunity. They are a passionate, worshipping generation, motivated by a vision of the greatness of God, for his name to be famous, and his glory to be exalted among the nations. Are you one of them?

No matter how the cultural or religious landscape of our particular nation may make us feel, our observations enable us to affirm with McGavran that we are in the sunrise, not the sunset of mission. God is on the move, working in new and thrilling and ancient ways. God has a mission that he will complete. Will we be on the move with him?

Henry Blackaby in his popular study *Experiencing God* encourages us to "look what God is doing and join him." When the Perspectives course originated, it joined a movement of God already in progress in that generation. It advanced from nation to nation and generation to generation to become what it is today: a global movement. What future chapters of the Perspectives story will be written? Will you write one?

You and I are living in days in which the words of Habakkuk proclaim loudly, "Look among the nations! Observe! Be astonished! Wonder! Because I am doing something in your days that you would not believe if you were told." What chapter is your life writing in the ultimate Story of God's glory?

Perspectives participants are *propelled by hope*: a certainty of the glorious conclusion of God's great Story, and thereby the purposeful fulfillment of our labors for his name. Yet the beauty is that we are not alone in our labors. It is a relational work, both with others across the ages and nations, and most especially with God himself, who initiated his work and lovingly invites us to join him. No one can live for any purpose more worthy, more fulfilling, more arduous, surer of great reward. This great hope propels us onward.

Join us! Together let us not just make history, let's fulfill it!

Appendix A

Graphical Illustrations of the Unfinished Task

THE UNFINISHED TASK

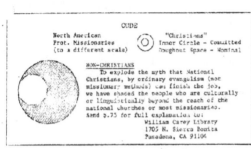

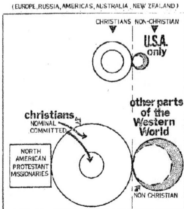

WESTERN WORLD
(EUROPE, RUSSIA, AMERICAS, AUSTRALIA, NEW ZEALAND)

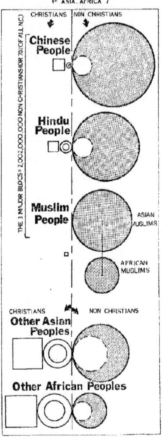

NON-WESTERN WORLD
(= ASIA, AFRICA)

World Pop. (in millions) (Scale drawings taken from these estimates)	Committed Christians — Nominal Christians — Reachable by ordinary E-1 Evangelism — Reachable only by E-2, E-3 Cross-Cultural Evangelism — No. American Protestant Missionaries				
	CHRISTIANS	NON-CHRISTIANS	TOTALS	(actual count)
WESTERN WORLD					
USA ONLY	62 130	15 11	218	16,118
OTHER WESTERN	68 738	173 142	1121	
NON-WESTERN WORLD					
CHINESE	2 1	38 803	844	1,317
HINDUS	5 10	42 524	561	1,000
MUSLIMS –Asia	.11 .05	15 434	449	100
–Africa	-- --	-- 146	146	36
OTHER ASIANS	38 56	142 252	488	9,677
OTHER AFRICANS	47 88	42 93	276	9,838
TOTALS	222 1023	467 2411	4123	36,930
STATISTICS AS OF MID 1977		16% 54%		

(Statistics on this page were assembled and derived by Dr. Ralph D. Winter of the U.S. Center for World Mission, 1605 Elizabeth St. Pasadena, CA 91104, 213-681-7959)

Winter, "The Grounds for a New Thrust in World Mission," 8–9, 24–25.

The Remaining Pioneer Mission Task Today

This chart shows the distribution of Christians and non-Christians in the world today, including the Unreached, and the Frontier People Groups still needing pioneer work. Note particularly the 25% represented in black—these Frontier People Groups are mostly in Muslim-majority countries, and in India.

Pray for the people groups living in the areas of the world shown in darker gray and black. No prior generation has had opportunity for such a great harvest. With the world's population at 8 billion, today's harvest could eclipse the total harvest of all previous generations combined. Pray that our generation will rise up and embrace this incredible opportunity God has given us.

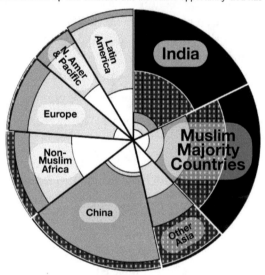

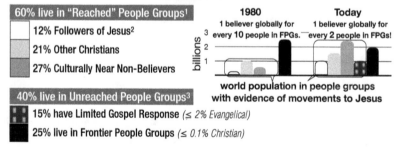

60% live in "Reached" People Groups[1]

- 12% Followers of Jesus[2]
- 21% Other Christians
- 27% Culturally Near Non-Believers

40% live in Unreached People Groups[3]

- 15% have Limited Gospel Response (≤ 2% Evangelical)
- 25% live in Frontier People Groups (≤ 0.1% Christian)

1980
1 believer globally for every 10 people in FPGs.

Today
1 believer globally for every 2 people in FPGs!

world population in people groups with evidence of movements to Jesus

[1] 60% of the world live in people groups where the gospel is well known and has had significant impact. (greater than 2% Evangelical or greater than 5% Christian Adherent)

[2] Estimate based on published figures for Evangelicals, Charismatics & Pentecostals.

[3] Less than or equal to 2% Evangelical AND less than or equal to 5% Christian Adherent.

Percentages based on a global population of 8 billion people, using data from JoshuaProject.net/frontier

This page adapted with permission from the Go31.org Prayer Guide—for the 31 largest Frontier People Groups

Coalition of Prayer and Mission Leaders, Pray for the Thirty-One Largest Frontier People Groups, 5.

Appendix B
Perspectives 16 Core Ideas

The core of the Perspectives course is a framework of ideas that serves as a paradigm of understanding for joining with God's work throughout history. These ideas were first articulated in 1997 as a foundational reference for developing the Third Edition of the Perspectives course. We look to the Lausanne Covenant as an expression of basic theology and missiology. It is hoped that this summation of the vision of the Perspectives course will help in the development of the Perspectives curriculum for different languages, audiences, and cultures.

1. God initiates and advances work in history to accomplish His purpose.

2. God calls His people to join Him in fulfilling His purpose.

3. God's purpose is to bless all peoples so that Christ will be served and glorified among all peoples.

4. God accomplishes His purpose by triumphing over evil in order to rescue and bless people and to establish His kingdom rule throughout the earth.

5. The Bible is a unified story of God's purpose.

6. God's work in history has continuity and will come to an ultimate culmination.

7. The Christian movement has brought about positive social transformation.

8. The mission task can and will be completed.

9. The world's population can be viewed in terms of people groups.

10. The progress of world evangelization can be assessed in terms of church planting movements within people groups.

11. Completing the mission task requires the initiation and growth of church planting movements that follow social avenues of influence.

12. Completing the task requires effective cross-cultural evangelism that follows communication patterns within cultures.

13. Completing the task requires strategic holism in which community development is integrated with church planting.

14. Completing the task requires collaborative efforts of churches and mission agencies from diverse cultures and traditions.

15. God calls His people to embrace strategic sacrifice and suffering with Christ in order to accomplish His global purpose.

16. By participating in the world Christian movement, every believer can find a way to live with vital, strategic significance in God's global purpose.

Appendix C
Changing of the Guard
The Passing Of Influential Mission Leaders

This is not a comprehensive list; rather it is representative to illustrate the shoulders upon which much of the frontier mission movement stands. Most of these mission leaders are mentioned within the text of this book, and/or contributed directly or indirectly to the *Perspectives on the World Christian Movement* course. The date given is year of death.

Adeney, David H., 1994

Barrett, David B., 2011

Beaver, R. Pierce, 1987

Butler, Phill, 2023

Cho, David J., 2020

Coggins, Wade T., 2013

Conn, Harvie, 1999

Covell, Ralph, 2013

Cunningham, Loren, 2023

Dayton, Edward R., 2002

Eshleman, Paul, 2023

Frizen, Edwin L. (Jack), 2012

Glasser, Arthur F., 2009

Graham, Billy, 2018

Greenway, Roger S., 2016

Gren, Elisabeth Elliot, 2015

Hannum, Walter, 2012

Hesselgrave, David J., 2018

Hiebert, Paul G., 2007

Howard, David M., 2022

Kane, Herbert J., 1988

Love, Rick, 2019

McClung, Floyd L. Jr., 2021

McGavran, Donald A., 1990

McKaughn, Paul, 2018

McQuilkin, J. Robertson, 2016

Moffett, Samuel H., 2015

Montgomery, Jim, 2006

Mulholland, Kenneth B., 2003

Nida, Eugene A., 2011

Orr, J. Edwin, 1987

Padilla, C. René, 2021

Palau, Luis, 2021

Patterson, George, 2022

Reapsome, James W., 2017

Richardson, Don, 2018

Siemens, Ruth, 2005

Smalley, William A., 1997

Stott, John R., 2011

Tippett, Alan R., 1988

Verwer, George, 2023

Wagner, C. Peter, 2016

Wang (Wang Yongxin), Thomas, 2018

Ward, Ted W., 2016

Webster, Warren, 2007

Willis, Avery T., 2010

Wilson, J. Christy, 1999

Wilson, Samuel, 2014

Winter, Ralph D., 2009

Winter, Roberta, 2001

Appendix D
Nigeria Communiqué

Nigeria Evangelical Missions Association (NEMA)
*A Networking Association and Fellowship Forum
for Missions Movement in Nigeria*

A COMMUNIQUÉ at the end of the
PERSPECTIVES STUDY PROGRAM on WORLD EVANGELIZATION
HELD IN JOS, NIGERIA IN AUGUST 2002

PREAMBLE:

Forty-one (41) participants from twenty-seven (27) different churches, mission agencies and institutions gathered in Jos, Nigeria on August 19–30, 2002 to attend the PERSPECTIVES STUDY PROGRAM tagged Perspectives on the World Christian Movement sponsored by the Nigeria Evangelical Missions Association (NEMA) in partnership with the United States Center for World Mission (USCWM)

OBSERVATIONS:

At the end of the program, all participants expressed their thanks for the opportunity to participate in this course of study and testified thus:

- That the program is richly instructive and biblically sound on issues concerning global evangelization and cross-cultural communication of the gospel of the kingdom of God;

- That this study program reveals the need for missionaries and church planters to be more knowledgeable of the peoples they are reaching so that peoples that are yet unreached may hear the message of the gospel clearly and find appropriate ways to follow Jesus in the context of their culture;

- We, the pioneer participants of the Perspectives study program in Nigeria, believe that this Perspectives study program is relevant and most needed in the Church in Nigeria today.

IMPACT:

As a result of this course we have seen:

- The Bible as a unified story that reveals God's purpose for all ages which will be fulfilled when he is received and worshipped in all peoples;

- How the Lord has raised up leaders throughout history who have understood his purpose and have labored sacrificially to see the Lamb receive the reward of his suffering;

- That an understanding of cultural differences is needed to communicate the gospel effectively across cultural boundaries and for the church to expand rapidly within a people;

- The need to think strategically and cooperatively to respond to the great needs and opportunities the Lord is giving us today to fulfill his promise to all peoples.

RESOLUTIONS:

In light of the foregoing, all participants hereby passionately call on the church in Nigeria to:

i. Acknowledge the harm to the task of evangelization caused by the rift between mission agencies and the churches;

ii. Find a basis for unity in pursuing together the fulfillment of God's promise to bless all the peoples of the earth through his people;

iii. Incorporate the Perspectives study program in all schools of missions;

iv. Encourage all theological institutions to recognize the value of the Perspectives study program by giving credit for it in their programs;

v. Promote the program among all church and mission leaders and encourage all of them to attend in order to sharpen focus and vision for global evangelization;

vi. Create awareness of the Perspectives program in all churches and mission conferences, councils, synods and conventions.

CONCLUSION:

We commit ourselves to be faithful in our walk and work with the Lord and pledge our support to the leadership of the church in Nigeria as they lead His people to "declare His glory among the nations, His marvelous deeds among all peoples."

Appendix E
Perspectives Family Covenant

On December 12-14, 2003, about 50 leaders who have used the Perspectives course or courses derived from Perspectives expressed a desire to strengthen ongoing collaboration by drafting a Perspectives Family covenant. The following items were voiced at that time. You are welcome to join. Look for supporting documents at www.perspectves.org/global.

In recognition of God's desire to engage all of His people in the completion of the missionary task with the hope of fulfilling all of His global purposes, we covenant to work together to mobilize the church for missions using education.

Specifically:

We will seek to convey frontier missiology as expressed in the Perspectives Core Ideas. We affirm the beliefs and hopes of the Lausanne Covenant.

We will seek to co-labor with others in the evangelical missions movement and especially with others in the Perspectives Family. We will seek to communicate with one another in ongoing ways. We will seek creative ways to share curricular resources.

We will seek to honor copyrights, trademarks and distribution rights of published materials. We will use the names "Perspectives" and/or "Perspectives Family" according to established guidelines.

Signed: _____

Date: _____

BIBLIOGRAPHY

24:14 Multiplying Movements Together. "Global Dashboard December 2022." Accessed June 15, 2023. https://2414now.net/wp-content/uploads/2023/01/dashboard-template-english.pdf.

Addison, Steve. "Advancing Perspectives Globally." *Mission Frontiers*, March–April 2004. http://www.missionfrontiers.org/issue/article/advancing-perspectives-globally.

Becker, John. "What Must Be Done? The Birth of a Vision and Its Network." *Mission Frontiers*, March–April 2017. https://www.missionfrontiers.org/issue/article/what-must-be-done.

Boot, Kevin. "Perspectives in Brazil." Speech, Perspectives Global Huddle, São Paulo, Brazil, December 7, 2019.

Bosch, David J. *Transforming Mission: Paradigm Shifts in Theology of Mission*. Maryknoll, NY: Orbis Books, 1991.

Bryant, David. *In the Gap: What It Means to Be a World Christian*. Ventura, CA: Regal Books, 1979.

Bryant, David. "Personal Recollections." Perspectives Thirtieth Anniversary Celebration, Pasadena, CA, July 13, 2004. Audio tape recording.

Bustamante, Claudia. "Perspectives in Argentina." Speech, Perspectives Global Huddle, São Paulo, Brazil, December 8, 2019.

Butler, Robby. "A Decade's Progress in Just One Year!" *Mission Frontiers*, November–December 2018. https://www.missionfrontiers.org/issue/article/a-decades-progressin-just-one-year.

Caleb Project. "Caleb Declaration." June 24, 2004. http://www.calebproject.org/main.php/about_us/the_caleb_declaration.

Caleb Project. "Libya To Libya: Twenty-Five Years of Prayer for A Nation." January 13, 2005. http://www.calebproject.org/main.php/the_good_report_newsletter/libya_to_libya_-_twenty-five.

Caleb Project. "Caleb Declaration." June 24, 2004.

Camp, Bruce. "The Evangelical Free Church Launches a Bold New Adopt-A-People Strategy." *Mission Frontiers*, July–August 1992. https://www.missionfrontiers.org/issue/article/the-evangelical-free-church-launches-a-bold-new-adopt-a-people-strategy.

The Center for the Study of Global Christianity. *Christianity in Its Global Context, 1970–2020: Society, Religion and Mission*. South Hamilton, MA: Center for the Study of Global Christianity, June 2013. https://www.gordonconwell.edu/wp-content/uploads/sites/13/2019/04/2ChristianityinitsGlobalContext.pdf.

The Center for the Study of Global Christianity. *The Inquiry*, issue 12, April 2020. https://www.gordonconwell.edu/center-for-global-christianity/wp-content/uploads/sites/13/2020/04/CSGC-Newsletter-Spring-2020-Online-Version.pdf.

Chismon, Max. "Introducing the Condensed World Mission Course." Speech, Global Perspectives Consultation, Pasadena, CA, December 12, 2003.

Coalition of Prayer and Mission Leaders. Pray for the Thirty-One Largest Frontier People Groups. https://joshuaproject.net/assets/media/handouts/the31-en.pdf, 5.

Coggins, Wade T. "COWE: An Assessment of Progress and Work Left Undone." *Evangelical Missions Quarterly*, October 1980.

Coghlan, Warwick. "Perspectives in Australia." Speech, Perspectives USA National Conference, Dallas, June 14, 2008.

Crawley, Winston. *World Christianity: 1970–2000*. Pasadena, CA: William Carey Library, 2001.

Create Taiwan International. "United Missions of Taiwan." Accessed August 29, 2020. https://www.createtaiwan.com/post/_umot.

Daniels, Gene, and John Becker. "Abide, Bear Fruit: Combining the Spiritual, Strategic, and Collaborative Dimensions of Reaching the Muslim World." *International Journal of Frontier Missiology* 35, no. 1 (Spring 2018): 39–41. https://www.ijfm.org/PDFs_IJFM/35_1_PDFs/IJFM_35_1-DanielsandBecker.pdf.

Ebarb, Tracy. "Nonprofits Fail: Here's Seven Reasons Why." NANOE (National Association of Nonprofit Organizations & Executives) website. September 7, 2019. https://nanoe.org/nonprofits-fail/.

Eshleman, Paul. "Reaching the Unengaged: It's Time to Act." *Mission Frontiers*, January–February 2013. http://www.missionfrontiers.org/issue/article/reaching-the-unengaged.

Farah, Warrick, ed. *Motus Dei: The Movement of God to Disciple the Nations*. Littleton, CO: William Carey Publishing, 2021.

Finishing the Task. "2020 Global Update." August 2020. https://finishingthetask.com/wp-content/uploads/FTT-Global-2020-Update.pdf, 19.

Flynn, Dave. "Perspectives 4th Edition Tour Comes to an End!" *Mission Frontiers*, January–February 2008. https://www.missionfrontiers.org/pdfs/30-1.pdf.

Garrison, David. *Church Planting Movements*. Midlothian, VA: WIGTake Resources, 2000.

Garrison, David. *Church Planting Movements: How God is Redeeming a Lost World*. Midlothian, VA: WIGTake Resources, 2004.

Garrison, David. *A Wind in the House of Islam: How God Is Drawing Muslims around the World to Faith in Jesus Christ*. Monument, CO: WIGTake Resources, 2014.

Gary, Jay. "Perspectives Marks 30th Anniversary." *ChristianFutures.com: Empowering Christians to Create the Future*, July 13, 2004. https://www.christianfutures.com/perspectives-30th/.

Glasser, Arthur F. "Personal Recollections." Perspectives Thirtieth Anniversary Celebration, Pasadena, CA, July 13, 2004. Audio tape recording.

Glasser, Arthur F., Paul G. Hiebert, C. Peter Wagner, and Ralph D. Winter, eds. *Crucial Dimensions in World Evangelization*. Pasadena, CA: William Carey Library, 1976.

Glasser, Arthur F., Paul G. Hiebert, C. Peter Wagner, and Ralph D. Winter, eds. *Understanding World Evangelization: Cultural Dimensions in International Development*. Pasadena, CA: William Carey Library, 1977.

Graham, Bruce. "Personal Recollections." Perspectives Thirtieth Anniversary Celebration, Pasadena, CA, July 13, 2004. Audio tape recording.

Gray, Naomi. "Perspectives in the United Kingdom." Speech, Perspectives USA National Conference, Dallas, June 14, 2008.

Green, Tim. "Conversion in Light of Identity Theories." In *Longing for Community*, edited by David Greenlee. Pasadena, CA: William Carey Library, 2013. Quoted in L. D. Waterman, "LIFE Scale: Exploring Eight Dimensions of Life in Christ," *International Journal of Frontier Missiology* 31, no. 3 (Fall 2014): 149–57. https://www.ijfm.org/PDFs_IJFM/31_3_PDFs/IJFM_31_3-Waterman.pdf.

Hall, Bob. "Global Perspective Grabs New Zealand." *Mission Frontiers*, March–April 1990. http://www.missionfrontiers.org/issue/article/global-perspective-grabs-new-zealand.

Hall, Nick. Quoted by Mark A. Kellner in "U.S. Evangelist Working to Rescue Faith Workers in Ukraine." *The Washington Times*, March 10, 2022. https://m.washingtontimes.com/news/2022/mar/10/us-evangelist-working-rescue-faith-workers-ukraine/.

Han, Chulho. "Report on Perspectives in Korea." Speech, Perspectives Global Huddle, London, December 11, 2006.

Hawthorne, Steven C. "History of the Perspectives Course." Speech, Perspectives USA Coordinators Consultation, Pasadena, CA, July 14, 2004. Audio tape recording.

Hawthorne, Steven C. "The Rise of the Global Prayer Movement." *Prayer Connect*, issue 4 (2012): 11–16. https://waymakers.org/wp-content/uploads/2012/01/RiseofGlobal.pdf.

Hawthorne Steven C. "The Story of His Glory." In *Perspectives on the World Christian Movement: A Reader*, 4th ed., edited by Ralph D. Winter and Steven C. Hawthorne, 49–63. Pasadena: CA: William Carey Library, 2009.

Hawthorne, Steven C. "Working Together to Strengthen Our Global Curriculum." Speech, Perspectives Global Huddle, São Paulo, Brazil, December 9, 2019.

Holloway, Steve. "Personal Recollections." Perspectives Thirtieth Anniversary Celebration, Pasadena, CA, July 13, 2004. Audio tape recording.

Horn of Africa Evangelical Mission. "Meet Our Board and Staff." Accessed June 16, 2023. https://hornofafrica.org/dr-markos-zemede.

Howard, David M. "Editorial: A Moratorium on Missions?" *Evangelical Missions Quarterly*, January 1975.

Howard, David M. "The Road to Urbana and Beyond." *Evangelical Missions Quarterly*, January 1985.

Howard, David M. "Urbana '73 Theme Emphasizes Positive View of Missions." *Evangelical Missions Quarterly*, January 1973.

Howard, David M. "What Happened at Urbana—Its Meaning for Missions." *Evangelical Missions Quarterly*, July 1977.

Jenkins, Philip. *The New Faces of Christianity: Believing the Bible in the Global South*. New York: Oxford University Press, 2006.

Johnson, Shodankeh. "Passion for God—Compassion for People." *Mission Frontiers*, November–December 2017. https://www.missionfrontiers.org/pdfs/32_Shodankeh_39.6_1112-2017-8.pdf.

Johnson, Todd M., and Gina A. Zurlo, eds. *World Christian Database*. Leiden/Boston: Brill. Accessed April 2018. https://www.worldchristiandatabase.org.

Johnstone, Patrick. *The Future of the Global Church: History, Trends and Possibilities*. Colorado Springs: Biblica, 2011.

Johnstone, Patrick. *Operation World*, 5th ed. Grand Rapids: Zondervan, 1993.

Kane, J. Herbert. "Changes Observed in Missiological Studies." *Evangelical Missions Quarterly*, January 1974.

Lambert, John. "Catalyzing Kingdom Breakthrough." *Mission Frontiers*, March–April 2015. http://www.missionfrontiers.org/issue/article/catalyzing-kingdom-breakthrough.

Lewis, R. W. "Losing Sight of the Frontier Mission Task: What's Gone Wrong with the Demographics?" *International Journal of Frontier Missiology* 35, no. 1 (Spring 2018): 5–15. https://www.ijfm.org/PDFs_IJFM/35_1_PDFs/IJFM_35_1-LewisFMTask.pdf.

Lewis, R. W. "The Remaining Peoples with No Chance to Hear about Jesus." *Mission Frontiers*, November–December 2018. https://www.missionfrontiers.org/issue/article/the-remaining-peoples-with-no-chance-to-hear-about-jesus.

Mathew, Shibu. "India Perspectives Report." Speech, Perspectives USA National Conference, Dallas, June 14, 2008.

McGavran, Donald A. *The Bridges of God*. rev. ed. New York: Friendship Press, 1981. Original edition published in 1955 by World Dominion Press, London.

McGavran, Donald A. "Introducing Crucial Issues in Missions." In *Crucial Dimensions in World Evangelization*, edited by Arthur F. Glasser, Paul G. Hiebert, C. Peter Wagner, and Ralph D. Winter, 165–89. Pasadena, CA: William Carey Library, 1976.

Merrill, Dean. "It's Our 20th Birthday: Interviews with Wade Coggins and Edwin L. Jack Frizen, Jr." *Evangelical Missions Quarterly*, April 1984.

Mission Frontiers. "The Escalating Filipino Force for the Nations." September–December 1998. http://www.missionfrontiers.org/issue/article/the-escalating-filipino-force-for-the-nations.

Mission Frontiers. "IIS Builds Momentum!" April–May 1984. https://www.missionfrontiers.org/issue/article/iis-builds-momentum.

Mission Frontiers. "MF Celebrates 20 Years of Charting the Growth of the Frontier Mission Movement, 1979–1999." July–September 1999. http://www.missionfrontiers.org/issue/article/mf-celebrates-20-years-of-charting-the-growth-of-the-frontier mission-movem.

Mission Frontiers. "Mobilizers Meet in Amsterdam to Advance the Perspectives Movement." September–October 2003. http://www.missionfrontiers.org/issue/article/mobilizers-meet-in-amsterdam-to-advance-the-perspectives-movement.

Mission Frontiers. "1985 at the USCWM: Year in Retrospect." February 1986. https://www.missionfrontiers.org/issue/article/1985-at-the-uscwm.

Mission Frontiers. "Perspectives Course Revision Completed as Movement Reaches New Heights: A Conversation with Co-editor Steve Hawthorne." July–September 1999. https://www.missionfrontiers.org/issue/article/news34.

Olonade, Timothy. "Perspectives in Nigeria." Speech, Perspectives USA National Conference, Dallas, June 14, 2008.

Peng, Ray. "Transforming the Church to Be Missional." *Lausanne Global Analysis* 7: no. 6 (November 2018). www.lausanne.org/content/lga/2018-11/transforming-the-church-to-be-missional.

Pew Research Center. "Modeling the Future of Religion in America." September 13, 2022. https://www.pewresearch.org/religion/2022/09/13/modeling-the-future-of-religion-in-america/.

Purgason, Lee. "Personal Recollections." Perspectives Thirtieth Anniversary Celebration, Pasadena, CA, July 13, 2004. Audio tape recording.

Reapsome, James W. "Editorial: A Positive Outlook." *Evangelical Missions Quarterly*, January 1974.

Reapsome, James W. "Editorial: The Unexpected Turnaround." *Evangelical Missions Quarterly*, April 1975.

Reapsome, James W. "People Groups: Beyond the Push to Reach Them Lie Some Contrary Opinions." *Evangelical Missions Quarterly*, January 1984.

Reapsome, James W. "Urbana '70: One Man's Impression." *Evangelical Missions Quarterly*, April 1971.

Ritchie, Hannah, and Max Roser. "Urbanization." *OurWorldinData.org*, revised November 2019. https:// https://ourworldindata.org/urbanization.

Ritchie, Jeff. "Mentors on My Journey in Mission: Swailem and Sameera Hennein," *The Outreach Foundation*. September 29, 2015. https://www. theoutreachfoundation.org/blog/2015/9/29/mentors-on-my-journey-in-mission-swailem-and-sameera-hennein.

Rosales, Osvaldo Arancibia. "Perspectives in Bolivia." Speech, Perspectives Global Huddle, São Paulo, Brazil, December 8, 2019.

Schwas, Phil, and Rick Melick. "How to Close the Gap between Students and Missionaries." *Evangelical Missions Quarterly*, October 1970.

Shimron, Yonat. "Pew Report: Older US Christians Being Quickly Replaced by Young 'Nones.'" *Religion News Service*, October 17, 2019. https:// religionnews.com/2019/10/17/pew-report-older-u-s-christians-being-quickly-replaced-by-young-nones.

Simkin, Michael. "Perspectives in New Zealand." Speech, Perspectives USA National Conference, Dallas, June 14, 2008.

Swartley, Keith E., ed. *Encountering the World of Islam*. 2nd ed. Orlando, FL: BottomLine Media: 2014.

Taylor, David. "An Enduring Legacy: Reflections on the Contribution of Western Protestant Missions from a Frontier Mission Perspective." *International Journal of Frontier Missiology* 29, no. 3 (Fall 2012): 123–28. https://www.ijfm. org/PDFs_IJFM/29_3_PDFs/IJFM_29_3-Taylor.pdf.

Taylor, David. "Ghana 2013 Report." *Mission Frontiers*, January–February 2014. http://www.missionfrontiers.org/issue/article/ghana-2013-report.

Tichy, Nancy. "Outside the Lines: The Latest Addition to Mission Resources for Children." *Mission Frontiers*, January–February 2007. https://www. missionfrontiers.org/issue/article/outside-the-lines.

UN International Organization for Migration. "World Migration Report 2022," December 1, 2021. https://publications.iom.int/books/world-migration-report-2022-chapter-2.

VisionSynergy. "History and Impact." Accessed July 30, 2022. https:// visionsynergy.net/history-and-impact.

Wallstrom, Timothy C. *The Creation of a Student Movement to Evangelize the World*. Pasadena, CA: William Carey International University Press, 1980.

Walston, Vaughn J. "Ignite the Passion." *Mission Frontiers*, March–April 2000. https://www.missionfrontiers.org/issue/article/ignite-the-passion.

Walston, Vaughn J., and Robert J. Stevens, eds. *African-American Experience in World Mission: A Call Beyond Community*, rev. ed. Pasadena, CA: William Carey Library, 2009.

Winter, Ralph D. "The Grounds for a New Thrust in World Mission." In *Crucial Dimensions in World Evangelization*, edited by Arthur F. Glasser, Paul G. Hiebert, C. Peter Wagner, and Ralph D. Winter, 8–9, 24–25, 479–80. Pasadena, CA: William Carey Library, 1976.

Winter, Ralph D. "Is a Big New Student Mission Movement in the Offing?" *Christianity Today*, May 10, 1974.

Winter, Ralph D. "Learn from Our Mistakes." *Mission Frontiers*, May–June 2007. http://www.missionfrontiers.org/issue/article/learn-from-our-mistakes.

Winter, Ralph D. "The New Macedonia: A Revolutionary New Era in Mission Begins." In *Perspectives on the World Christian Movement: A Reader*, 4th ed., edited by Ralph D. Winter, and Steven C. Hawthorne, 347–60. Pasadena, CA: William Carey Library, 2009.

Winter, Ralph D. "1980: Year of Three Mission Congresses." *Evangelical Missions Quarterly*, April 1980.

Winter, Ralph D. "Personal Recollections." Perspectives Thirtieth Anniversary Celebration, Pasadena, CA, July 13, 2004. Audio tape recording.

Winter, Ralph D. *The Twenty-Five Unbelievable Years, 1945–1969*. Pasadena, CA: William Carey Library, 1970.

Winter, Roberta H. *I Will Do a New Thing*. Pasadena, CA: William Carey Library, 1987.

Wood, Rick. "The Path Forward Is Clearer Than Ever Before. Will We Have the Courage to Take It?" *Mission Frontiers*, November–December 2018. https://www.missionfrontiers.org/issue/article/the-path-forward-is-clearer-than-ever-before.

Woodberry, J. Dudley, ed. *From Seed to Fruit: Global Trends, Fruitful Practices, and Emerging Issues among Muslims*. 2nd ed. Pasadena, CA: William Carey Library, 2008.

Yeh, Allen. "Tokyo 2010 and Edinburgh 2010: A Comparison of Two Centenary Conferences." *International Journal of Frontier Missiology* 27, no. 3 (Fall 2010): 117–25. https://www.ijfm.org/PDFs_IJFM/27_3_PDFs/tokyo_2010_yeh.pdf.

Zurlo, Gina A., Todd M. Johnson, and Peter F. Crossing. "World Christianity and Mission 2020: Ongoing Shift to the Global South." *International Bulletin of Mission Research*, January 2020. https://journals.sagepub.com/doi/pdf/10.1177/2396939319880074.

INDEX

WILLIAM CAREY PUBLISHING

visit us at missionbooks.org

I Will Do a New Thing: Unreached Peoples and the Founding of the U.S. Center for World Mission

Roberta H. Winter

It all started when Ralph Winter gave an address at Lausanne called "The Unfinished Task," urging the missions world to focus on a new type of evangelism to reach "hidden" or "unreached" peoples. Soon he and his wife Roberta were founding a center to help mission agencies fulfill that task. Around them gathered a group of experienced missionaries, computer scientists, and unusually dedicated young people in order to buy a college campus. This story, as told by Roberta, of their cliff-hanging prayer meetings and spiritual battles with a cult will reignite your determination to work with Jesus to "finish the Father's work" (John 4).

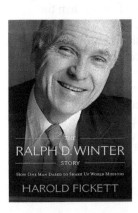

The Ralph D. Winter Story: How One Man Dared to Shake Up World Missions

Harold Fickett

Legendary missionary strategist Ralph D. Winter always provoked strong reactions, one way or another. This long overdue book captures both the genius and the controversy of a self-described "social engineer," named by *Time* magazine as one of the 25 Most Influential Evangelicals in America.

Perspectives on the World Christian Movement (Reader, 4th Ed)

Ralph D. Winter and Steven C. Hawthorne (Eds)

Perspectives on the World Christian Movement presents a multi-faceted collection of readings exploring the biblical, historical, cultural, and strategic dimensions of world evangelization. Writings from more than 150 mission scholars and practitioners portray the history and anticipate the potential of the global Christian movement. Every one of the 170 articles and side bars offers practical wisdom enabling Christians to labor together in bold, biblical hope to finish the task of seeing that Christ is named and followed among all the peoples of the earth.

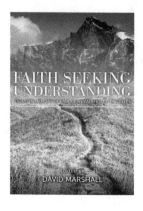

Faith Seeking Understanding: Essays in Memory of Paul Brand and Ralph Winter

David Marshall (Editor)

Notable Christian thinkers such as Philip Yancey, Alvin Plantinga, Rodney Stark, Allan Chapman, Don Richardson, Yuan Zhiming, and more share powerful insights that, from the perspective of Christian faith, help answer people's deepest questions in the twenty-first century. Inspired by the lives and accomplishments of Paul Brand and Ralph D. Winter, this book seeks to apply the curious, open-minded, and compassionate spirit these Christian leaders exhibited to key contemporary questions in science, history, philosophy, theology, and comparative religion. Readers will gain an appreciation for the intellectual challenges of the Christian faith, and some of the most fascinating and sometimes controversial ways in which those challenges are being met.

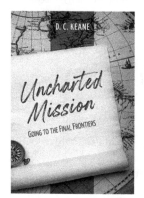

Uncharted Mission: Going to the Final Frontiers

D. C. Keane

Uncharted Mission is a book that is more than the history of the founding of Frontiers. D. C. Keane weaves together interviews with over one hundred missionaries who refused to accept the status quo in missions and were willing to go where no one had gone before—to the Muslim frontiers. In this inspiring true story, you'll meet pastors, engineers, artists, pilots, and others whose lives changed course when they discovered that Muslims were largely left out of historic missionary efforts. There are still "frontiers" of mission for the next generation of Christians who want to change the world, because it is too soon to celebrate and too soon to quit.

Printed in the USA
CPSIA information can be obtained
at www.ICGtesting.com
LVHW021030210224
772429LV00008B/128

9 781645 084648